BORUTO
-NARUTO NEXT GENERATIONS-

Creator/Supervisor
Masashi Kishimoto
Art by
Mikio Ikemoto
Script by
Ukyo Kodachi

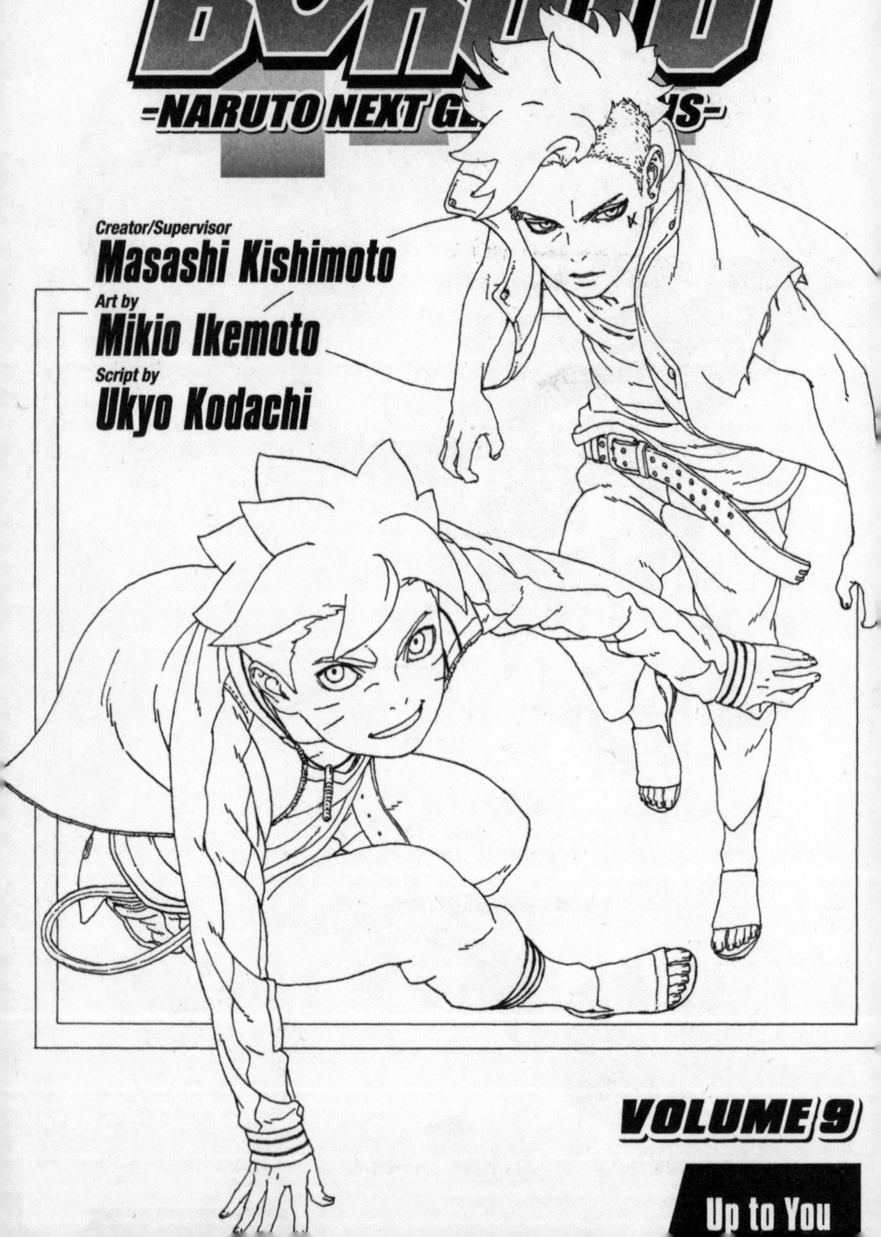

VOLUME 9

Up to You

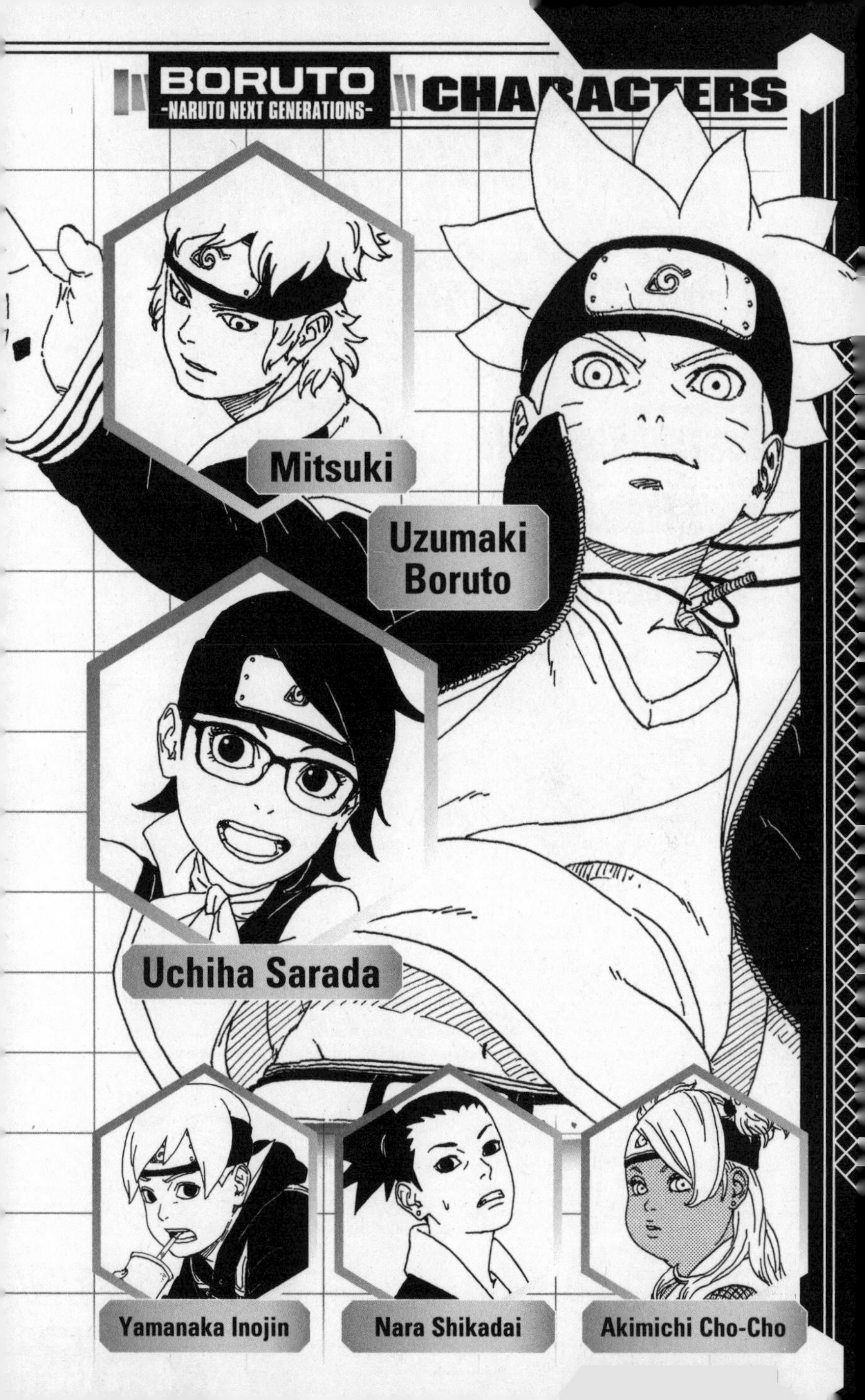
BORUTO
-NARUTO NEXT GENERATIONS-
CHARACTERS
Mitsuki
Uzumaki Boruto
Uchiha Sarada
Yamanaka Inojin
Nara Shikadai
Akimichi Cho-Cho

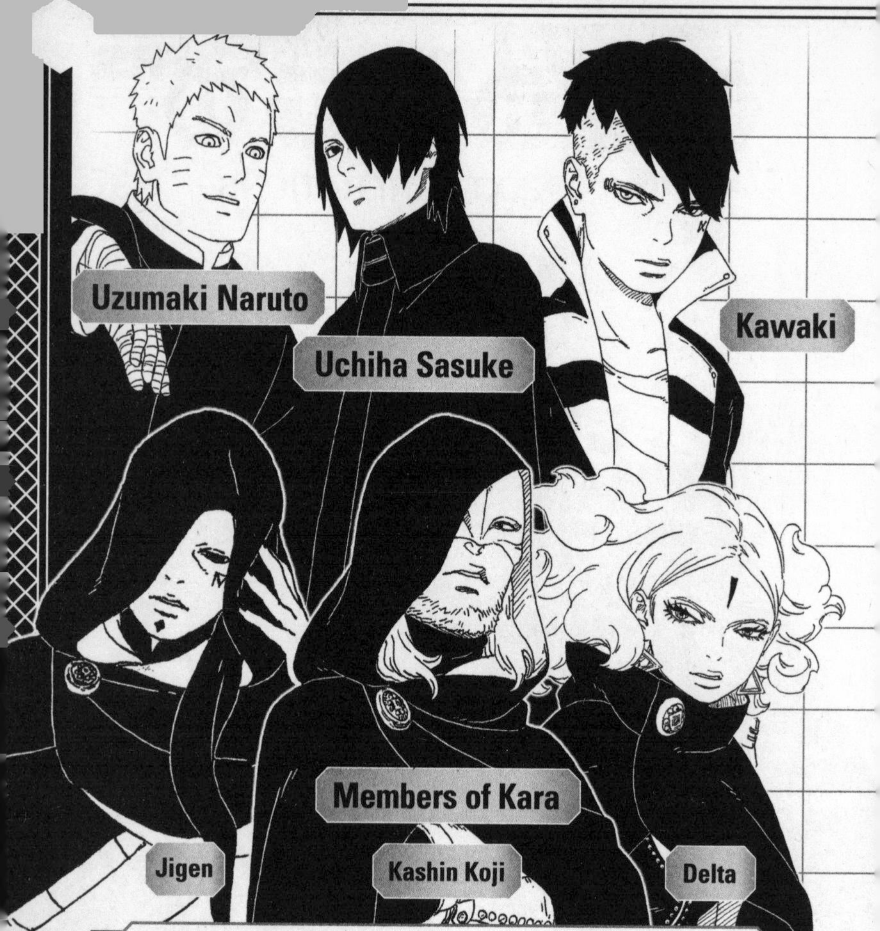
Uzumaki Naruto
Uchiha Sasuke
Kawaki
Members of Kara
Jigen
Kashin Koji
Delta

STORY

The Great Ninja War that shook the world and shed much blood is now history. Naruto has become the Seventh Hokage, and the people of Konohagakure Village are enjoying peace. Yet Naruto's son Uzumaki Boruto has a glum life, perhaps due to his father's too-great influence.

Rebelling against Naruto while simultaneously craving his praise, Boruto decides to enter the Chunin Exam along with his teammates Sarada and Mitsuki. However, Boruto ends up secretly using a prohibited Scientific Ninja Tool and is stripped of his shinobi status by his father.

Just then, members of the Ohtsutsuki Clan attack the arena! Boruto faces off against them alongside Naruto, Sasuke, and others, and they achieve victory with a Rasengan that father and son weave together. However, a strange mark appears on Boruto's right palm…

Afterward, Boruto happens upon a young man named Kawaki who bears the same Karma as himself. And it is he who is proven to be what Kara has been calling the Vessel.

In order to place Kawaki under his protection, Naruto moves him into his own home. Though Kawaki clashes with Boruto, his heart also starts to heal. However, Kara member Delta shows up and a fierce battle with Naruto ensues…

BORUTO

-NARUTO NEXT GENERATIONS-

VOLUME 9
UP TO YOU

CONTENTS

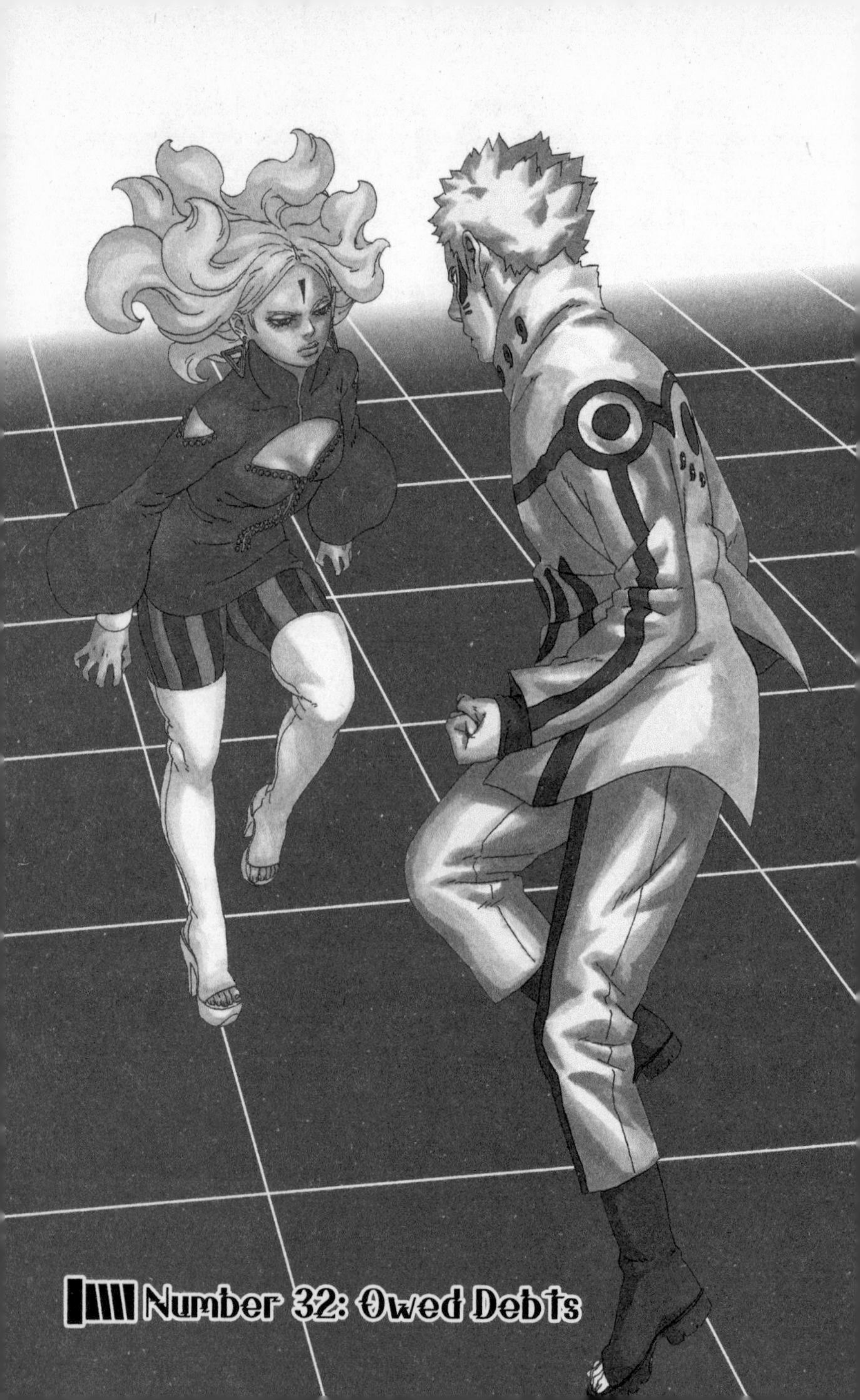

Number 32: Owed Debts

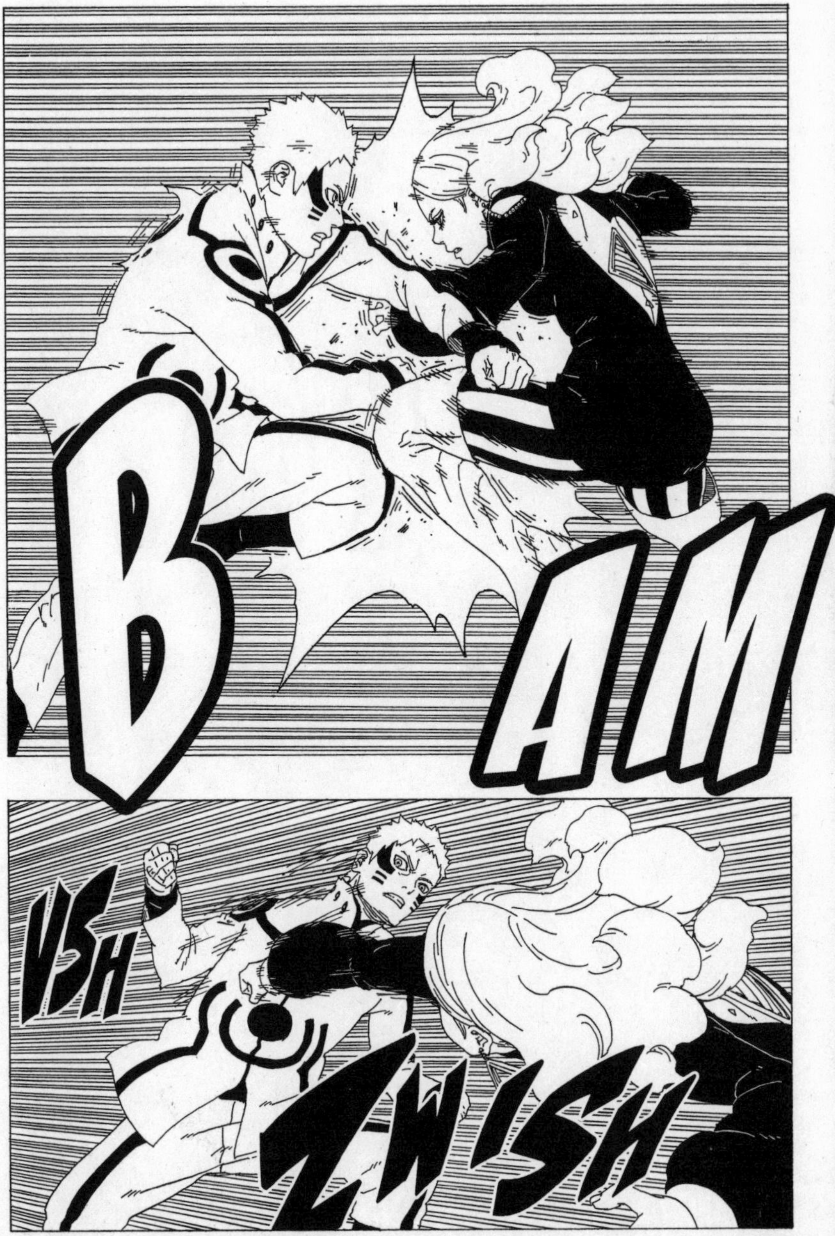
BAM
VSH
ZWISH

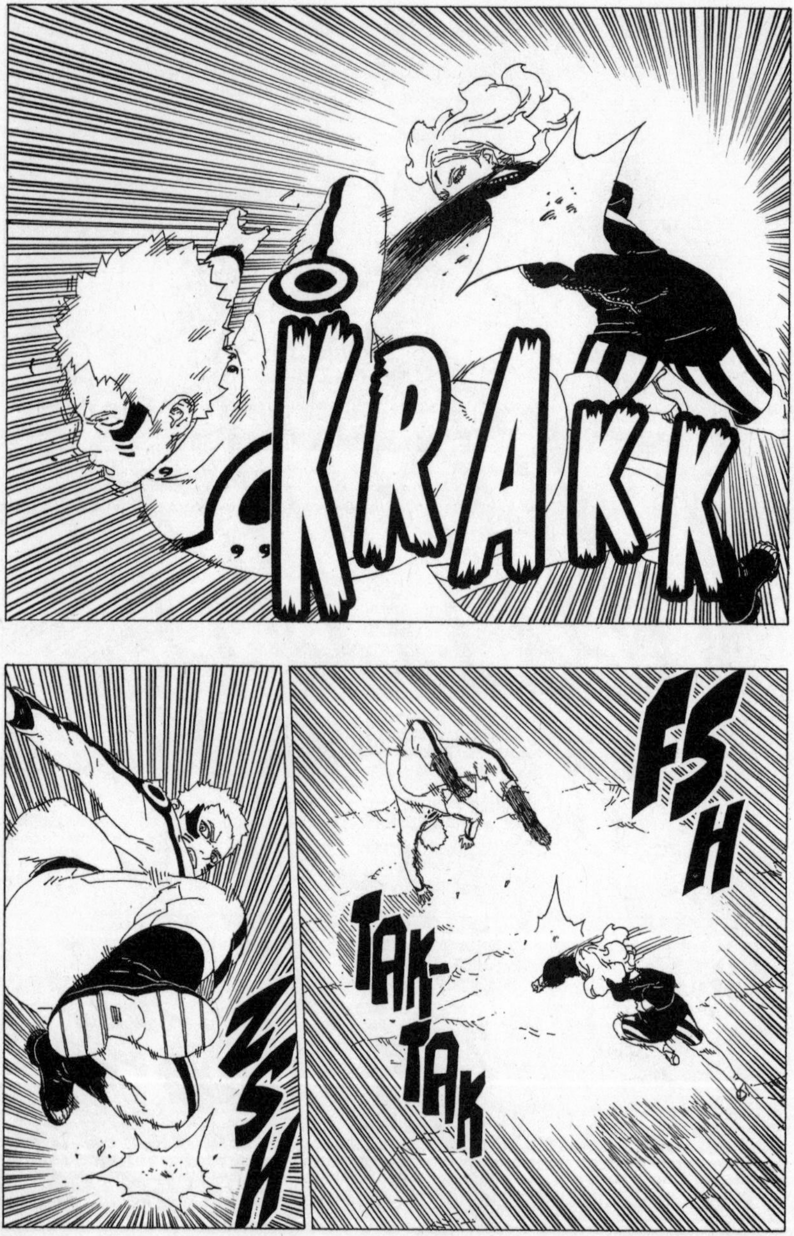
KRAKK
FSH
TAK-TAK
WSH

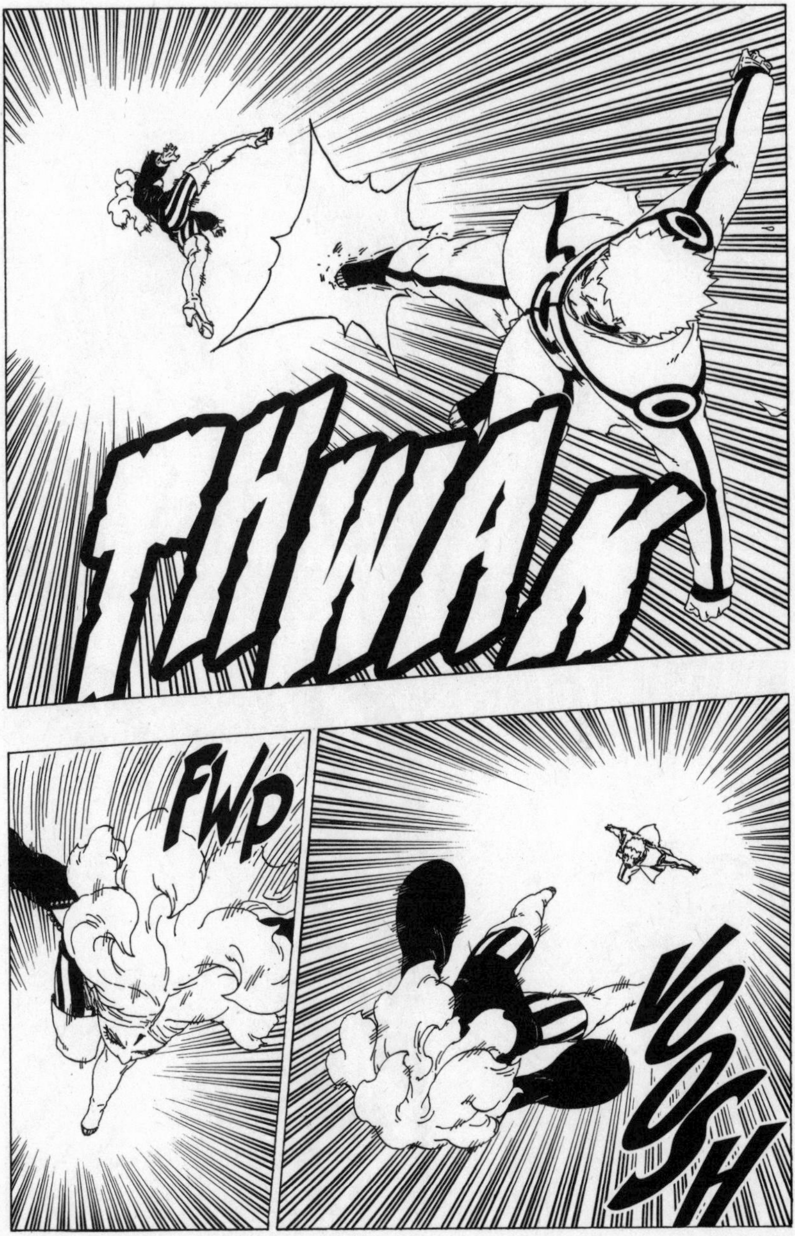
THWAK
SWOOSH
FWP

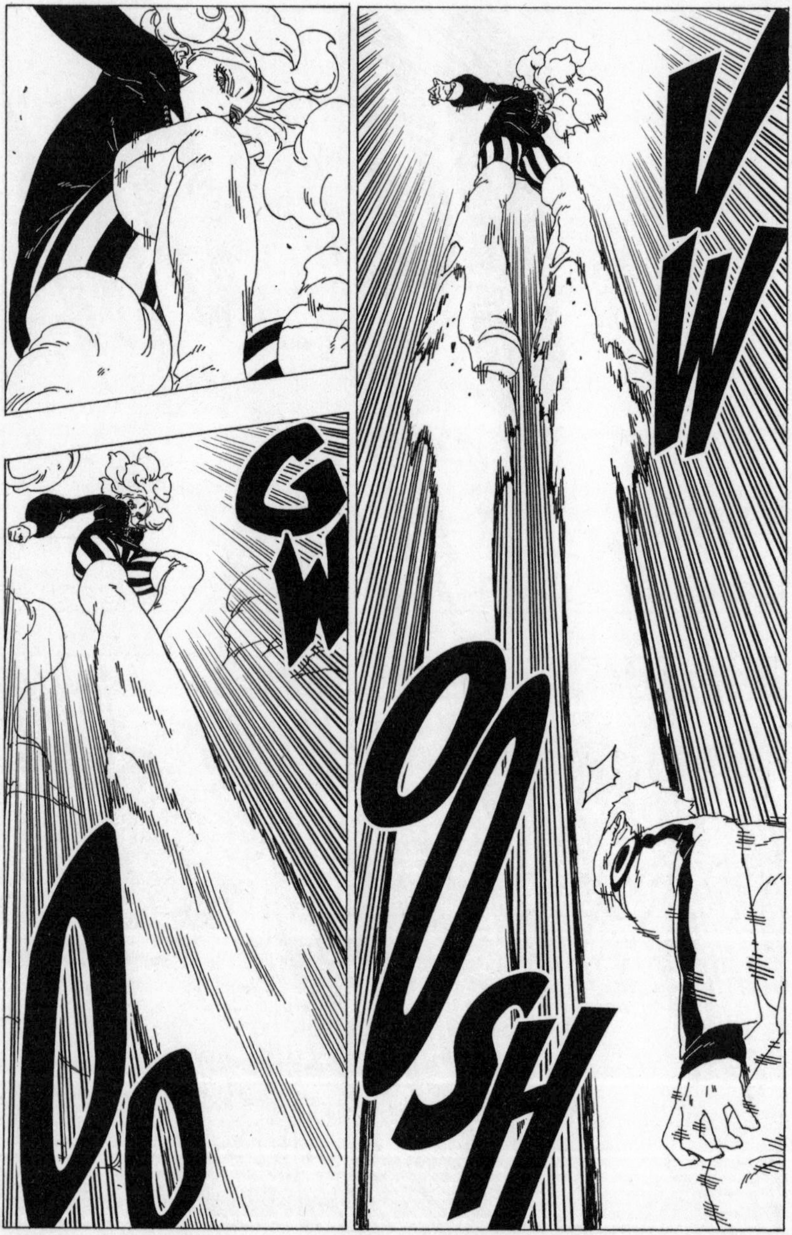

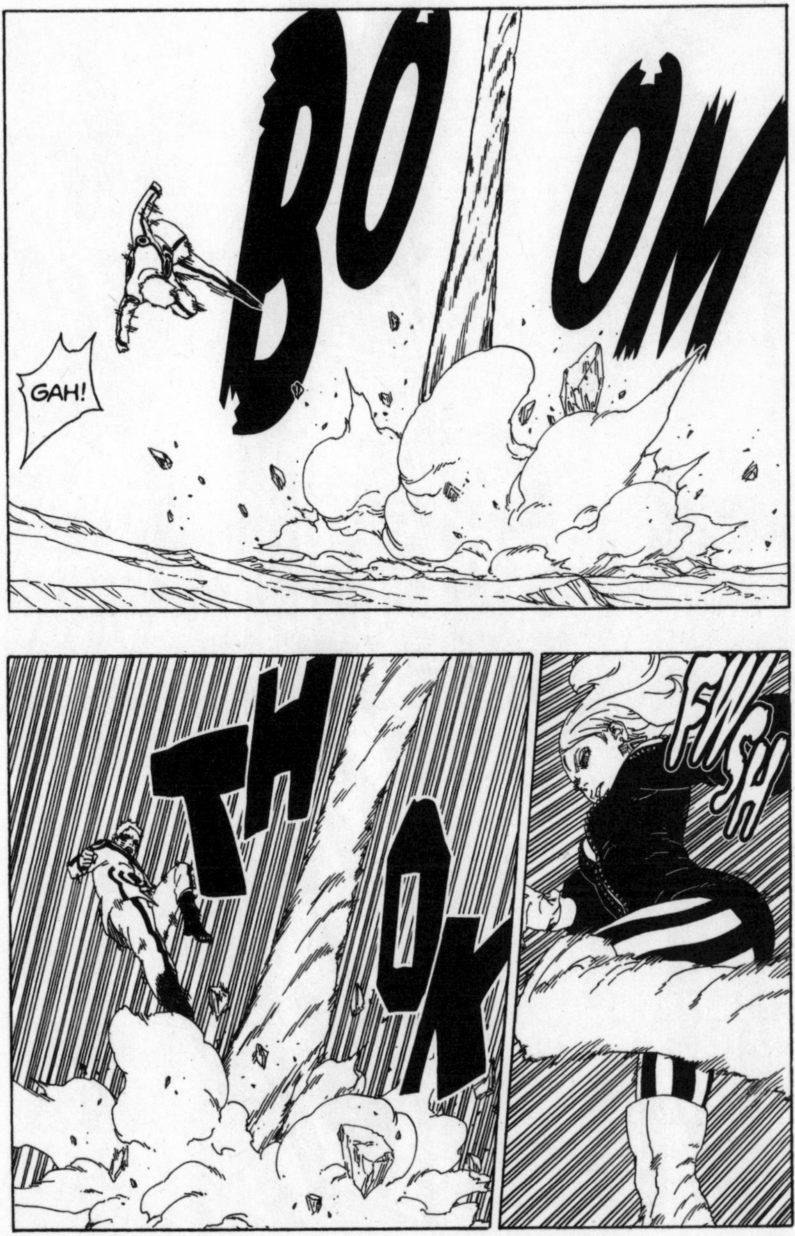
BOOM
GAH!
FWSH
THOK

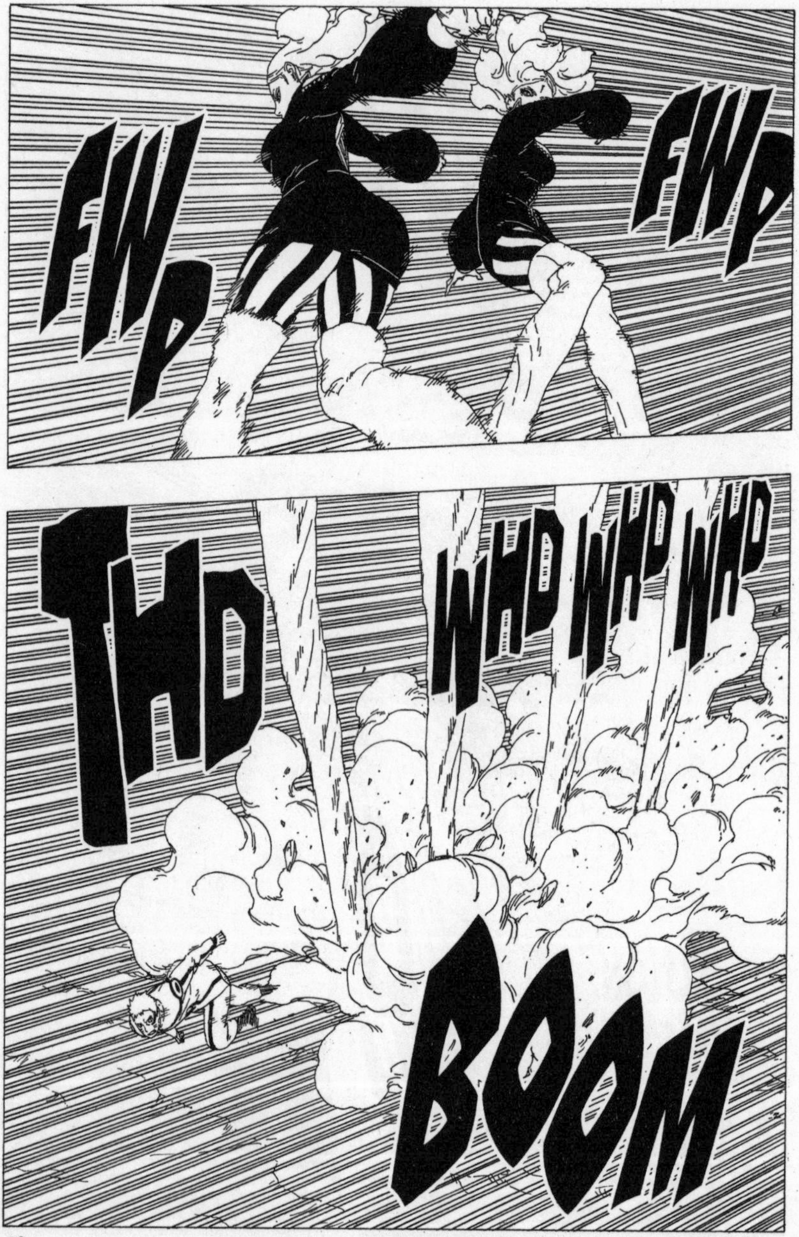
FWP
FWP
WHD WHD WHD
THD
BOOM

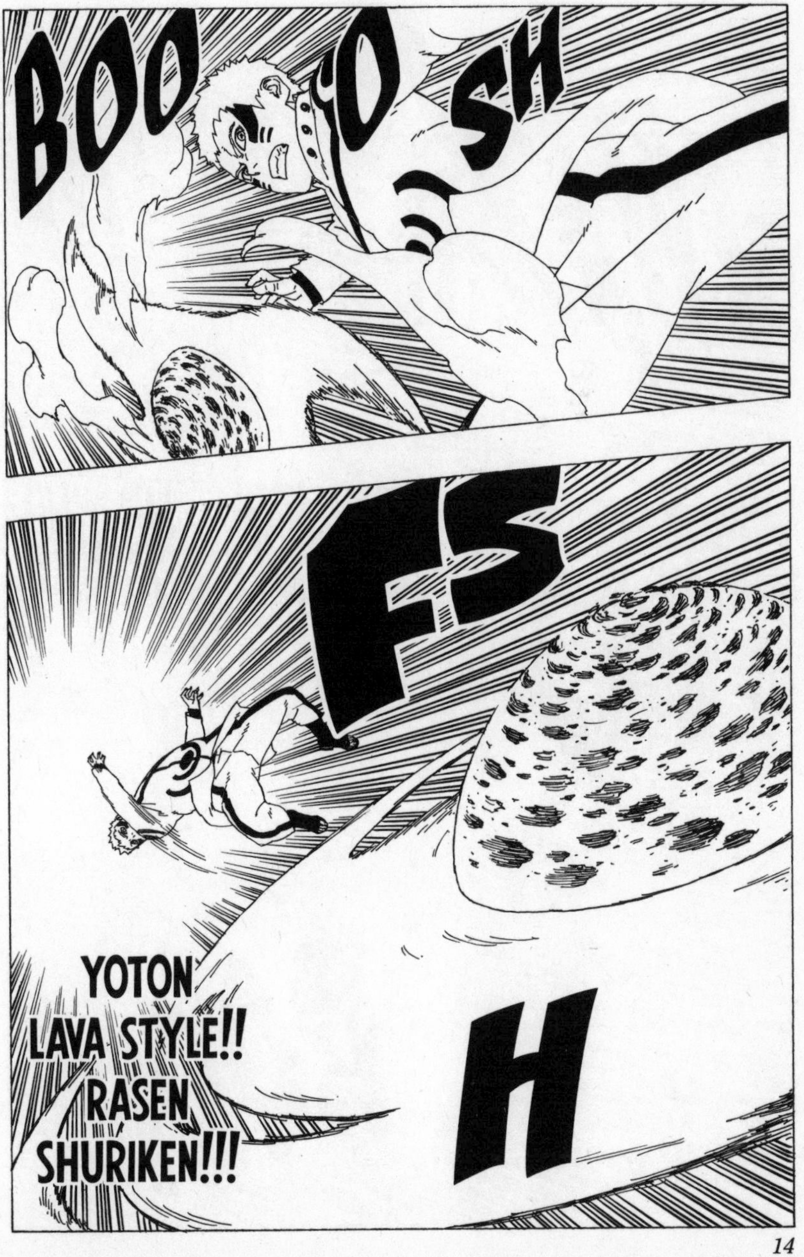
BOOOSH
FSH
YOTON LAVA STYLE!! RASEN SHURIKEN!!!

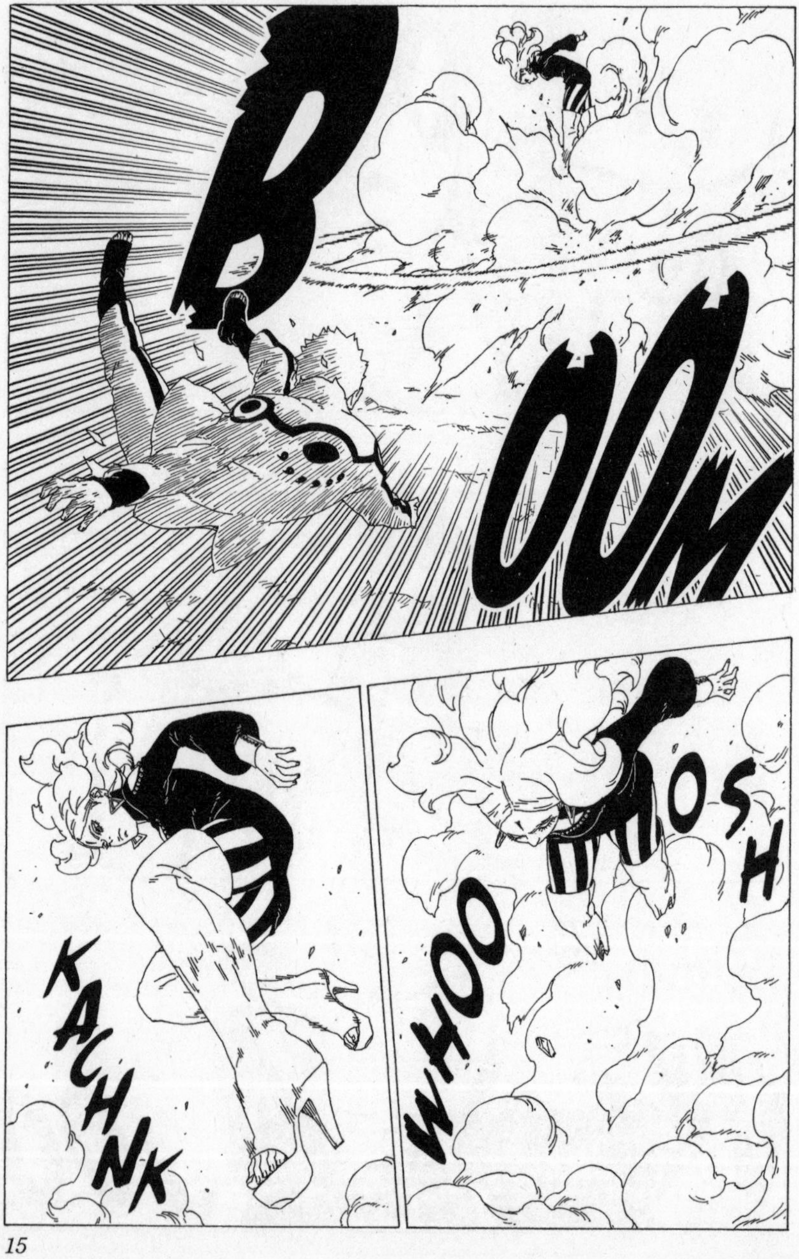
BOOM
WHOOOSH
KACHNK

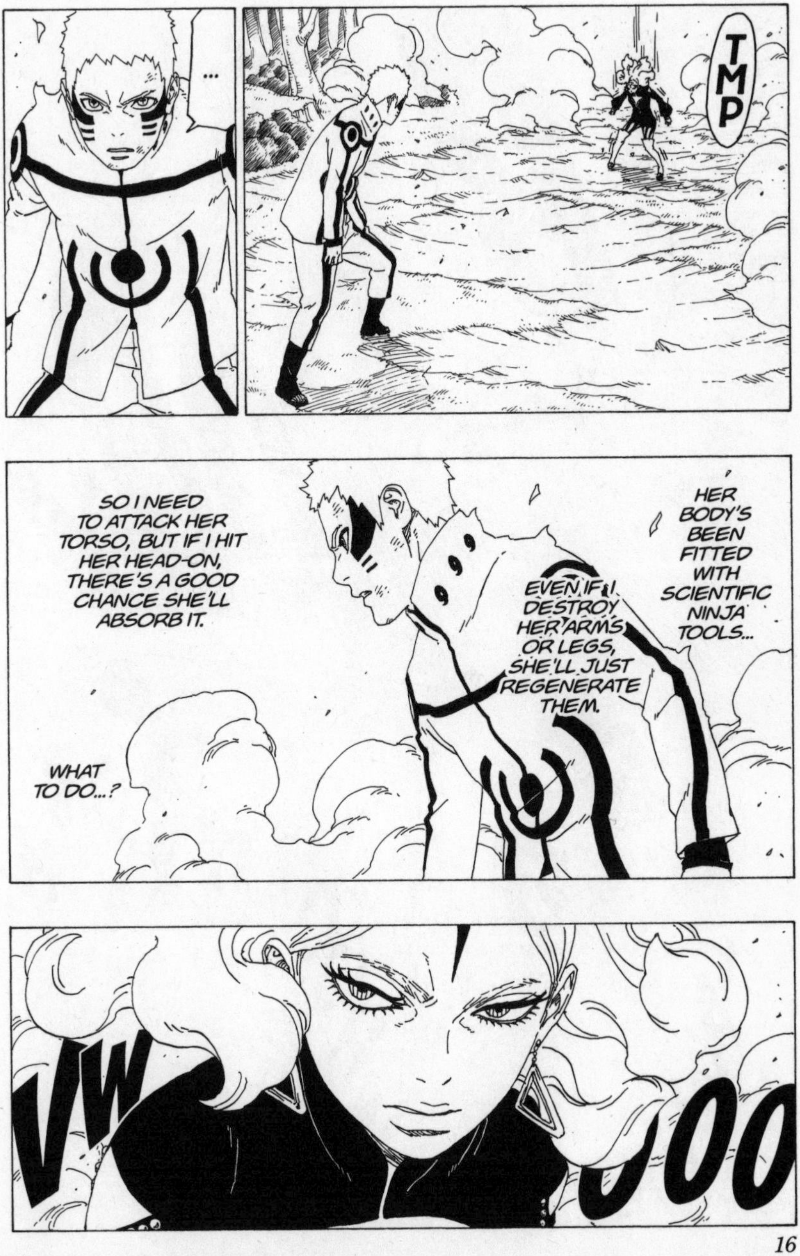
TMP
...
HER BODY'S BEEN FITTED WITH SCIENTIFIC NINJA TOOLS...
EVEN IF I DESTROY HER ARMS OR LEGS, SHE'LL JUST REGENERATE THEM.
SO I NEED TO ATTACK HER TORSO, BUT IF I HIT HER HEAD-ON, THERE'S A GOOD CHANCE SHE'LL ABSORB IT.
WHAT TO DO...?
VW
OOO

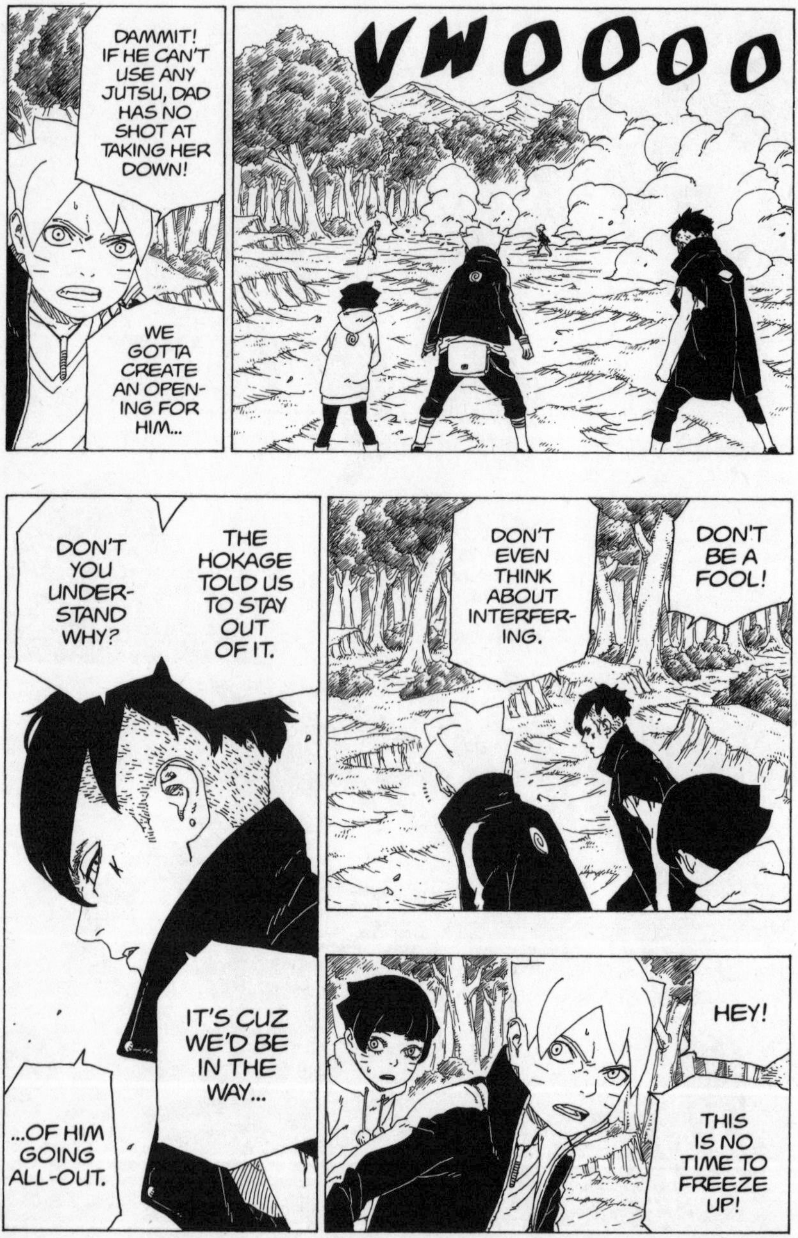
VWOOOO
DAMMIT! IF HE CAN'T USE ANY JUTSU, DAD HAS NO SHOT AT TAKING HER DOWN!
WE GOTTA CREATE AN OPENING FOR HIM...
DON'T BE A FOOL!
DON'T EVEN THINK ABOUT INTERFERING.
HEY!
THIS IS NO TIME TO FREEZE UP!
THE HOKAGE TOLD US TO STAY OUT OF IT.
DON'T YOU UNDERSTAND WHY?
IT'S CUZ WE'D BE IN THE WAY...
...OF HIM GOING ALL-OUT.

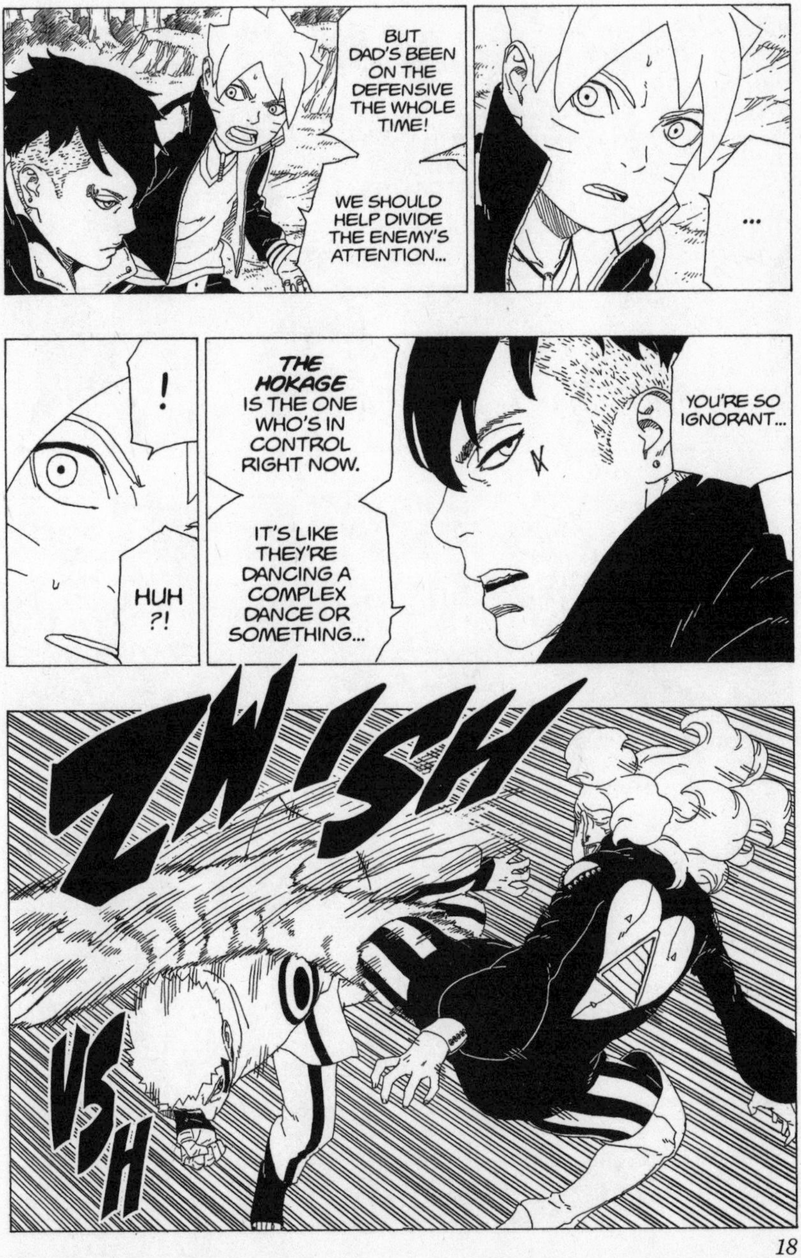
...
BUT DAD'S BEEN ON THE DEFENSIVE THE WHOLE TIME!
WE SHOULD HELP DIVIDE THE ENEMY'S ATTENTION...
YOU'RE SO IGNORANT...
THE HOKAGE IS THE ONE WHO'S IN CONTROL RIGHT NOW.
IT'S LIKE THEY'RE DANCING A COMPLEX DANCE OR SOMETHING...
!
HUH ?!
ZWISH
VSH

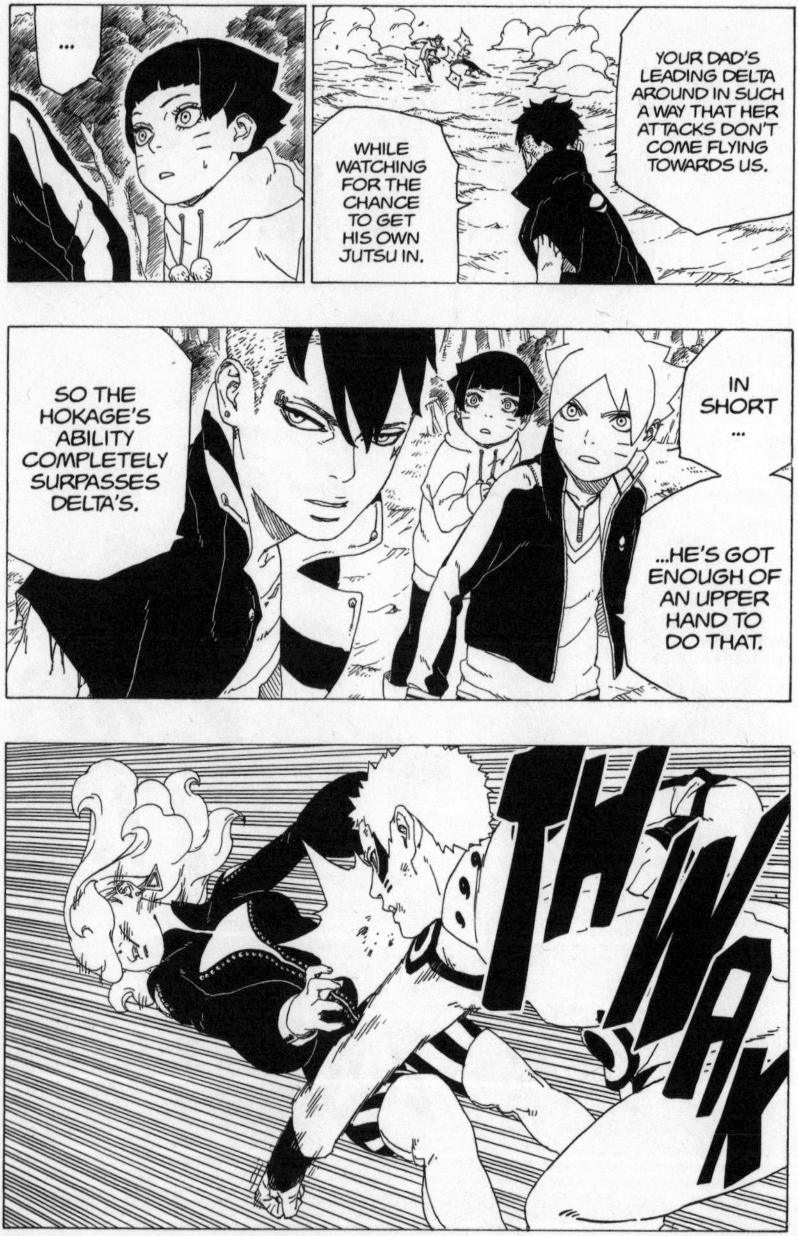
YOUR DAD'S LEADING DELTA AROUND IN SUCH A WAY THAT HER ATTACKS DON'T COME FLYING TOWARDS US.
WHILE WATCHING FOR THE CHANCE TO GET HIS OWN JUTSU IN.
...
IN SHORT ...
...HE'S GOT ENOUGH OF AN UPPER HAND TO DO THAT.
SO THE HOKAGE'S ABILITY COMPLETELY SURPASSES DELTA'S.
THWAK

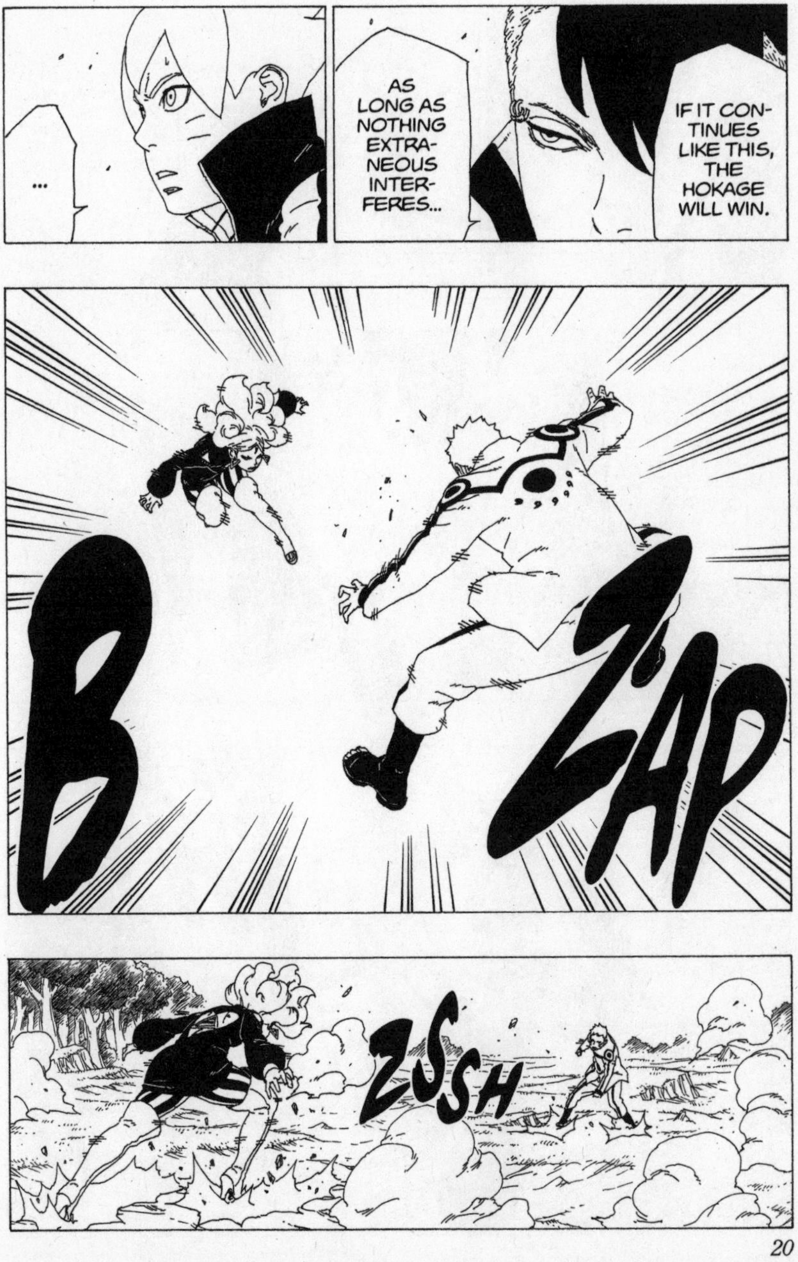
IF IT CONTINUES LIKE THIS, THE HOKAGE WILL WIN.
AS LONG AS NOTHING EXTRANEOUS INTERFERES...
...
BZAP
ZSSH

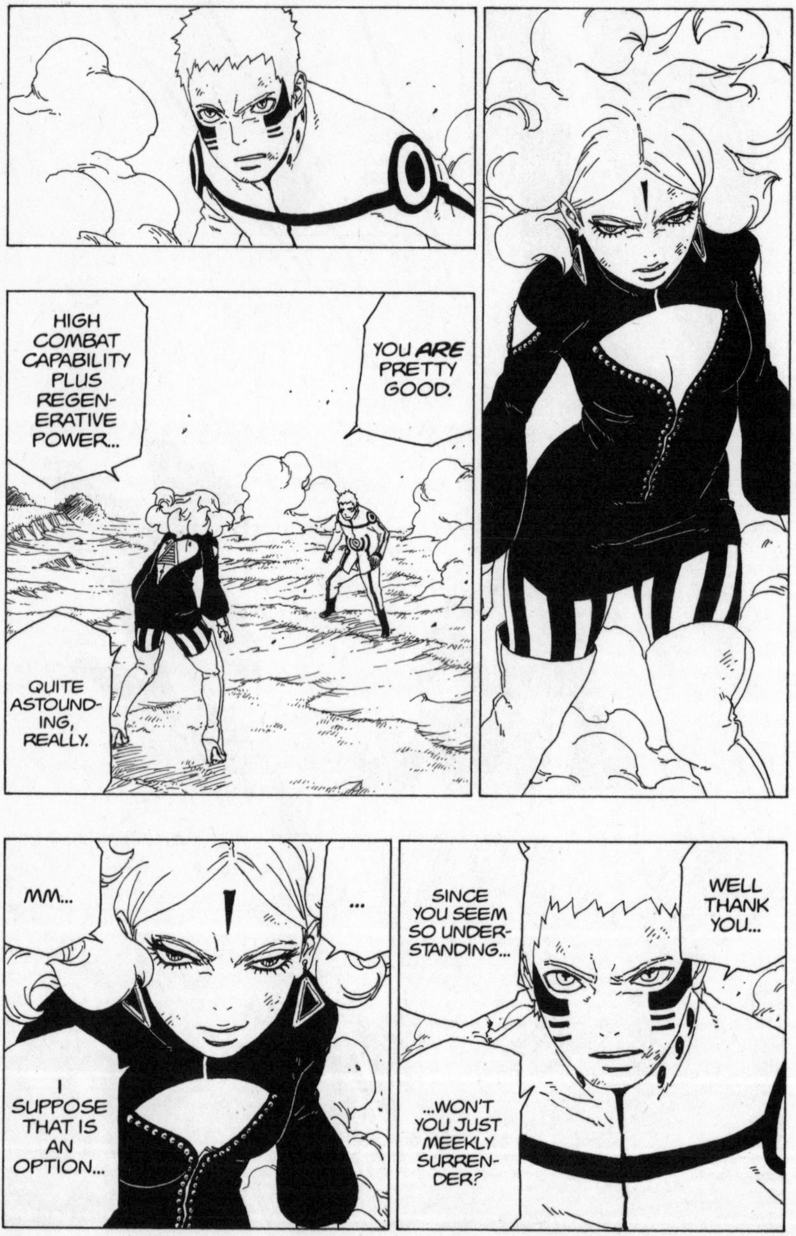
YOU *ARE* PRETTY GOOD.
HIGH COMBAT CAPABILITY PLUS REGENERATIVE POWER...
QUITE ASTOUNDING, REALLY.
WELL THANK YOU...
SINCE YOU SEEM SO UNDERSTANDING...
...WON'T YOU JUST MEEKLY SURRENDER?
...
MM...
I SUPPOSE THAT IS AN OPTION...

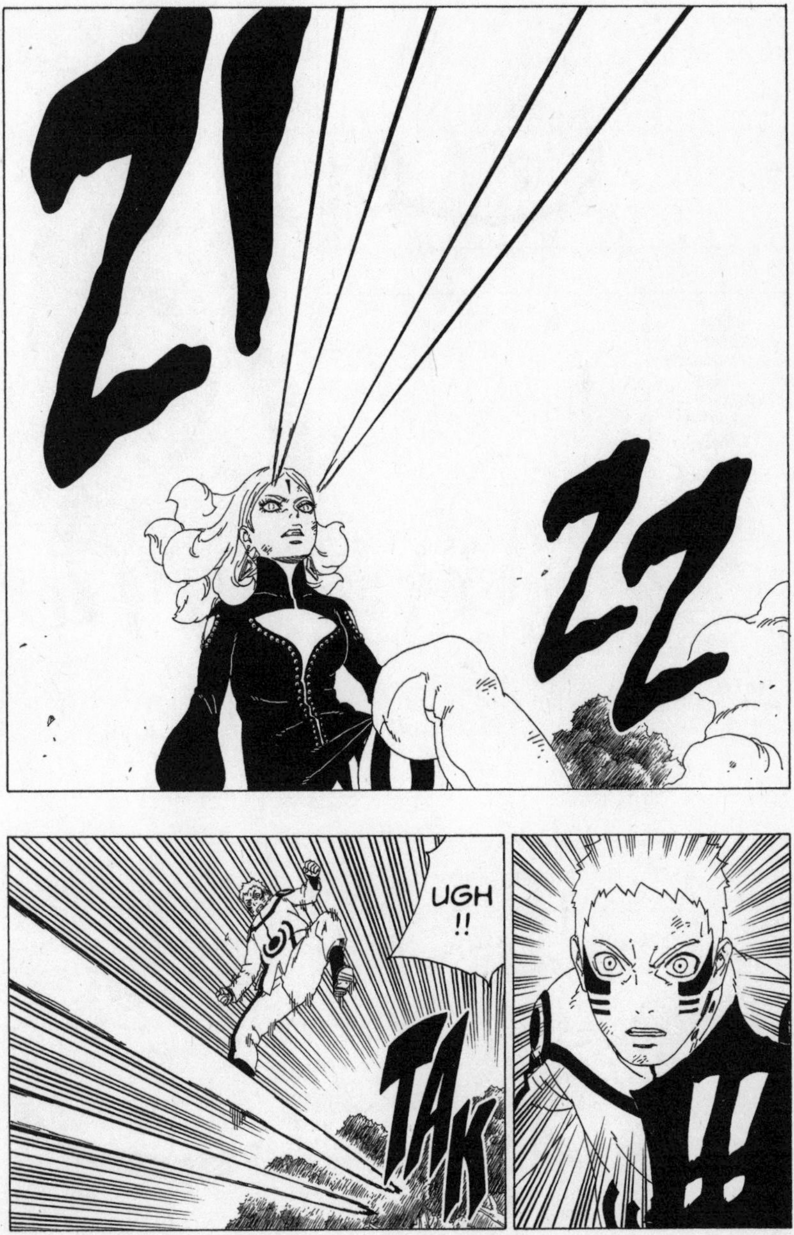
Z!
ZZ
!!
UGH !!
TAK

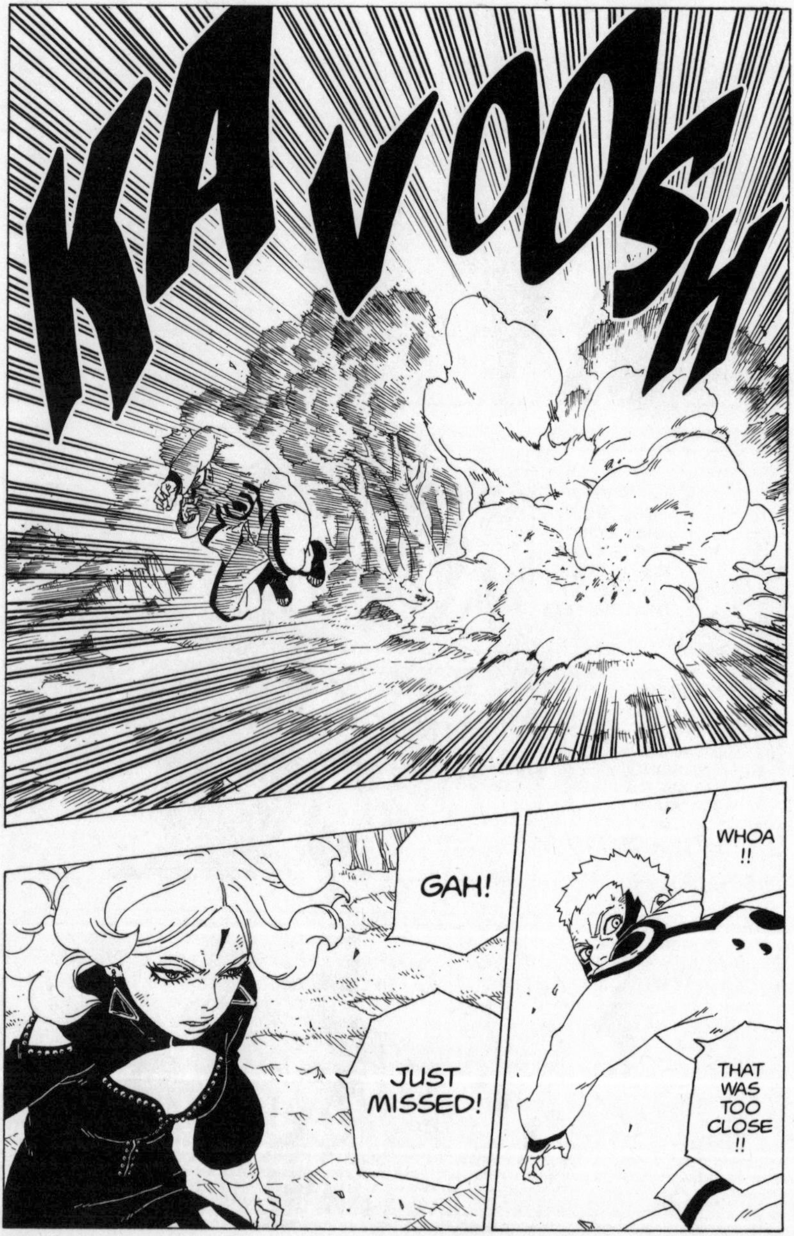
KAVOOSH
WHOA !!
THAT WAS TOO CLOSE !!
GAH!
JUST MISSED!

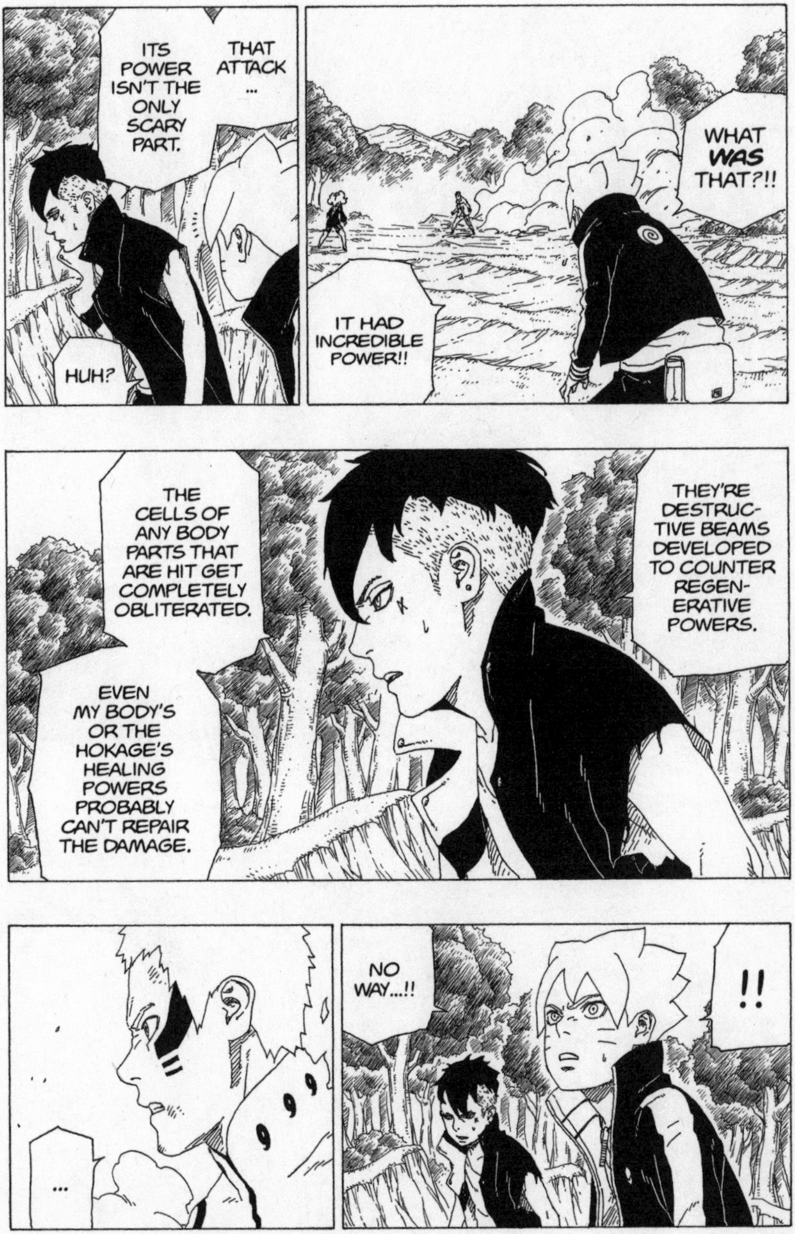
WHAT WAS THAT?!!
IT HAD INCREDIBLE POWER!!
THAT ATTACK ...
ITS POWER ISN'T THE ONLY SCARY PART.
HUH?
THEY'RE DESTRUC-TIVE BEAMS DEVELOPED TO COUNTER REGEN-ERATIVE POWERS.
THE CELLS OF ANY BODY PARTS THAT ARE HIT GET COMPLETELY OBLITERATED.
EVEN MY BODY'S OR THE HOKAGE'S HEALING POWERS PROBABLY CAN'T REPAIR THE DAMAGE.
!!
NO WAY...!!
...
...

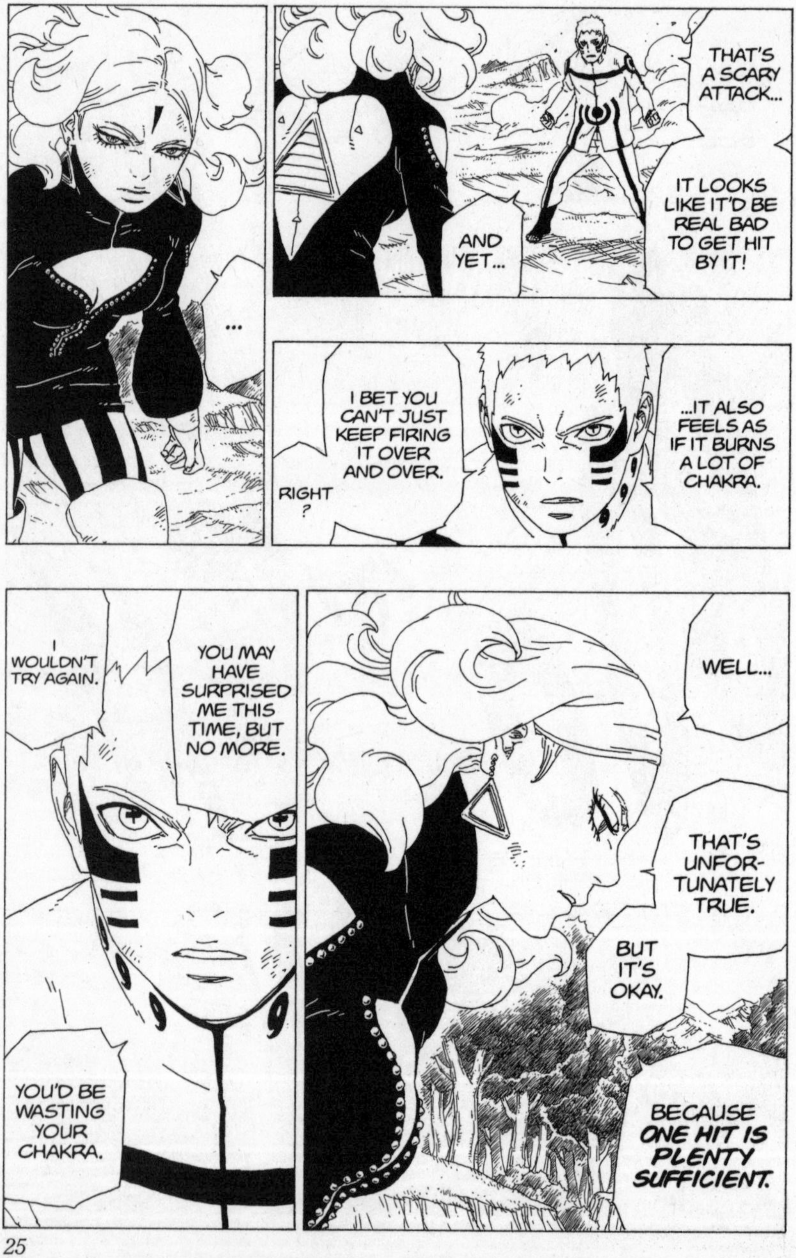
THAT'S A SCARY ATTACK...
IT LOOKS LIKE IT'D BE REAL BAD TO GET HIT BY IT!
AND YET...
...IT ALSO FEELS AS IF IT BURNS A LOT OF CHAKRA.
I BET YOU CAN'T JUST KEEP FIRING IT OVER AND OVER.
RIGHT?
...
WELL...
THAT'S UNFORTUNATELY TRUE.
BUT IT'S OKAY.
BECAUSE ***ONE HIT IS PLENTY SUFFICIENT.***
YOU MAY HAVE SURPRISED ME THIS TIME, BUT NO MORE.
I WOULDN'T TRY AGAIN.
YOU'D BE WASTING YOUR CHAKRA.

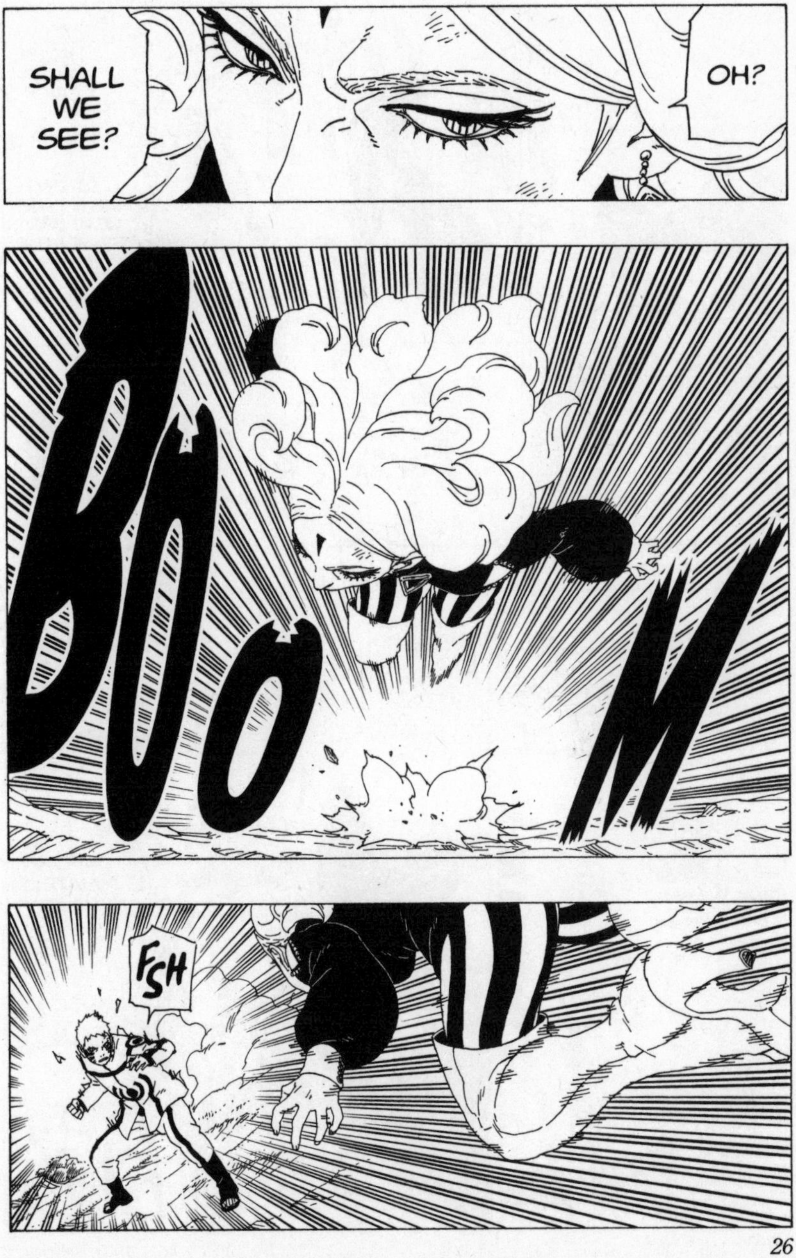
OH?
SHALL WE SEE?
BOOOM
FSH

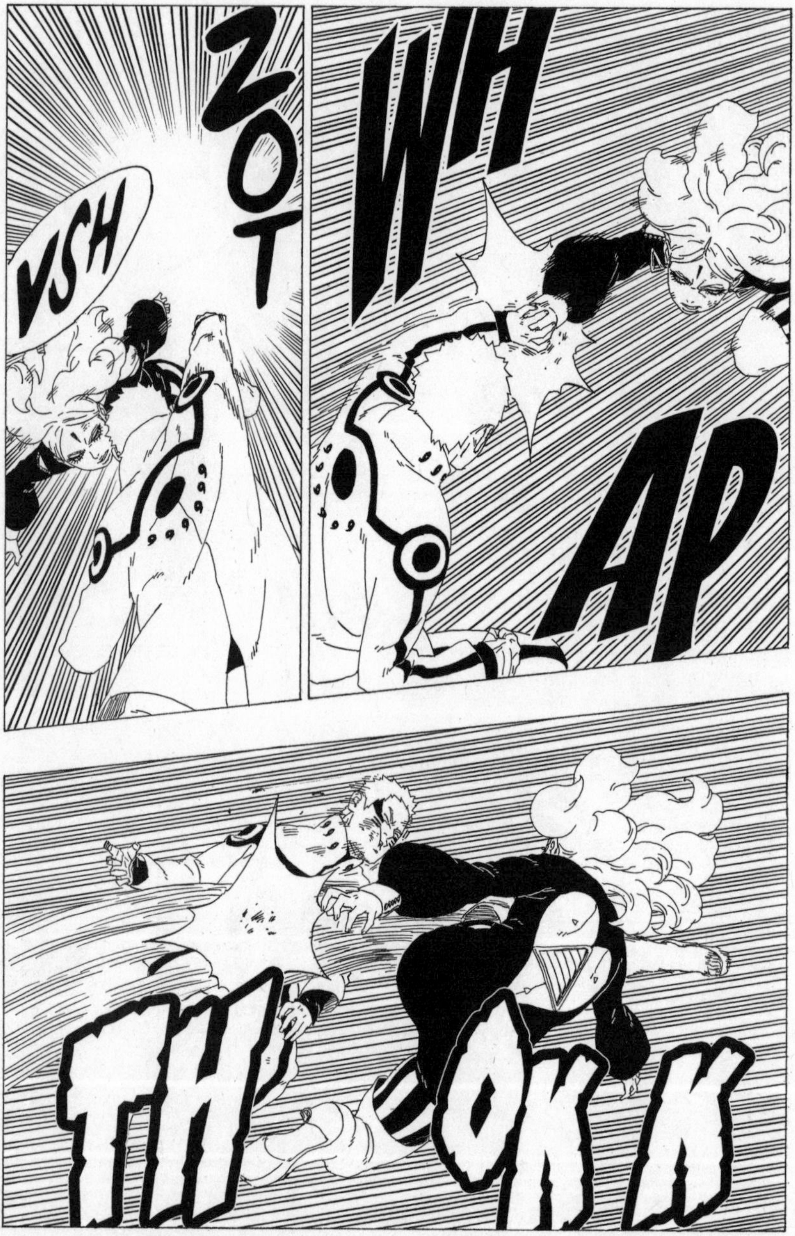
WHAP
VSH
ZOT
THOKK

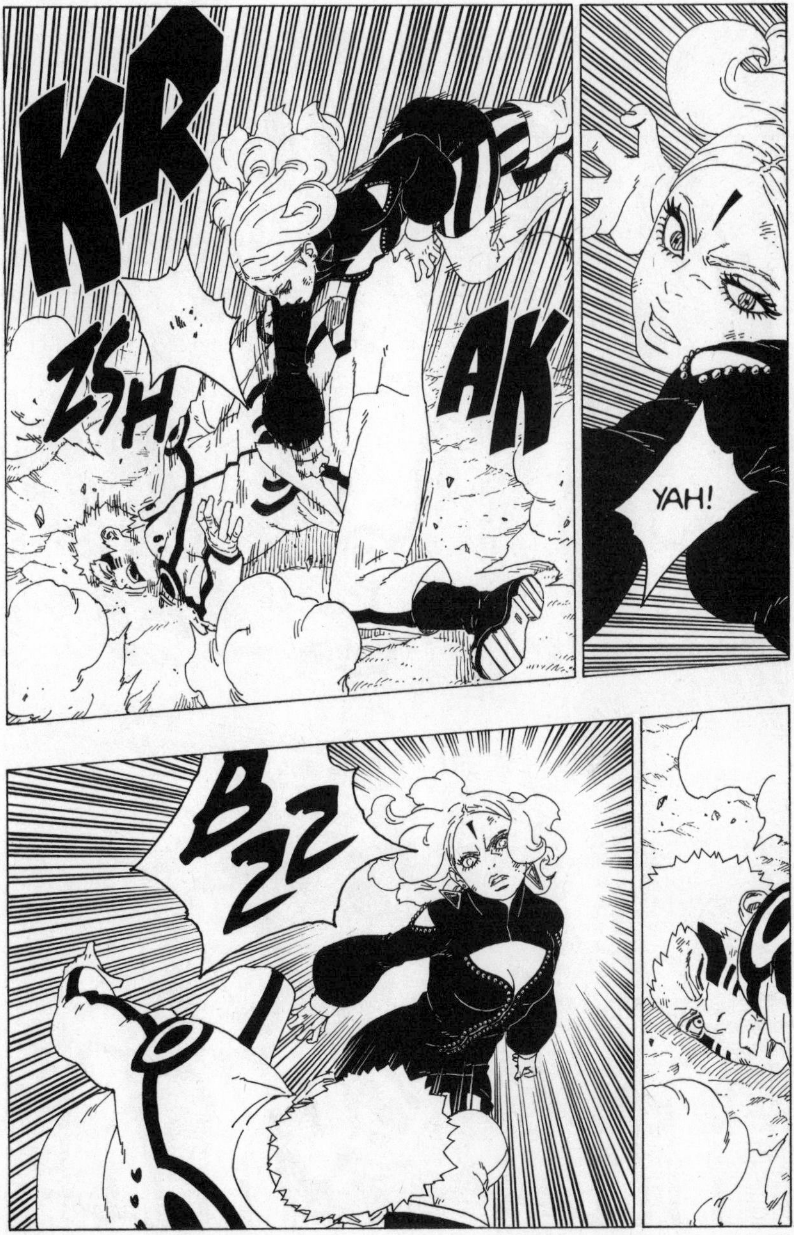
YAH!
KRAK
ZSH
BZZ

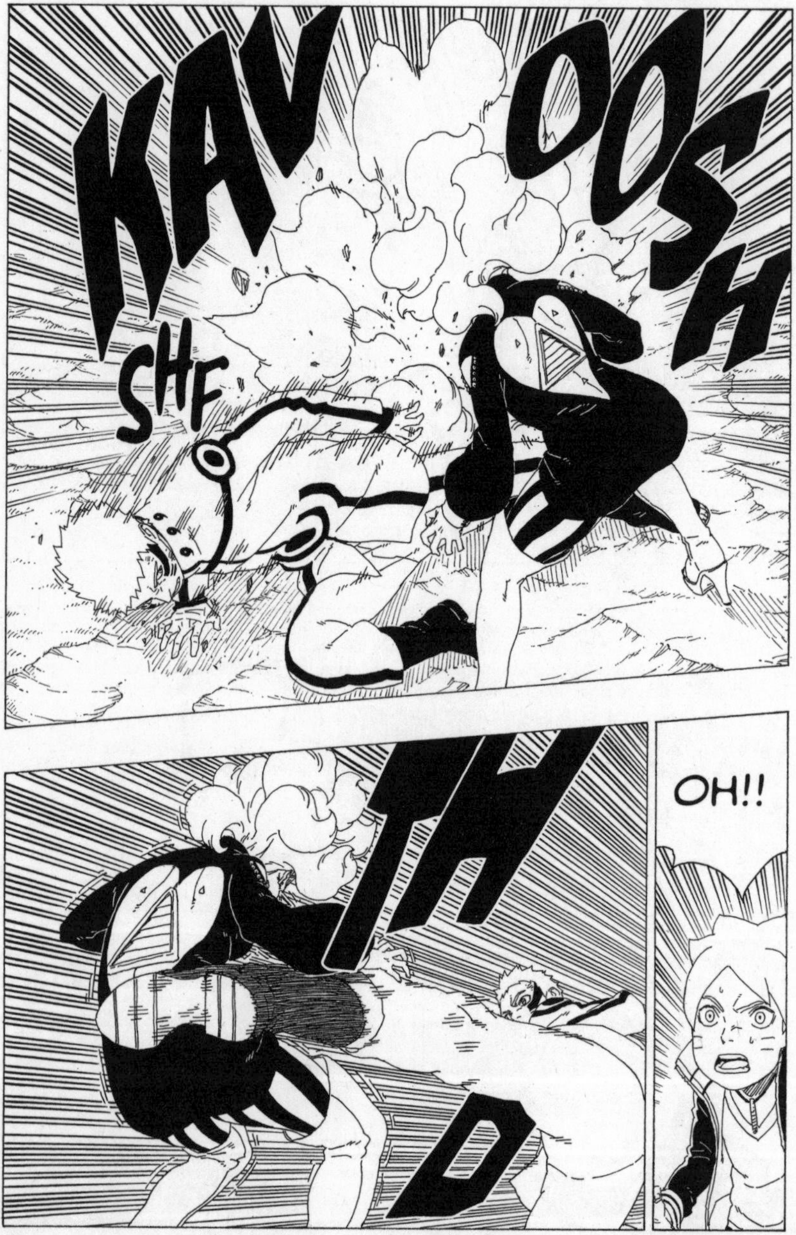
KAVOOSH
SHF
OH!!
THD

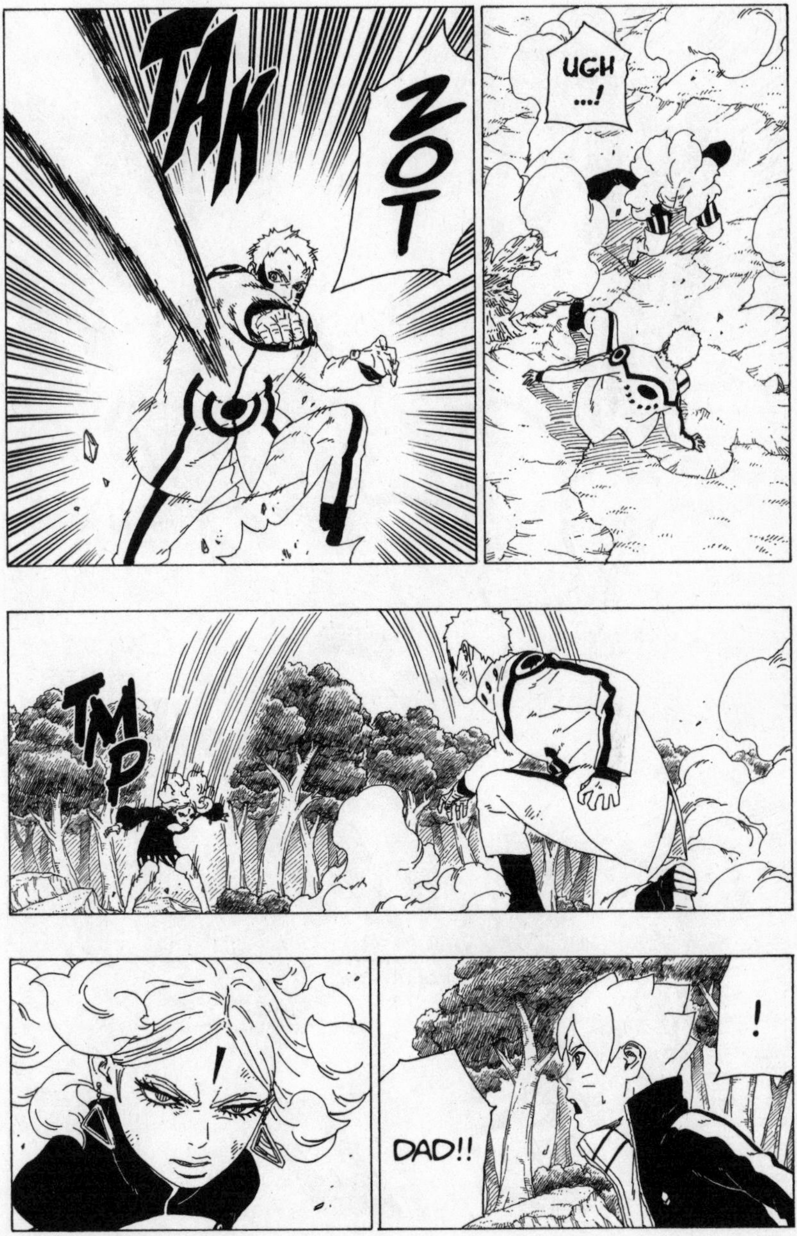
UGH ...!
TAK
ZOT
TMP
!
DAD!!

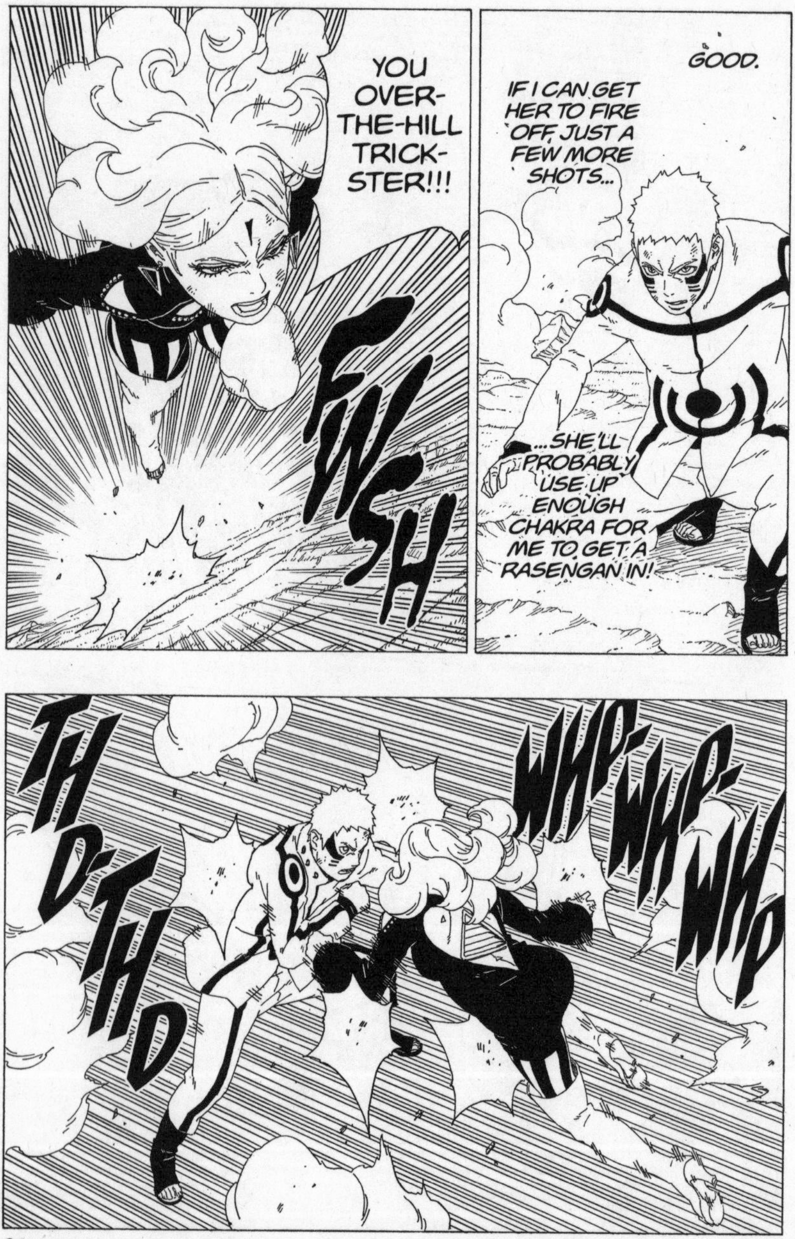
GOOD.
IF I CAN GET HER TO FIRE OFF, JUST A FEW MORE SHOTS...
...SHE'LL PROBABLY USE UP ENOUGH CHAKRA FOR ME TO GET A RASENGAN IN!
YOU OVER-THE-HILL TRICKSTER!!!
FWSH
WHP-WHP-WHP
THD-THD

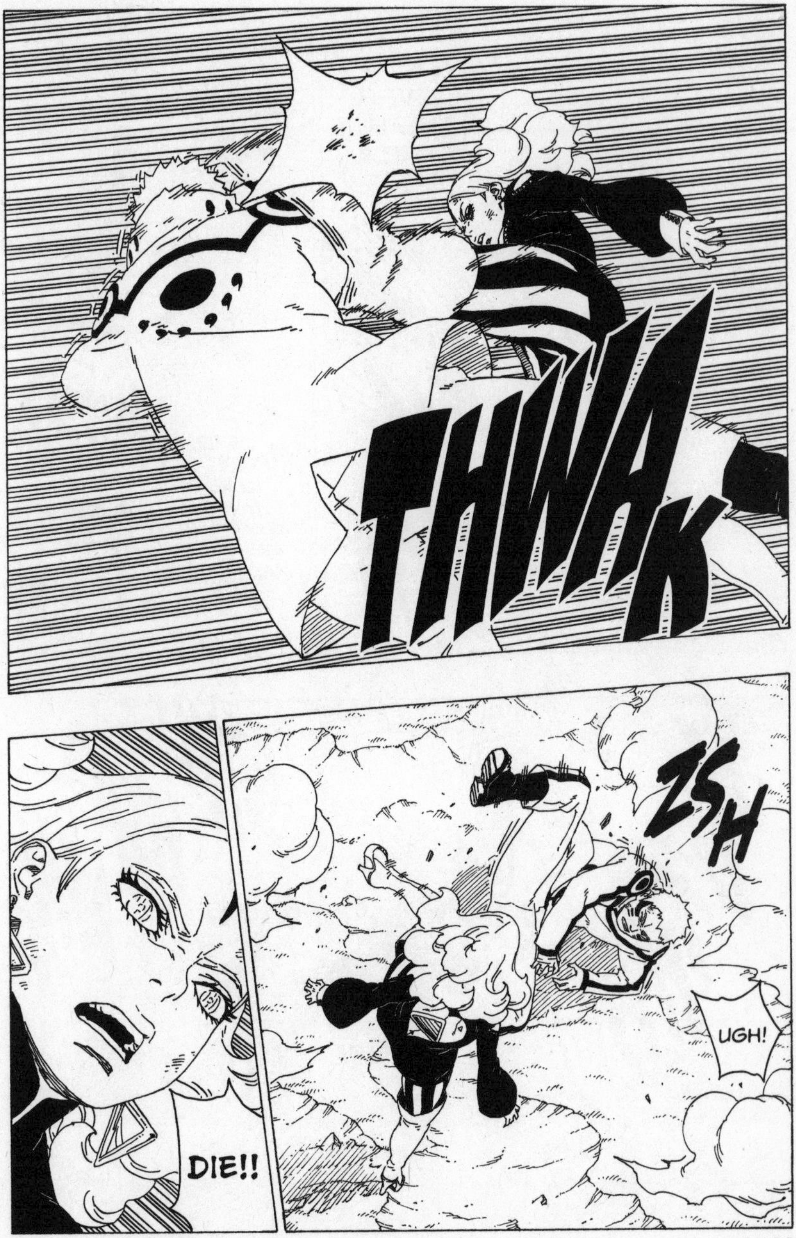
THWAK
ZSH
UGH!
DIE!!

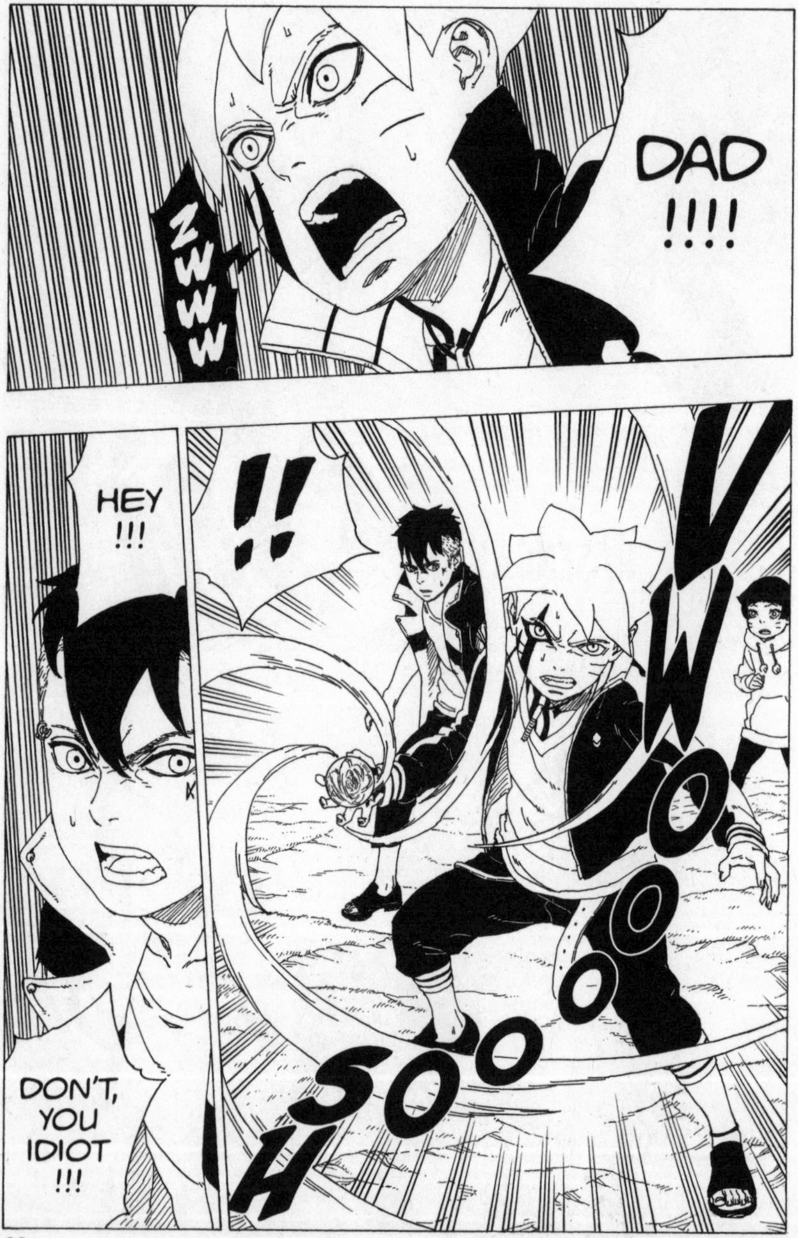

DAD !!!!
ZWWW
!!
VWOOOOOOOOSH
HEY !!!
DON'T, YOU IDIOT !!!

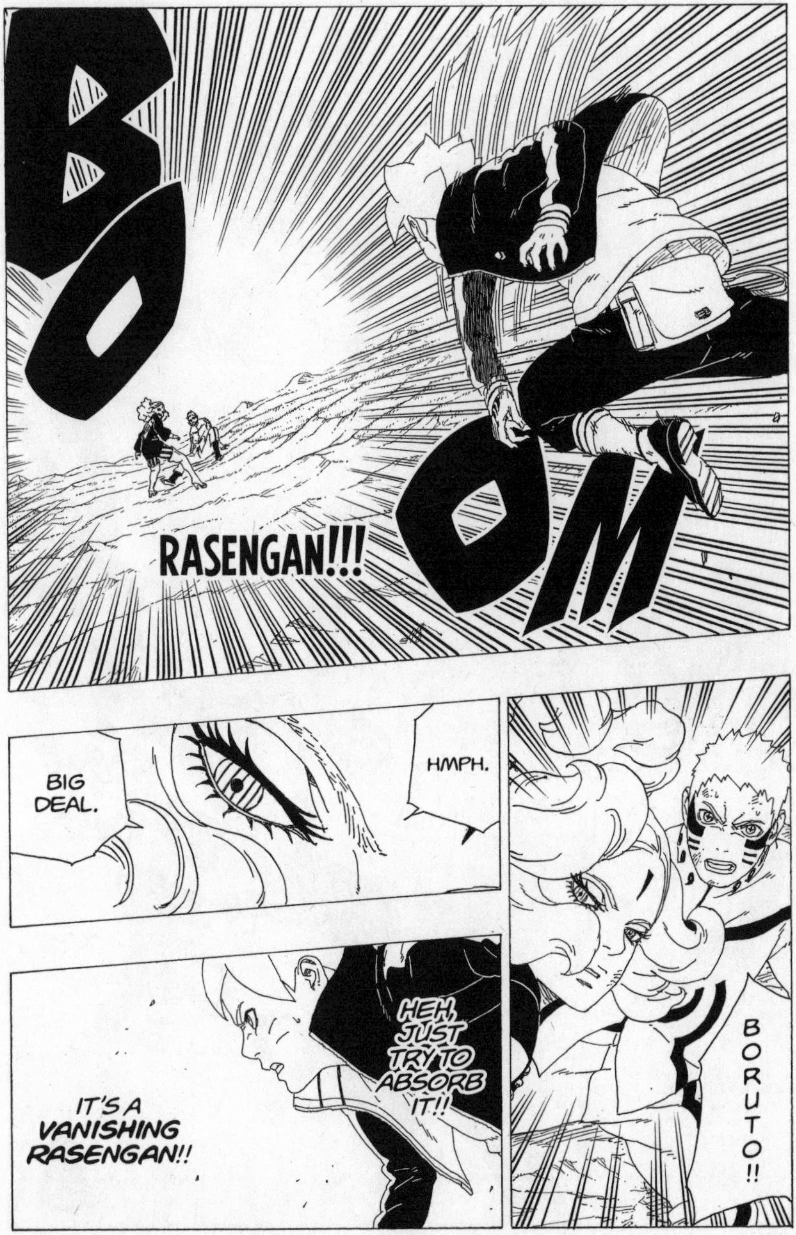
BOOM
RASENGAN!!!
BORUTO!!
HMPH.
BIG DEAL.
HEH, JUST TRY TO ABSORB IT!!
IT'S A VANISHING RASENGAN!!

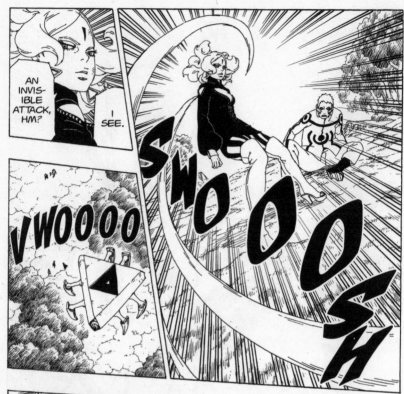

AN INVIS-IBLE ATTACK, HM?

I SEE.

SWOOOOSH

VWOOOO

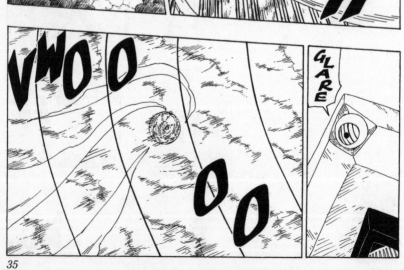

VWOO

OO

GLARE

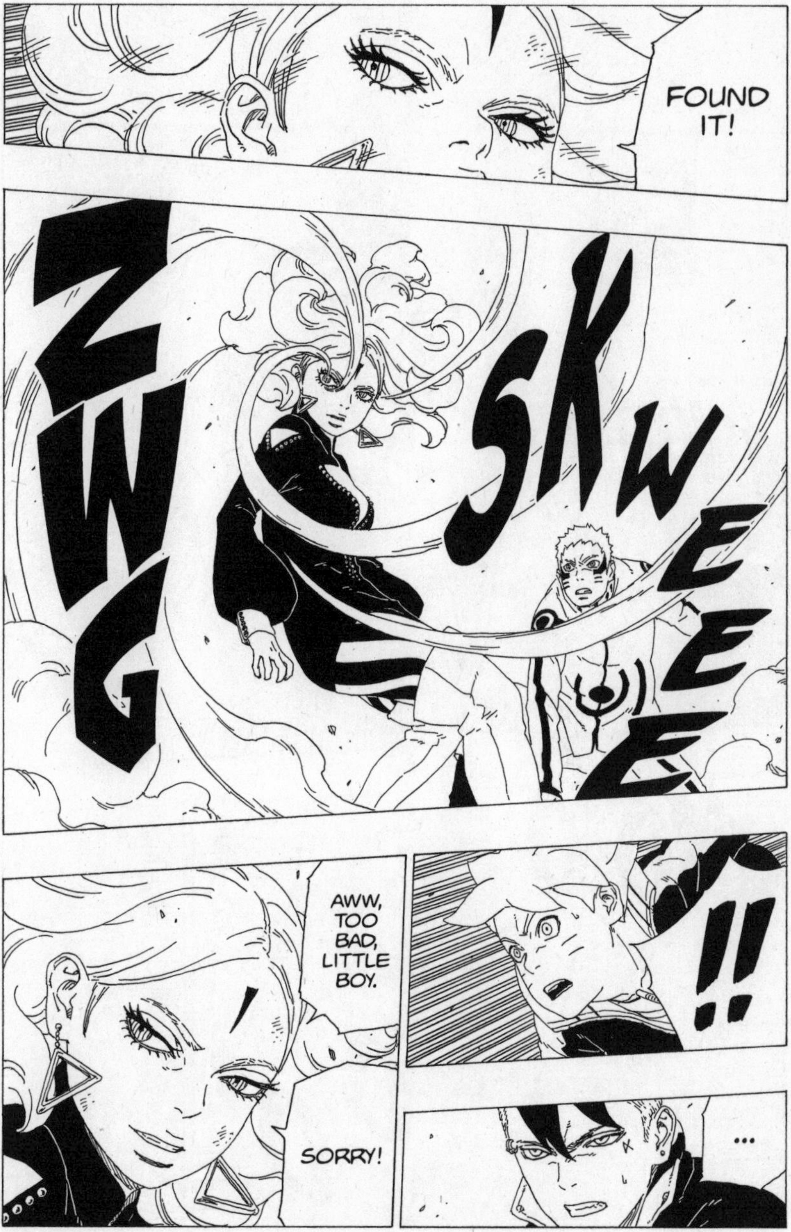
FOUND IT!
SKWEEEE
ZWG
!!
...
AWW, TOO BAD, LITTLE BOY.
SORRY!

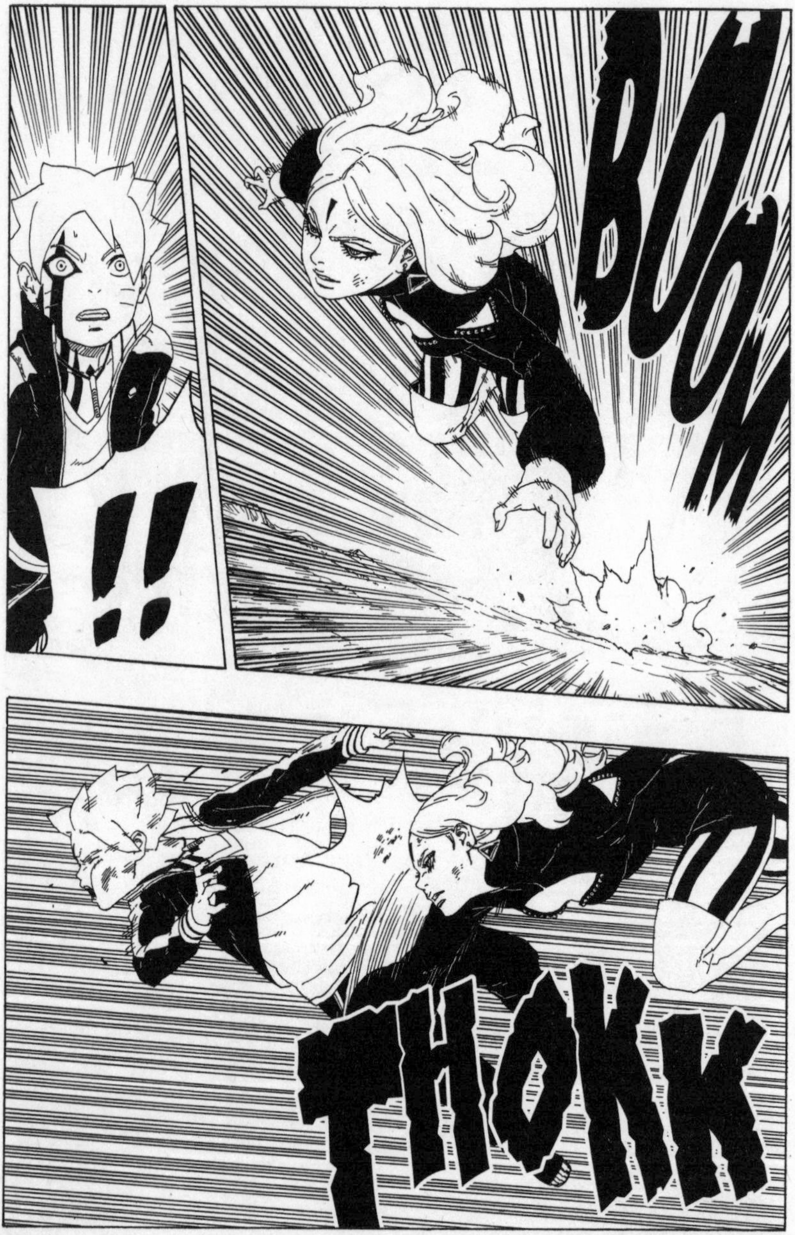
BOOM
!!
THOKK

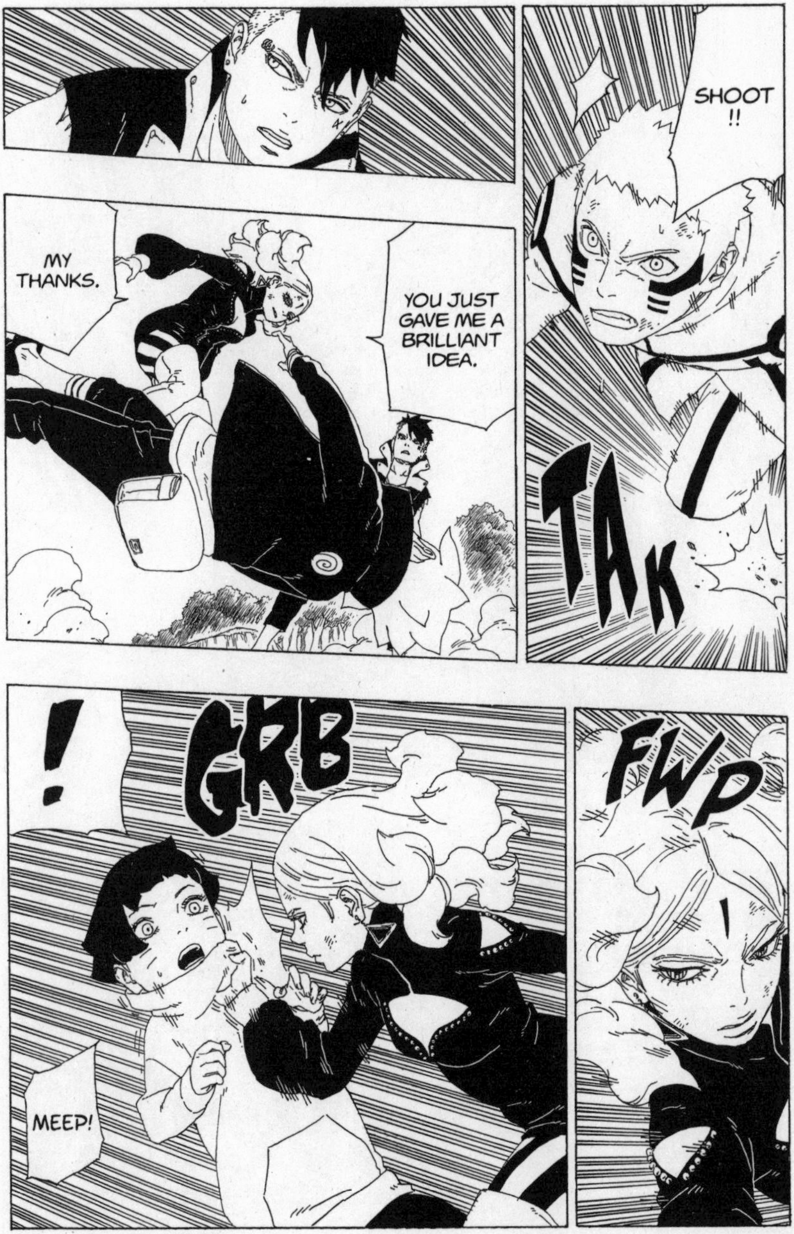

SHOOT
!!
TAK
MY THANKS.
YOU JUST GAVE ME A BRILLIANT IDEA.
FWD
!
GRB
MEEP!

!!
WHAT ?!
FSH
?!!
HIMA !!

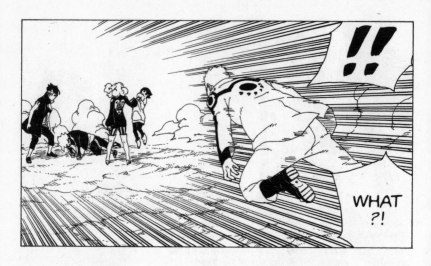

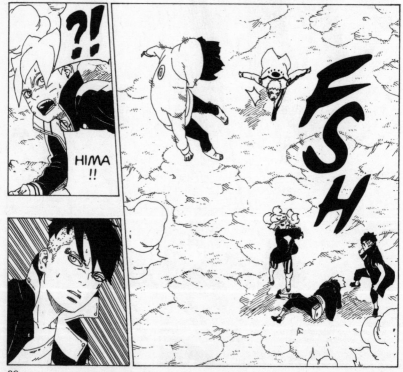

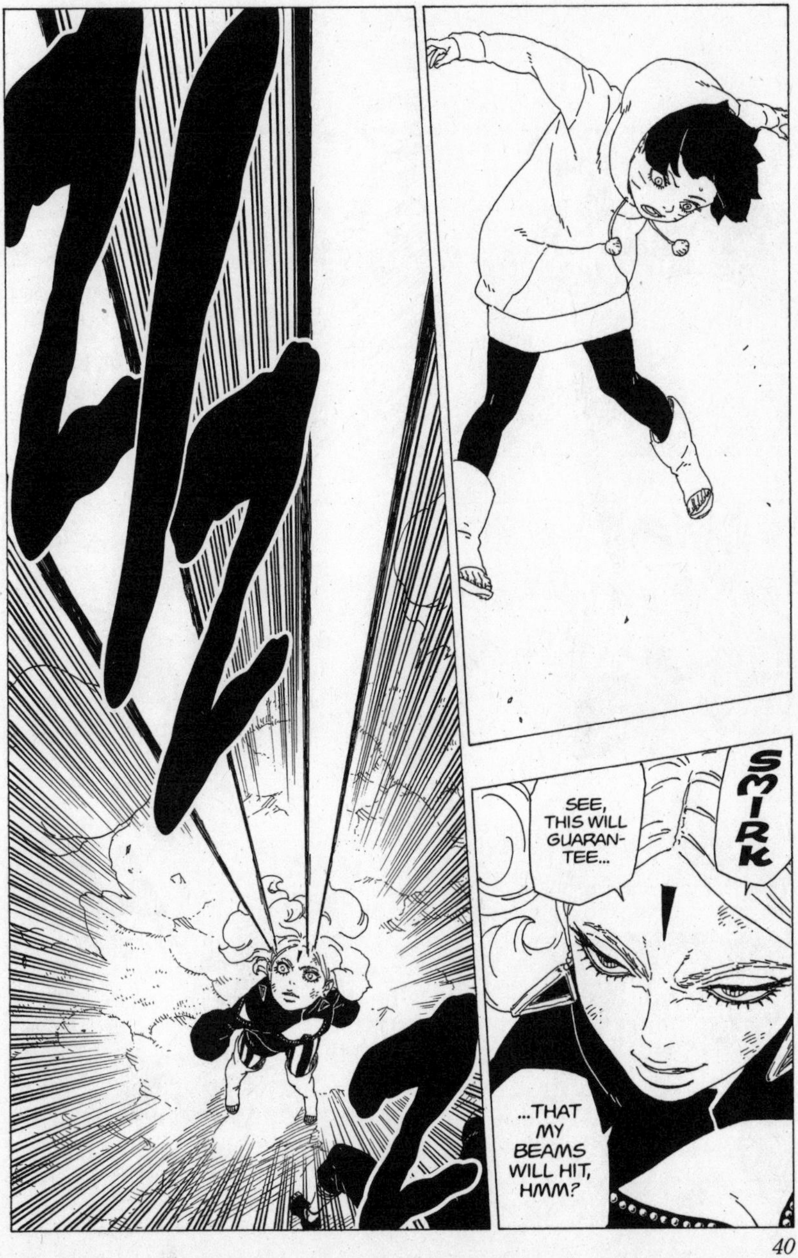
SMIRK
SEE, THIS WILL GUARANTEE...
...THAT MY BEAMS WILL HIT, HMM?

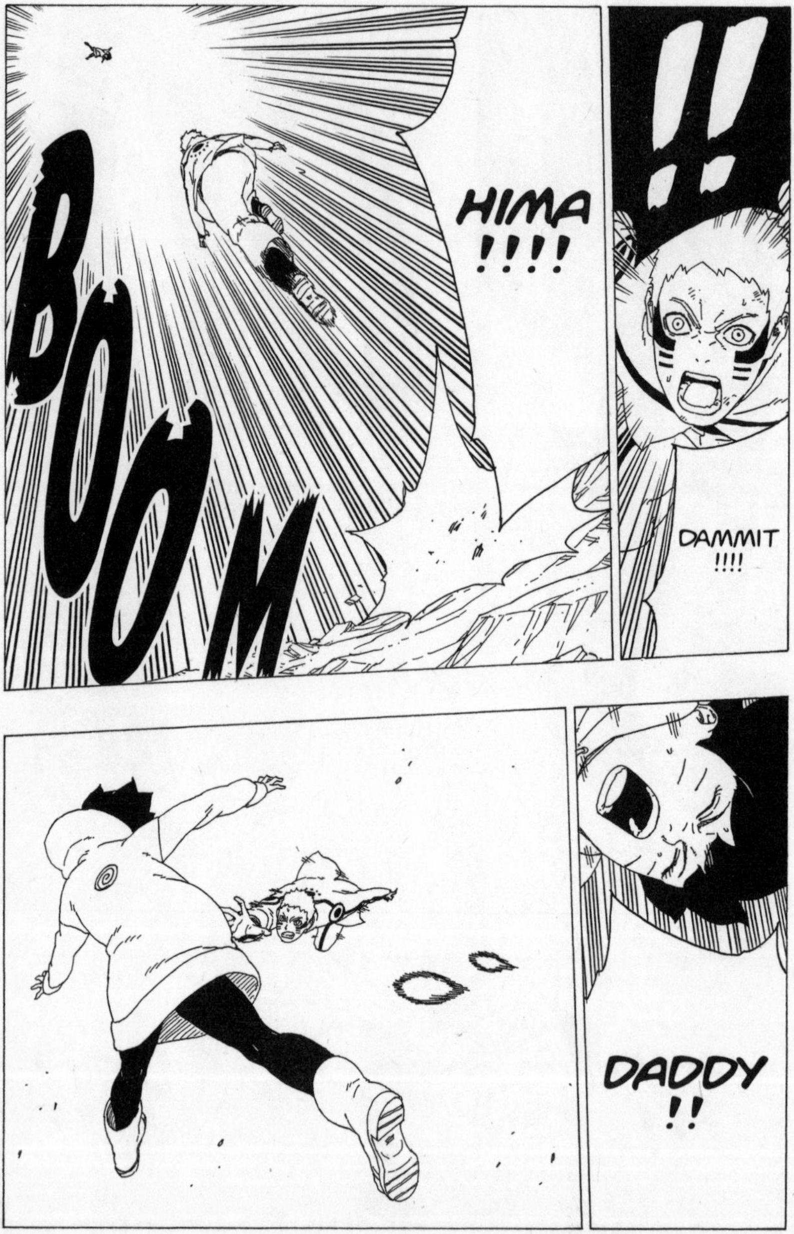
!!
DAMMIT !!!!
HIMA !!!!
BOOM
DADDY !!

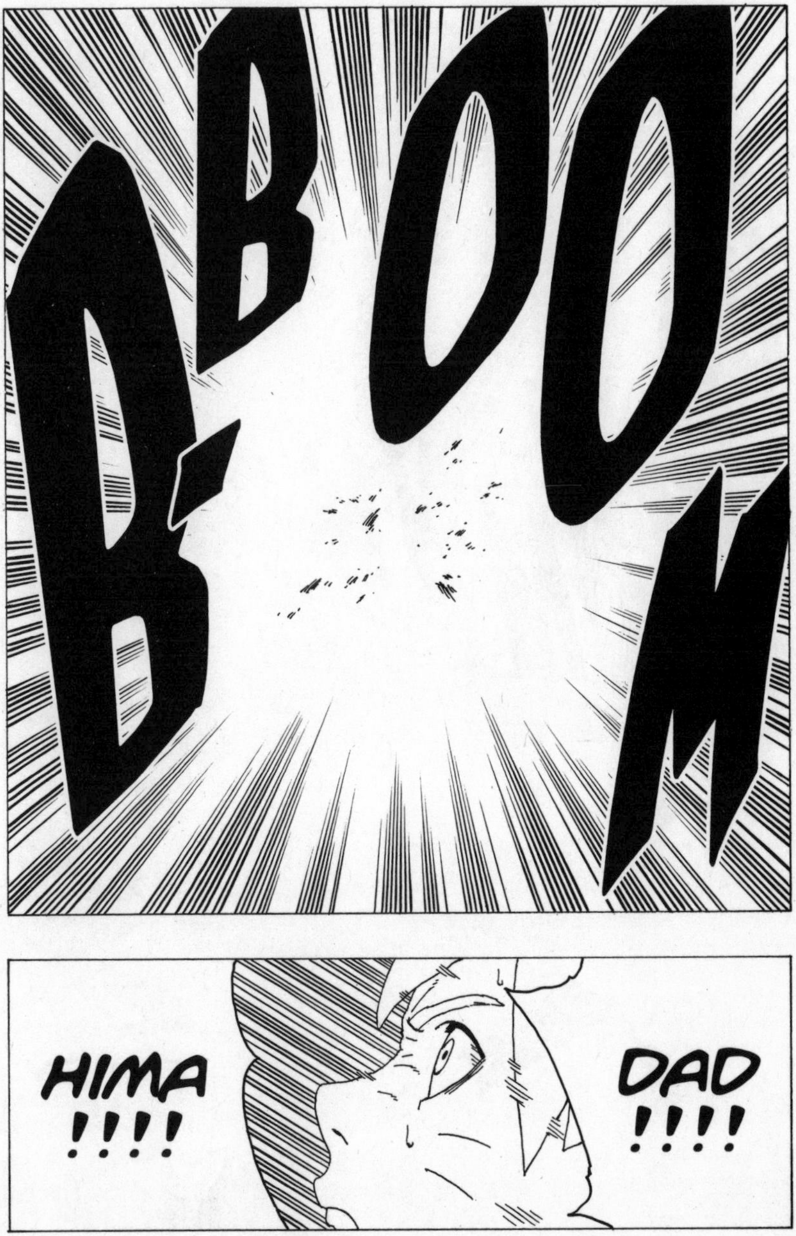
BBOOM
DAD !!!!
HIMA !!!!

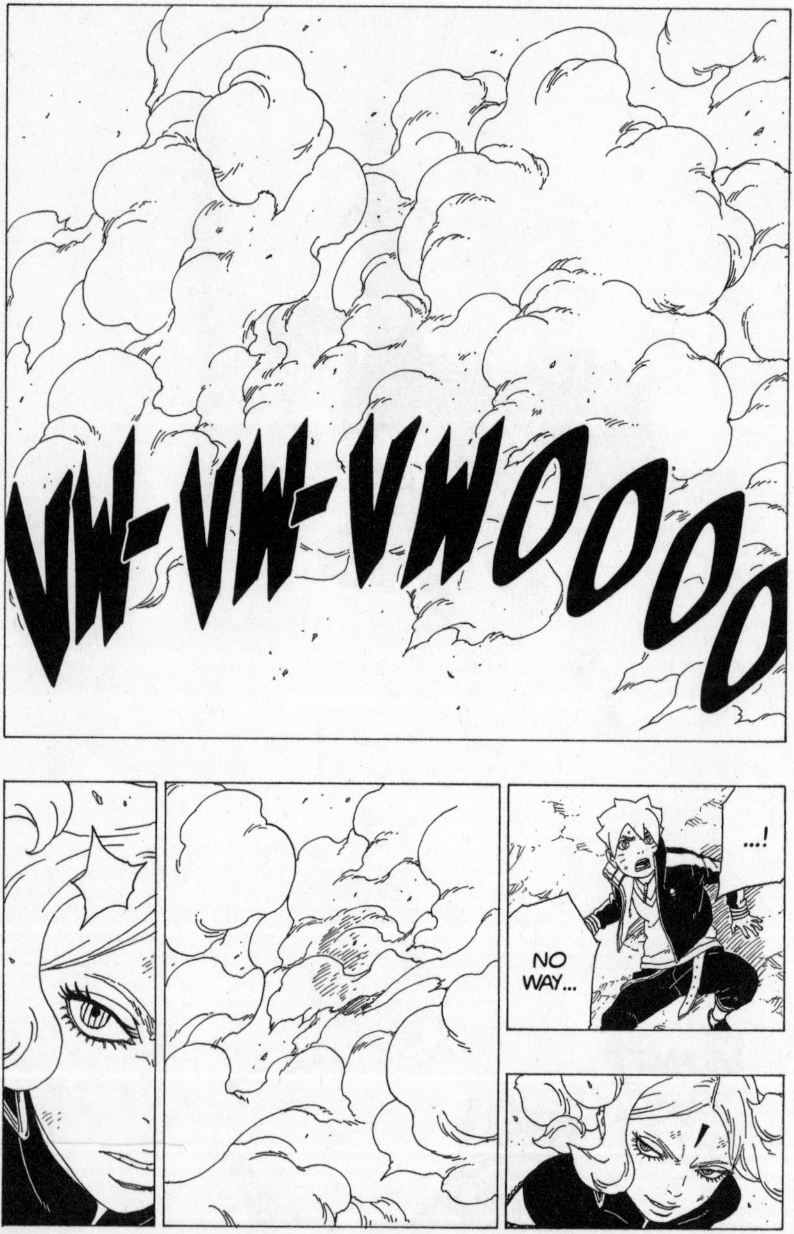
VW-VW-VWOOOO
...!
NO WAY...

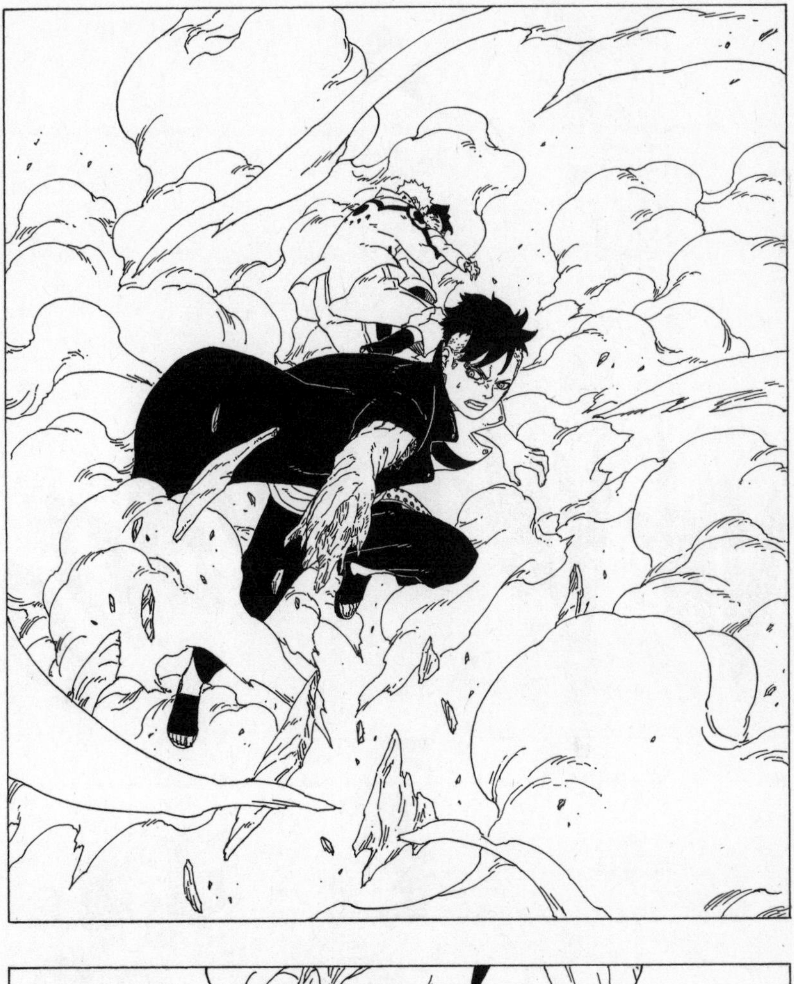

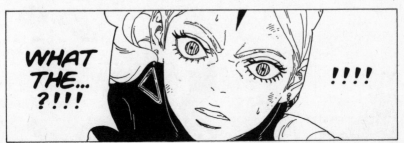

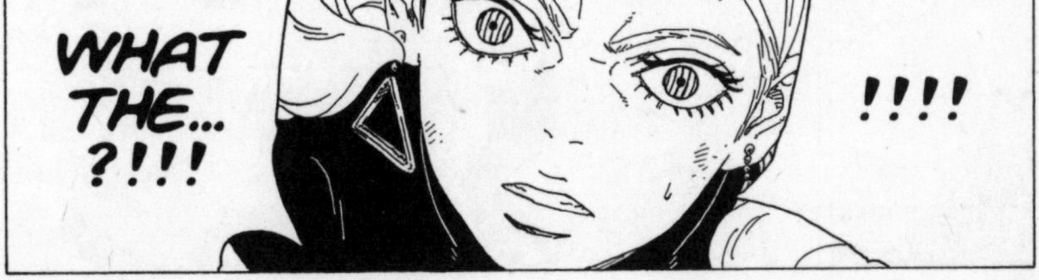
!!!!
WHAT THE...?!!!

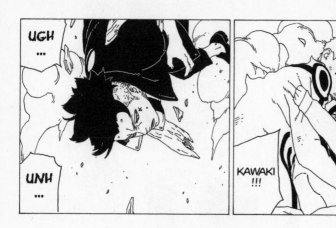

UGH
...

UNH
...

!

KAWAKI
!!!

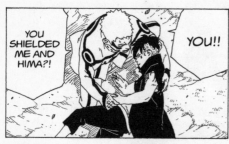

YOU SHIELDED ME AND HIMA?!

YOU!!

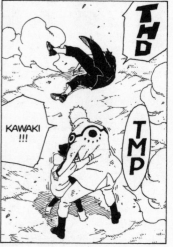

KAWAKI
!!!

THD

TMP

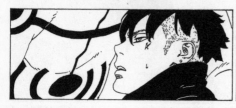

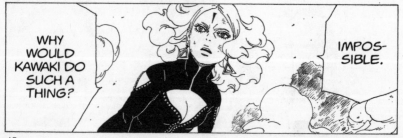

WHY WOULD KAWAKI DO SUCH A THING?

IMPOS-SIBLE.

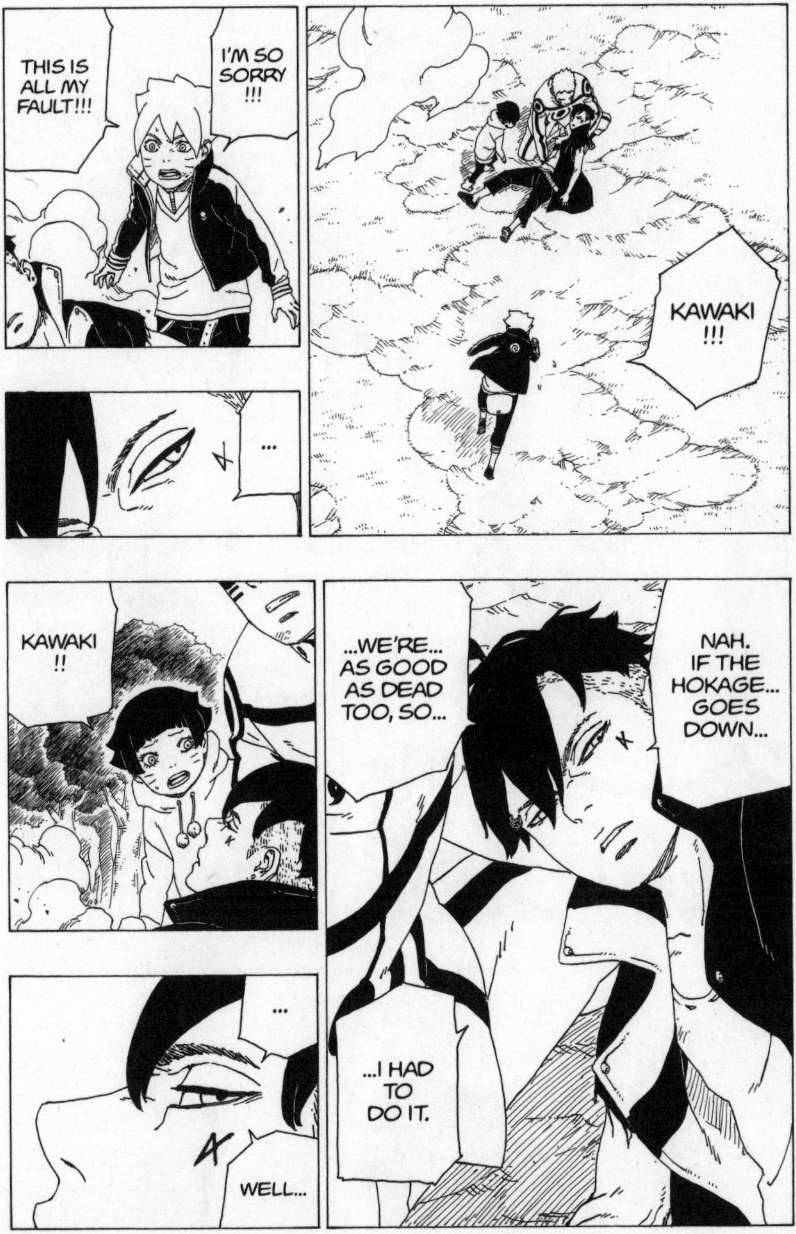
KAWAKI!!!
I'M SO SORRY!!!
THIS IS ALL MY FAULT!!!
...
NAH. IF THE HOKAGE... GOES DOWN...
...WE'RE... AS GOOD AS DEAD TOO, SO...
...I HAD TO DO IT.
KAWAKI!!
...
WELL...

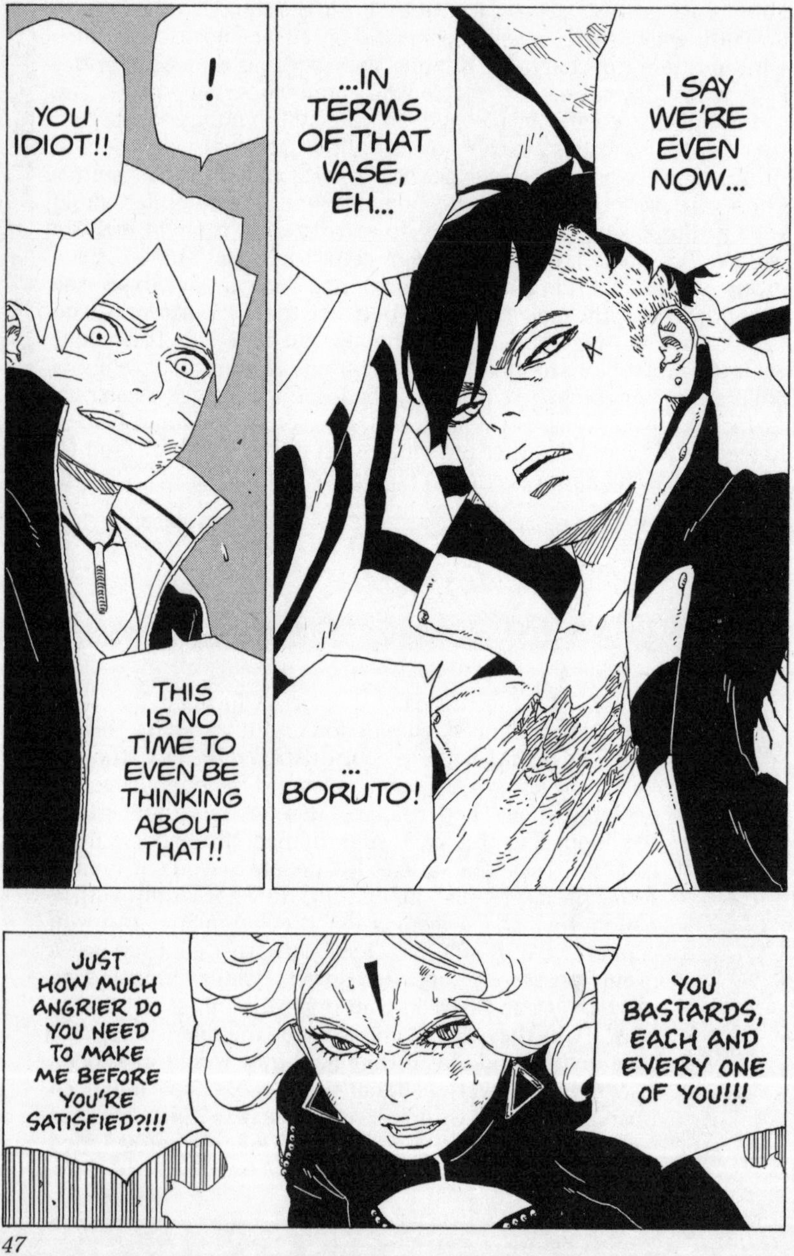
I SAY WE'RE EVEN NOW...
...IN TERMS OF THAT VASE, EH...
... BORUTO!
!
YOU IDIOT!!
THIS IS NO TIME TO EVEN BE THINKING ABOUT THAT!!
YOU BASTARDS, EACH AND EVERY ONE OF YOU!!!
JUST HOW MUCH ANGRIER DO YOU NEED TO MAKE ME BEFORE YOU'RE SATISFIED?!!!

Shinobi Hiden Column 1: Shinobi Society

Shinobi are intrinsically social entities. From the time that the Sage of Six Paths established Ninshu, the Shinobi Creed, and positioned those with aptitude for chakra as shinobi, they became the social entity known as ninja, not merely people who employ unusual powers. The same applies to rogue ninja. Rogue ninja are still shinobi, and whether they left their villages amicably or as fugitives, they are members of shinobi society nonetheless, just with "rogue" added to their status. There are various reasons why superhuman shinobi must mold society, but it fundamentally boils down to money. It might feel like we are discussing a somewhat disgraceful topic, but shinobi are a group of realists. Pride means nothing if one does not live to see the next day. That is the main difference between them and samurai, who faded away into legend. So why is money needed? This is because aside from a few extremely rare exceptions, superhuman shinobi abilities are unnecessary to daily life. Shadow doppelgangers can rival a whole army, and Fire Style jutsu are superior to bows and blades, indeed. However, will either put clothes on one's back? Put food on the table? Or put a roof over one's children's heads? Nay.

Shinobi skills intrinsically do not lie in manufacturing. Thus, shinobi need connections with common folk in order to maintain their own existence. In fact, the old Village of Konoha, which was impoverished and merely depleted their child soldiers, demonstrated something too appalling to call superhuman livelihood. It is commonly said that it takes 100 people to feed one human who specializes just in fighting. In short, only with a nation that has a population of one million can you support 10,000 shinobi. Deeply aware that they are a group possessing unusual powers, shinobi elected to position themselves within mainstream society. The reason why they did not choose to be the rulers is because they understood that if they had, they would have been rejected by an overwhelming majority of people and been unable to survive. By grabbing the niche within society of "professionals hired using money," shinobi safeguarded their existence.

Text: Ukyo Kodachi

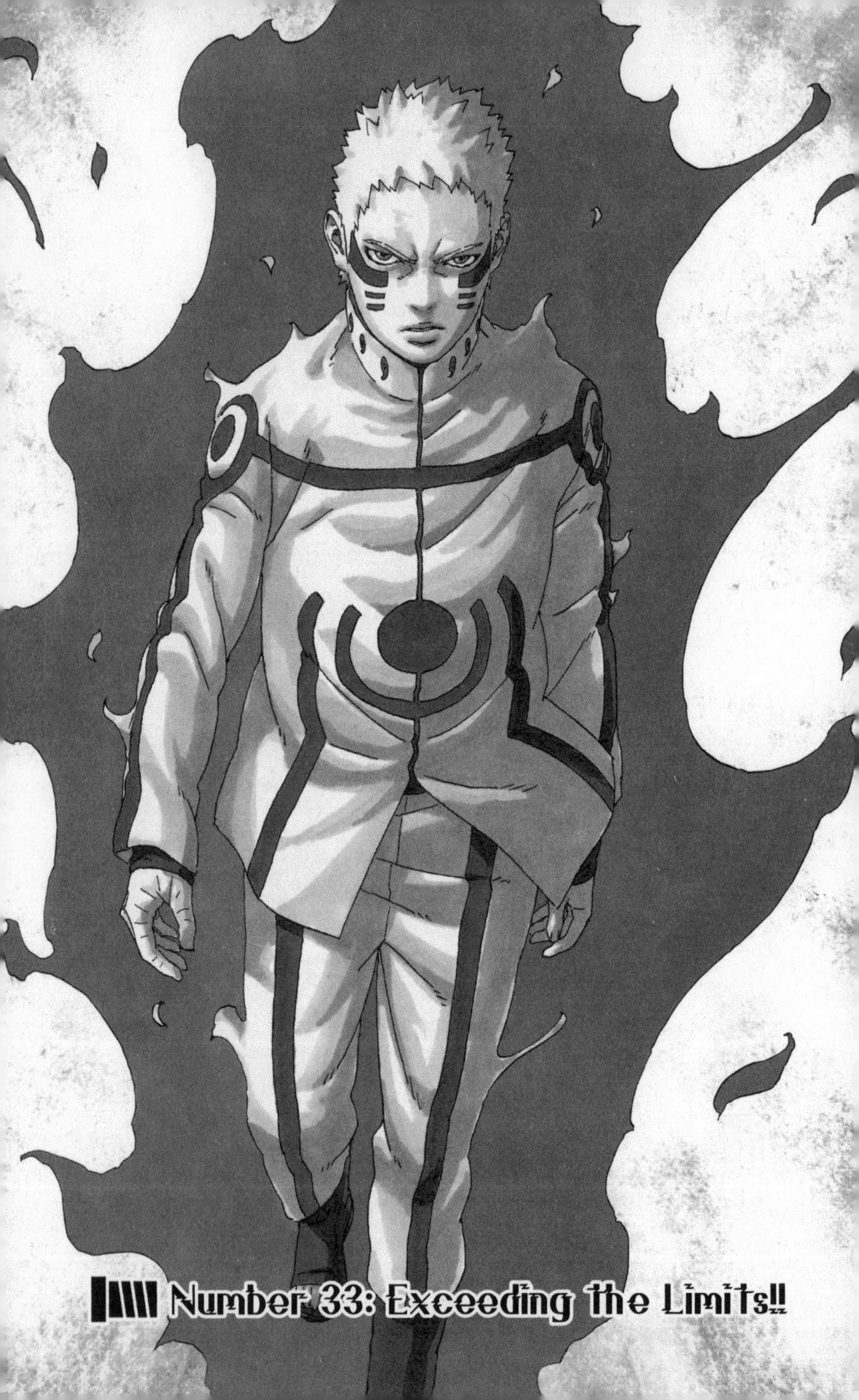

Number 33: Exceeding the Limits!!

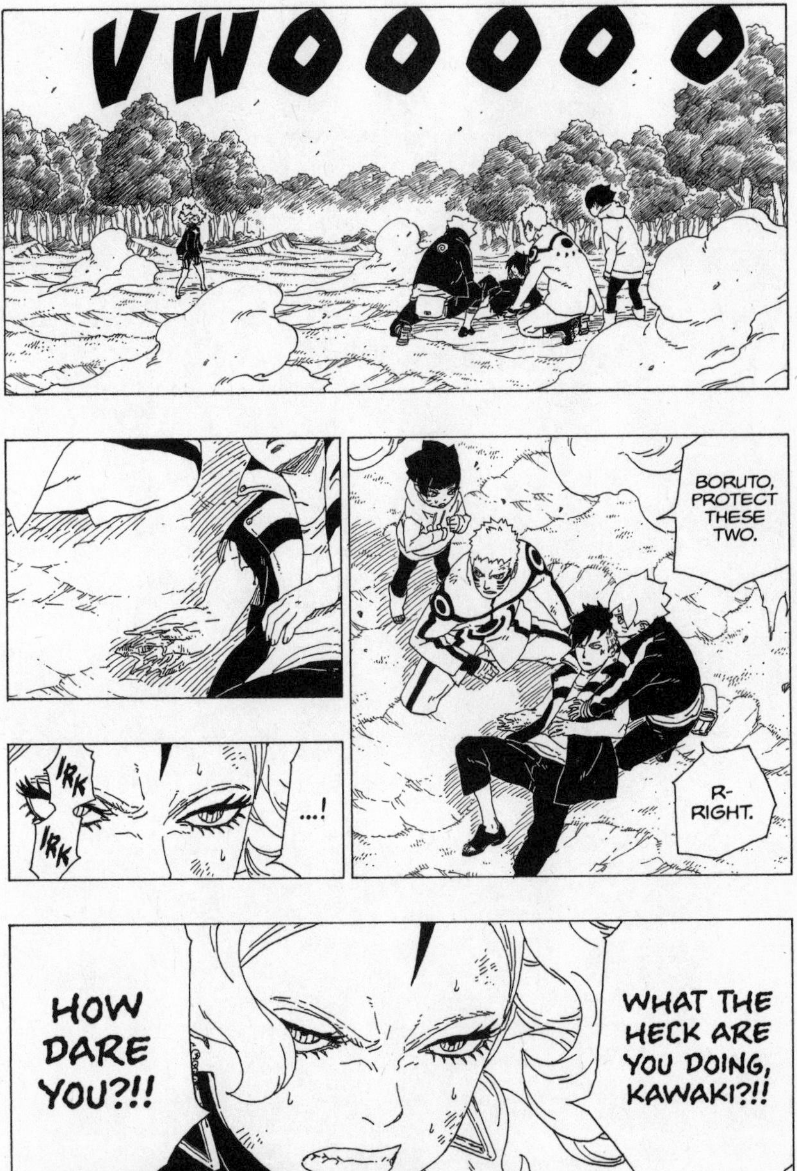
VWOOOOO
BORUTO, PROTECT THESE TWO.
R-RIGHT.
...!
IRK IRK
WHAT THE HECK ARE YOU DOING, KAWAKI?!!
HOW DARE YOU?!!

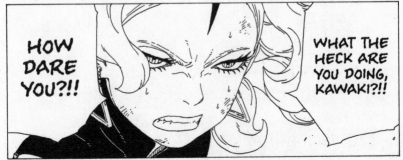

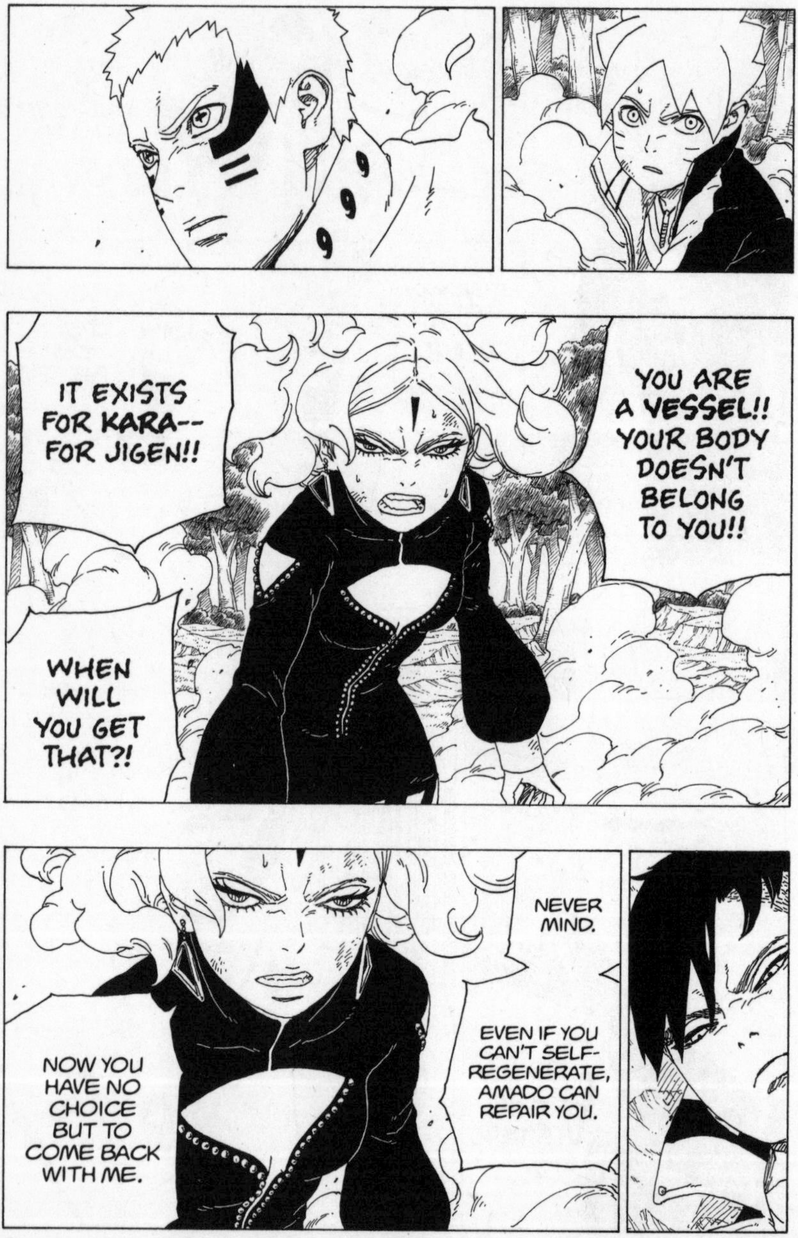
YOU ARE A VESSEL!! YOUR BODY DOESN'T BELONG TO YOU!!
IT EXISTS FOR KARA-- FOR JIGEN!!
WHEN WILL YOU GET THAT?!
NEVER MIND.
EVEN IF YOU CAN'T SELF-REGENERATE, AMADO CAN REPAIR YOU.
NOW YOU HAVE NO CHOICE BUT TO COME BACK WITH ME.

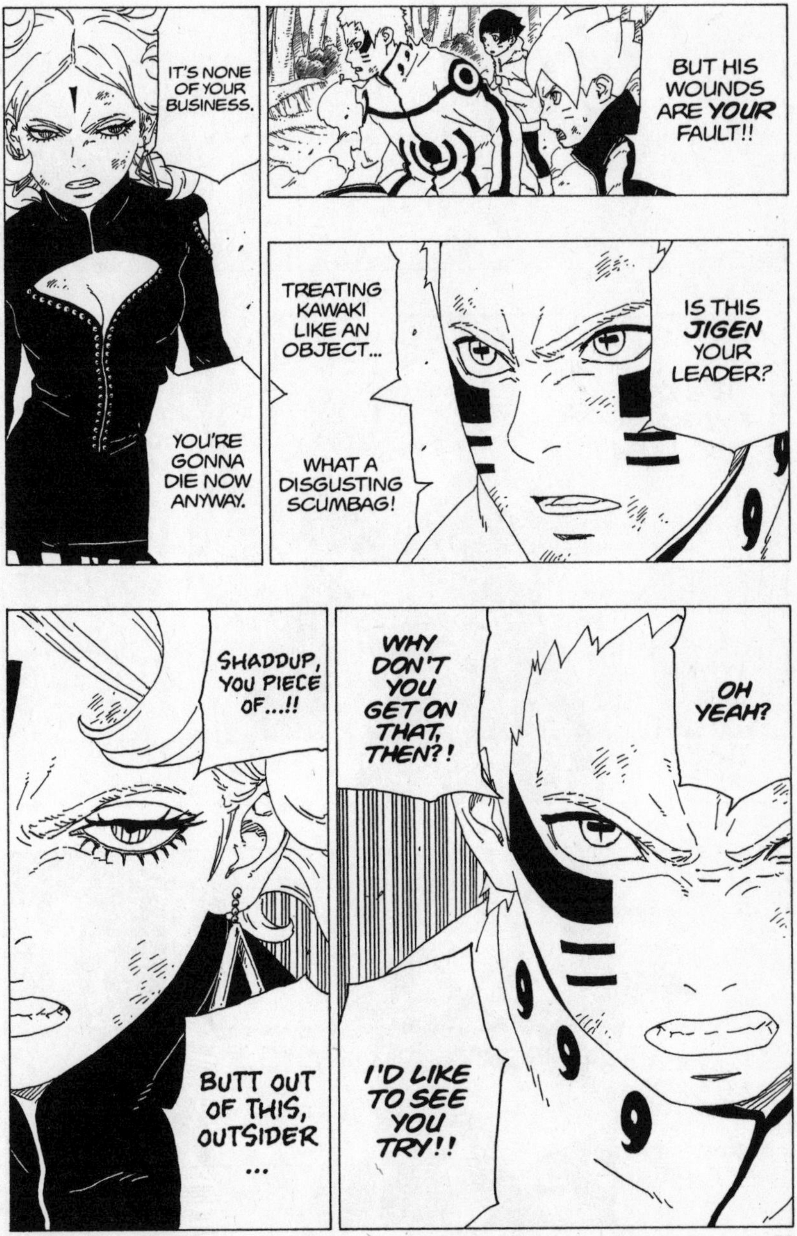
BUT HIS WOUNDS ARE YOUR FAULT!!
IS THIS JIGEN YOUR LEADER?
TREATING KAWAKI LIKE AN OBJECT...
WHAT A DISGUSTING SCUMBAG!
IT'S NONE OF YOUR BUSINESS.
YOU'RE GONNA DIE NOW ANYWAY.
OH YEAH?
WHY DON'T YOU GET ON THAT, THEN?!
I'D LIKE TO SEE YOU TRY!!
SHADDUP, YOU PIECE OF...!!
BUTT OUT OF THIS, OUTSIDER ...

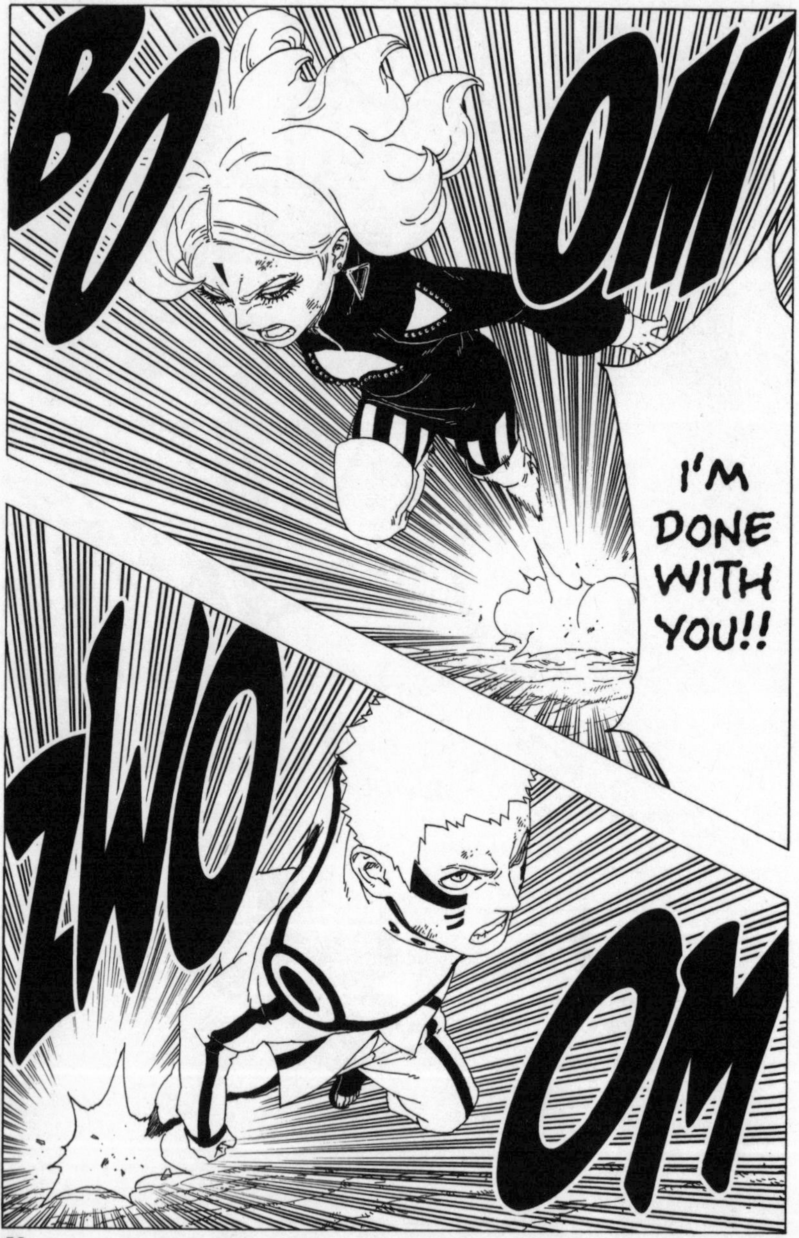
BOOM
I'M DONE WITH YOU!!
ZWOOM

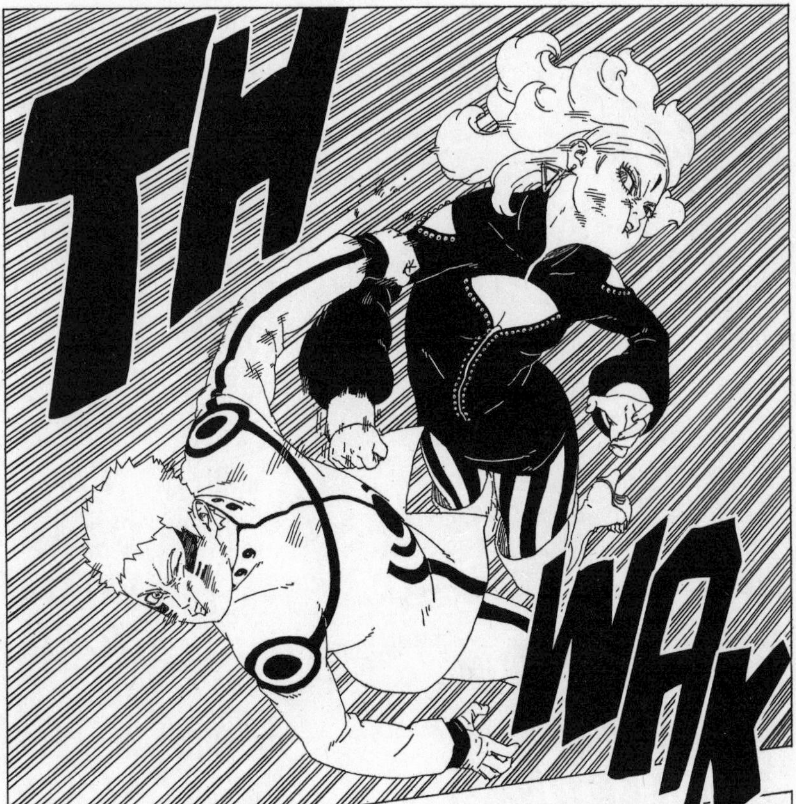
TH
WAK
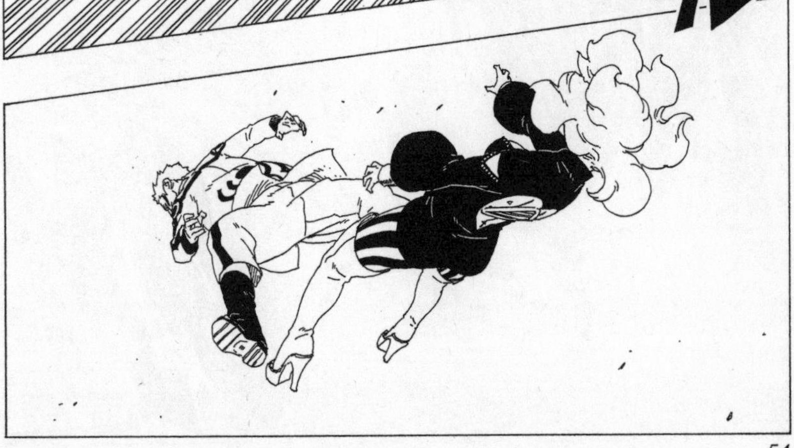

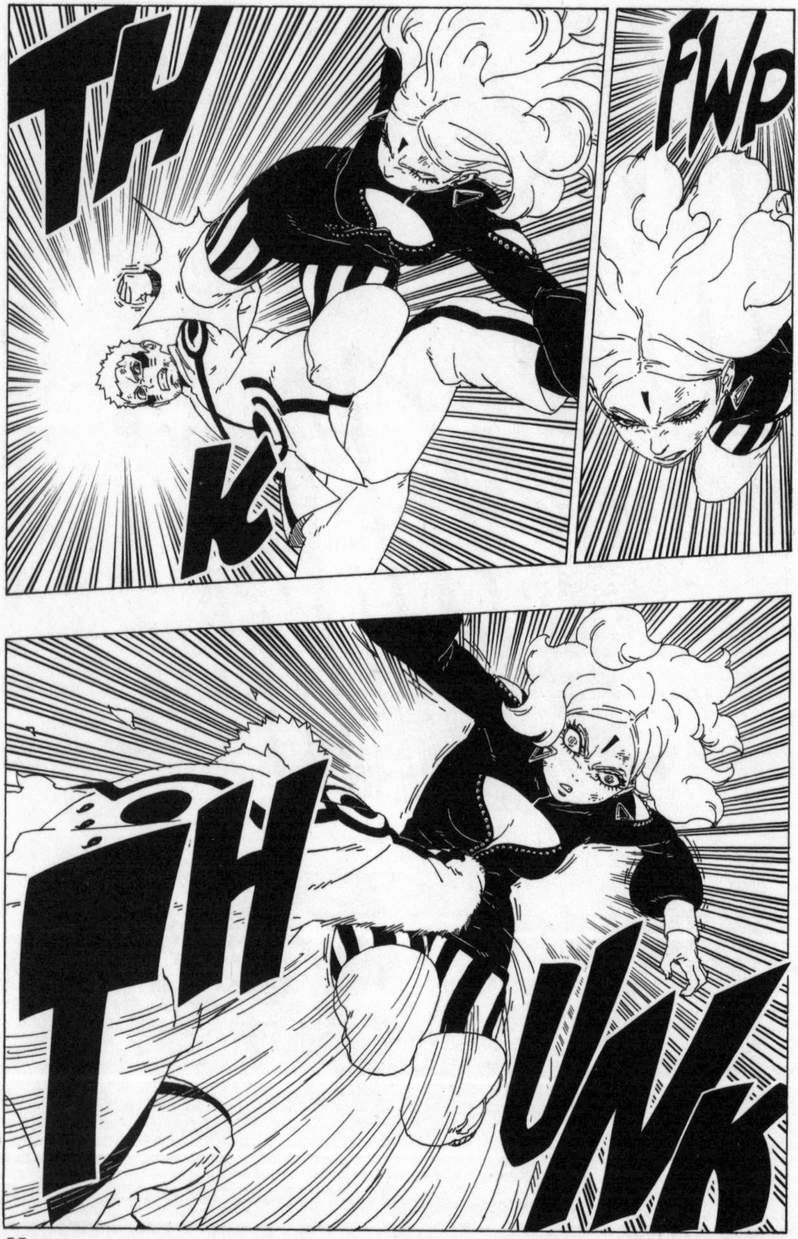
FWP
THK
THUNK

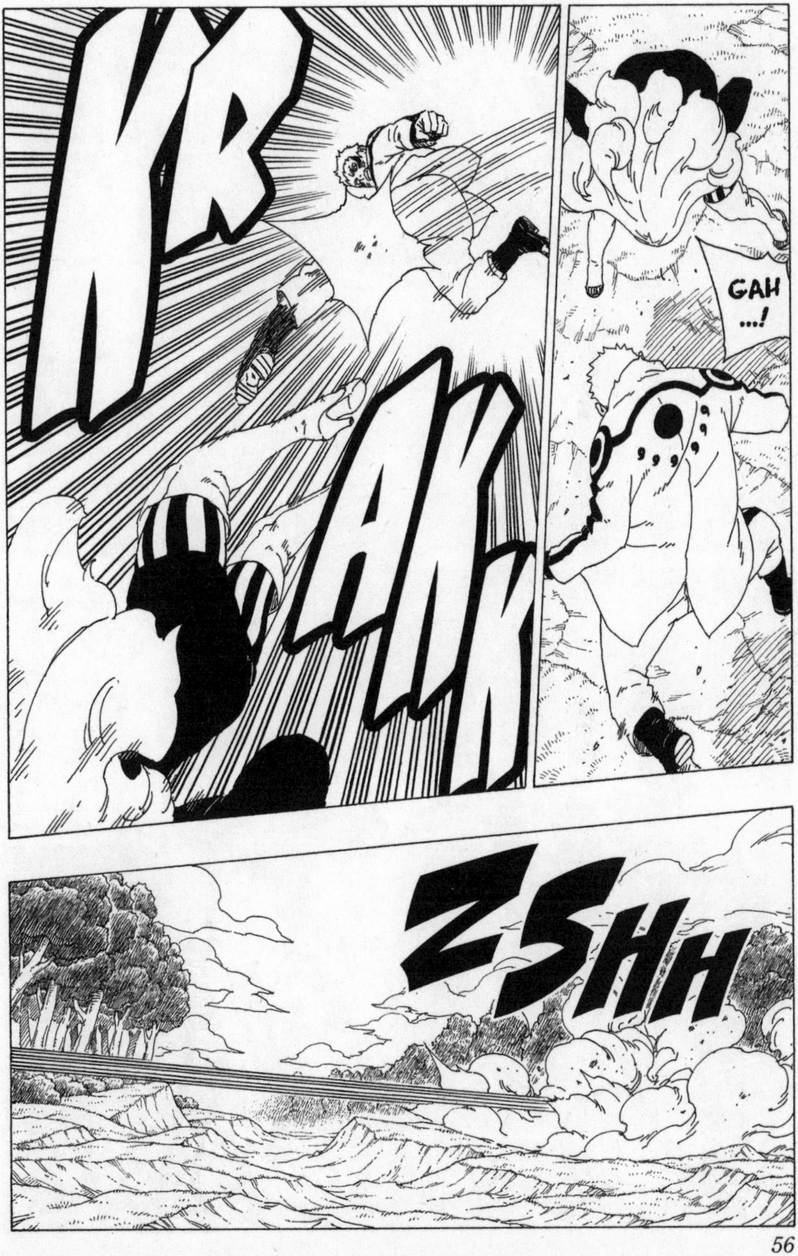
GAH ...!
KRAAK
ZSHH

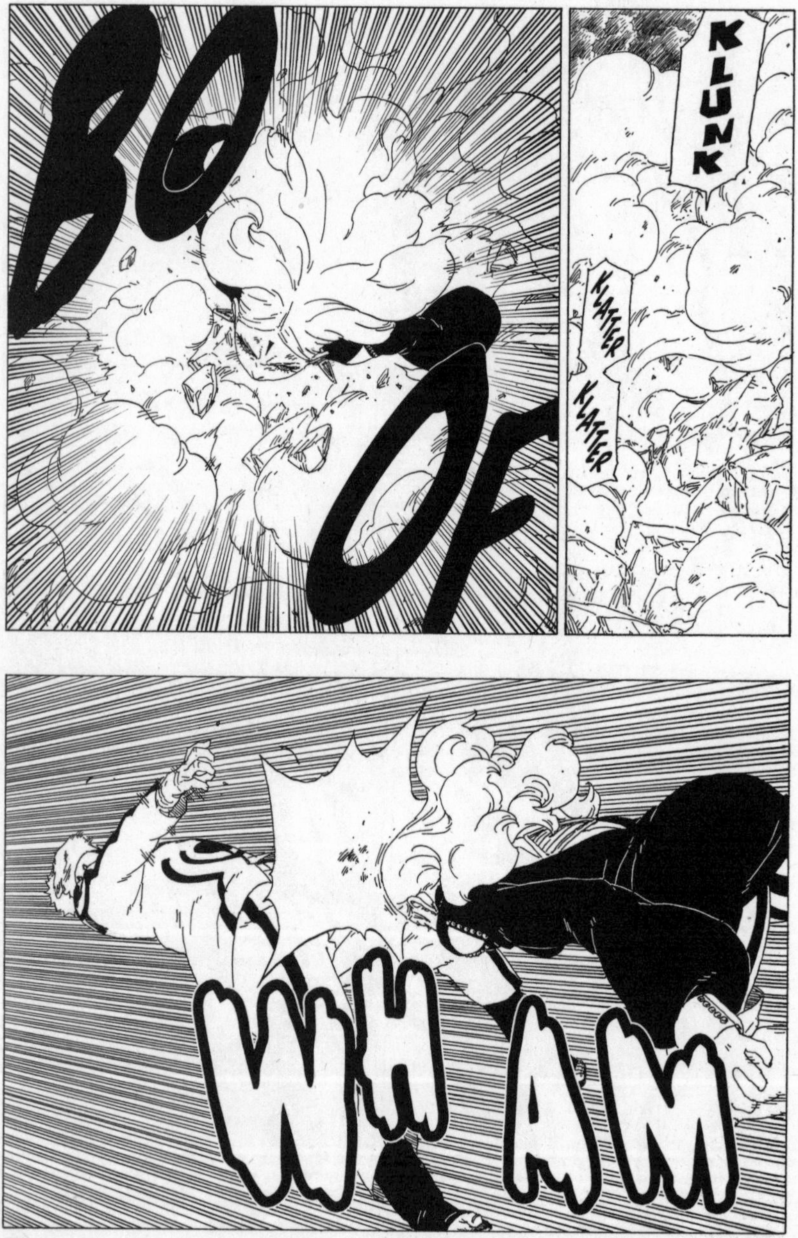
KLUNK
KLATTER
KLATTER
BOOF
WHAM

ZWISH
VSH
BAM
WHAK

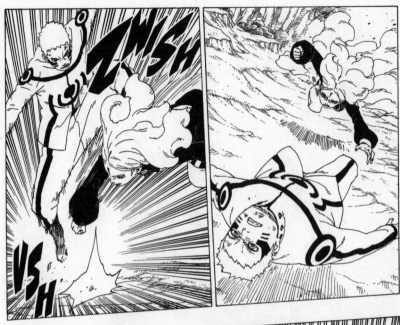

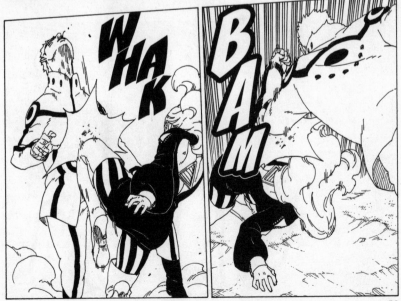

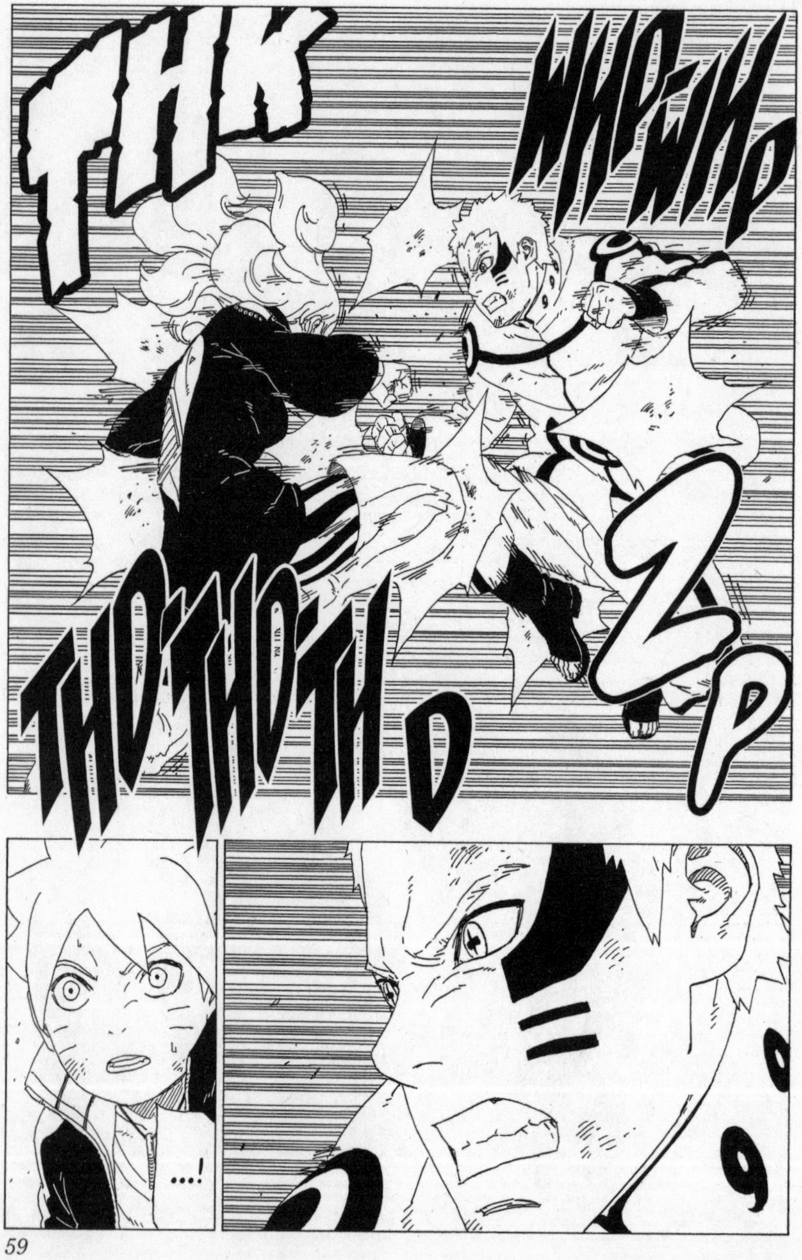
WHP-WHP
THK
ZIP
THD-THD-THD
...!

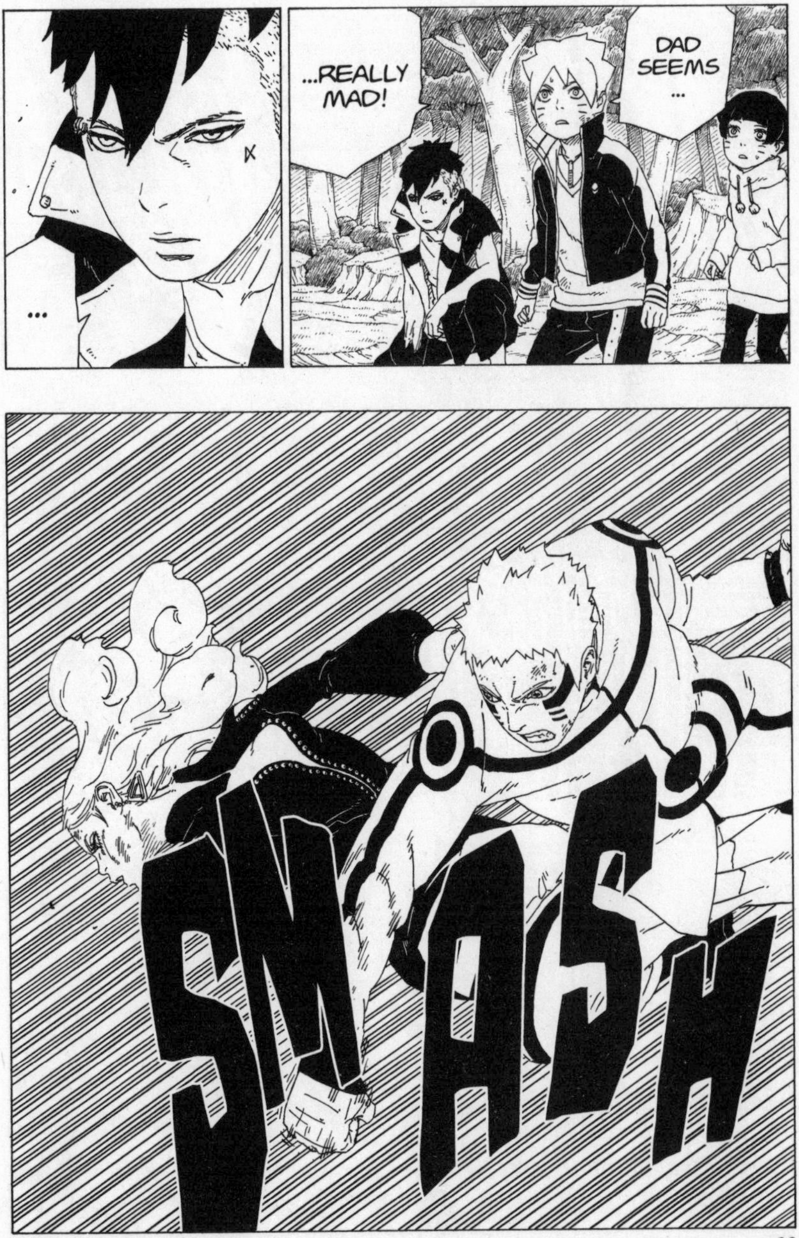
DAD SEEMS ...
...REALLY MAD!
...
SMASH

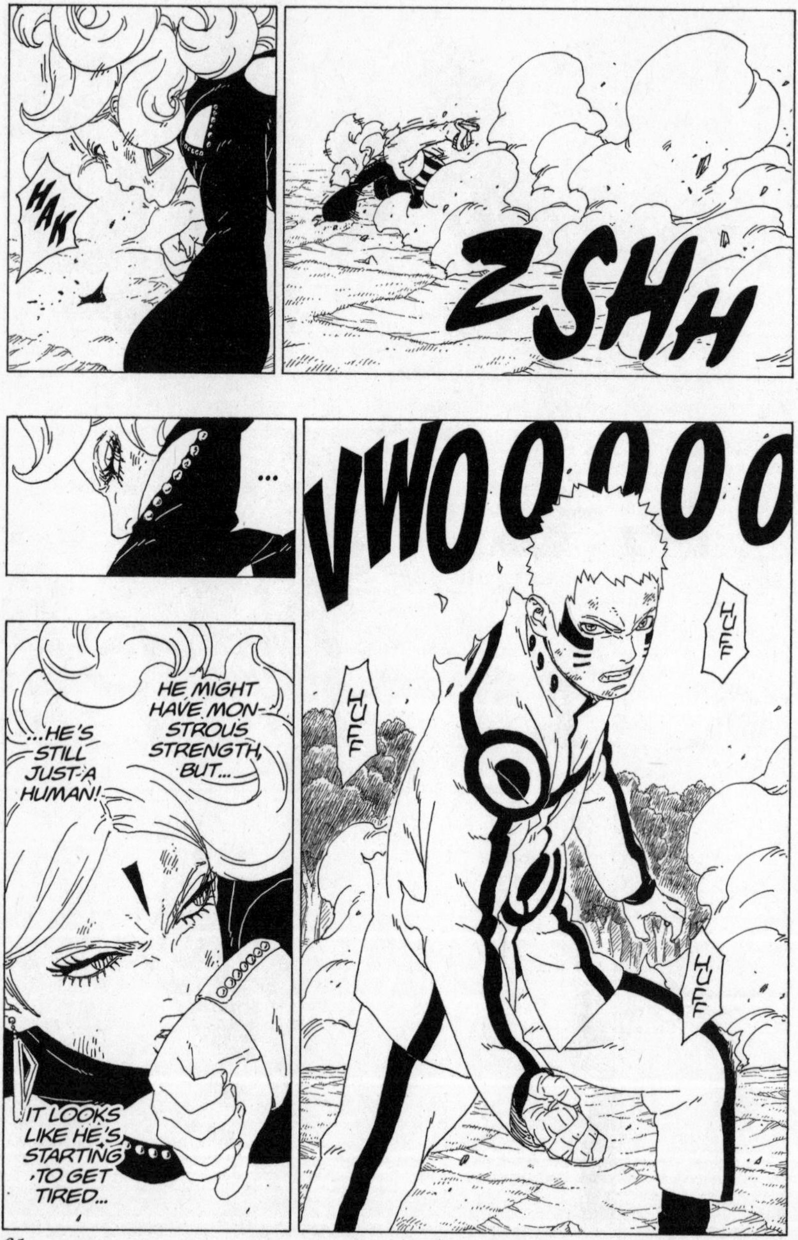
ZSHH
HAK
VWOOOOOO
HUFF
HUFF
HUFF
...
HE MIGHT HAVE MON-STROUS STRENGTH, BUT...
...HE'S STILL JUST A HUMAN!
IT LOOKS LIKE HE'S STARTING TO GET TIRED...

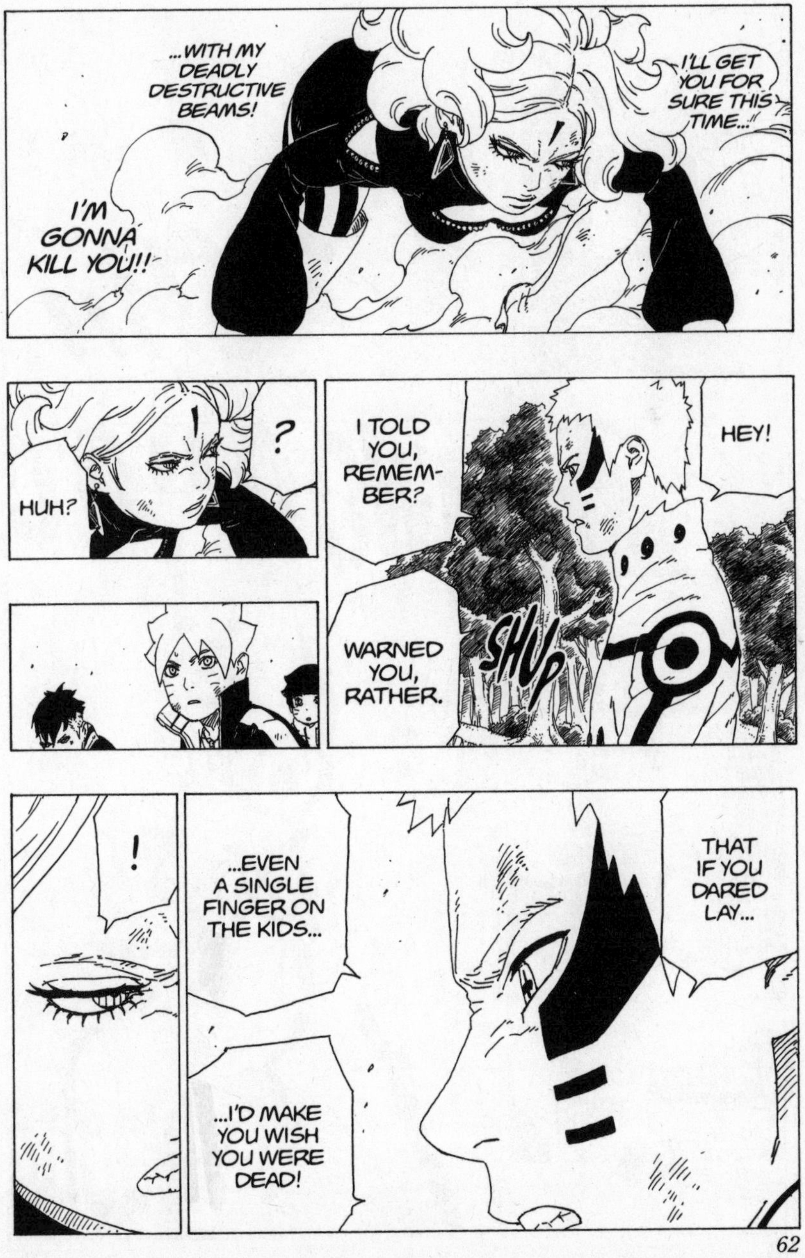
I'LL GET YOU FOR SURE THIS TIME...!
...WITH MY DEADLY DESTRUCTIVE BEAMS!
I'M GONNA KILL YOU!!
HEY!
I TOLD YOU, REMEMBER?
SHUP
WARNED YOU, RATHER.
?
HUH?
THAT IF YOU DARED LAY...
...EVEN A SINGLE FINGER ON THE KIDS...
...I'D MAKE YOU WISH YOU WERE DEAD!
!

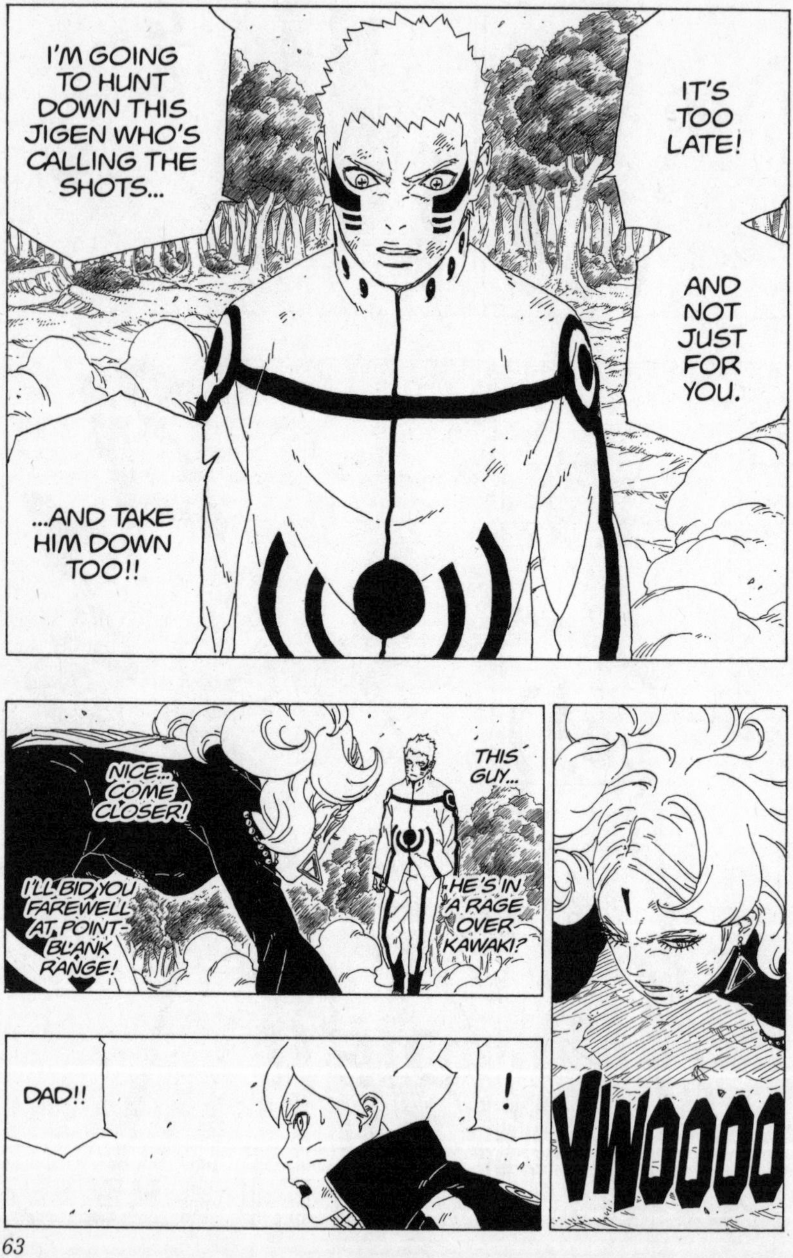
IT'S TOO LATE!
AND NOT JUST FOR YOU.
I'M GOING TO HUNT DOWN THIS JIGEN WHO'S CALLING THE SHOTS...
...AND TAKE HIM DOWN TOO!!
VWOOOO
THIS GUY...
HE'S IN A RAGE OVER KAWAKI?
NICE... COME CLOSER!
I'LL BID YOU FAREWELL AT POINT-BLANK RANGE!
!
DAD!!

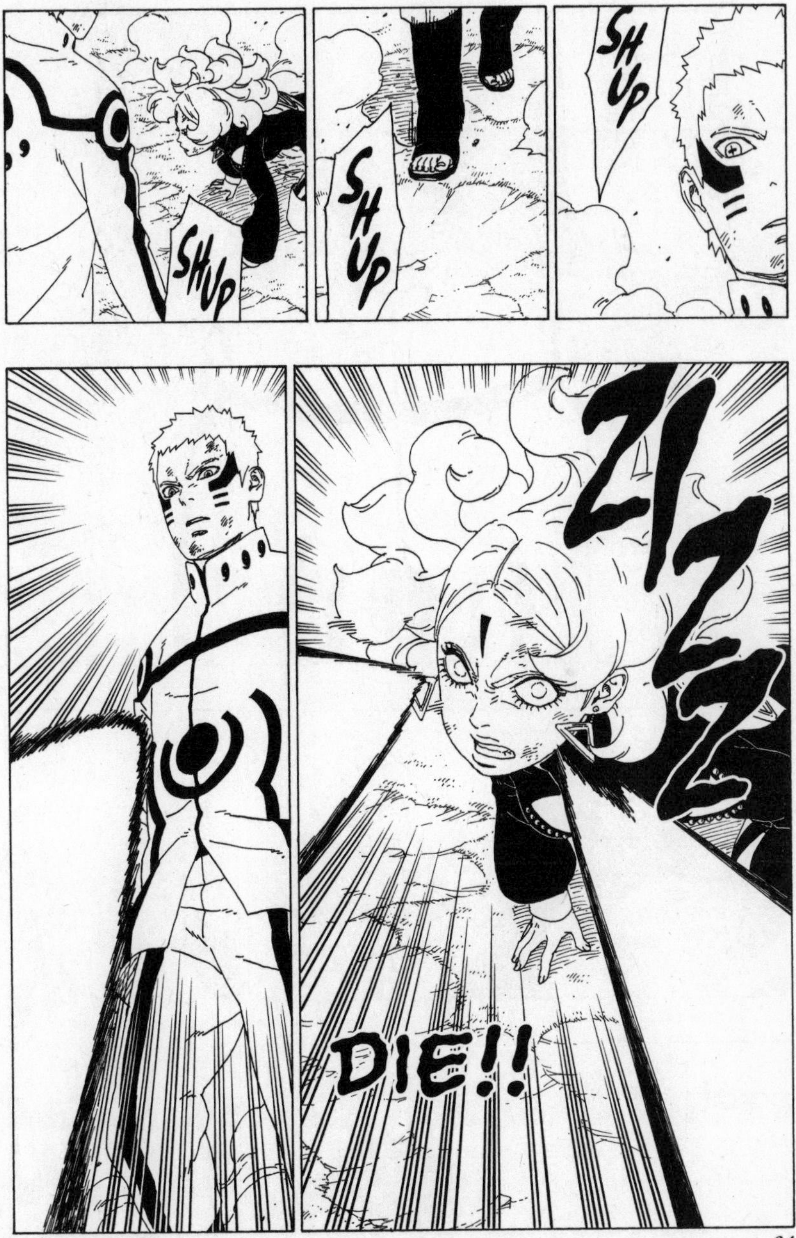
SHUP
SHUP
SHUP
DIE!!

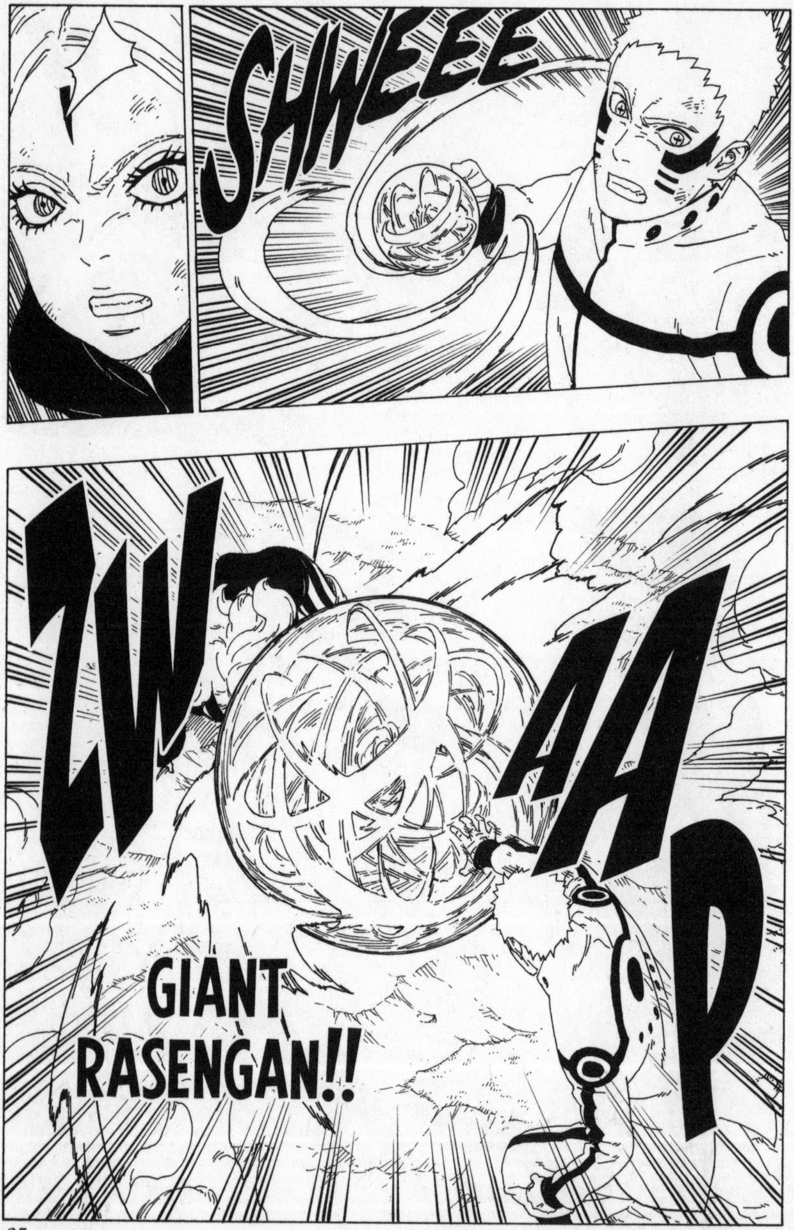
SHWEEE
ZWAAP
GIANT RASENGAN!!

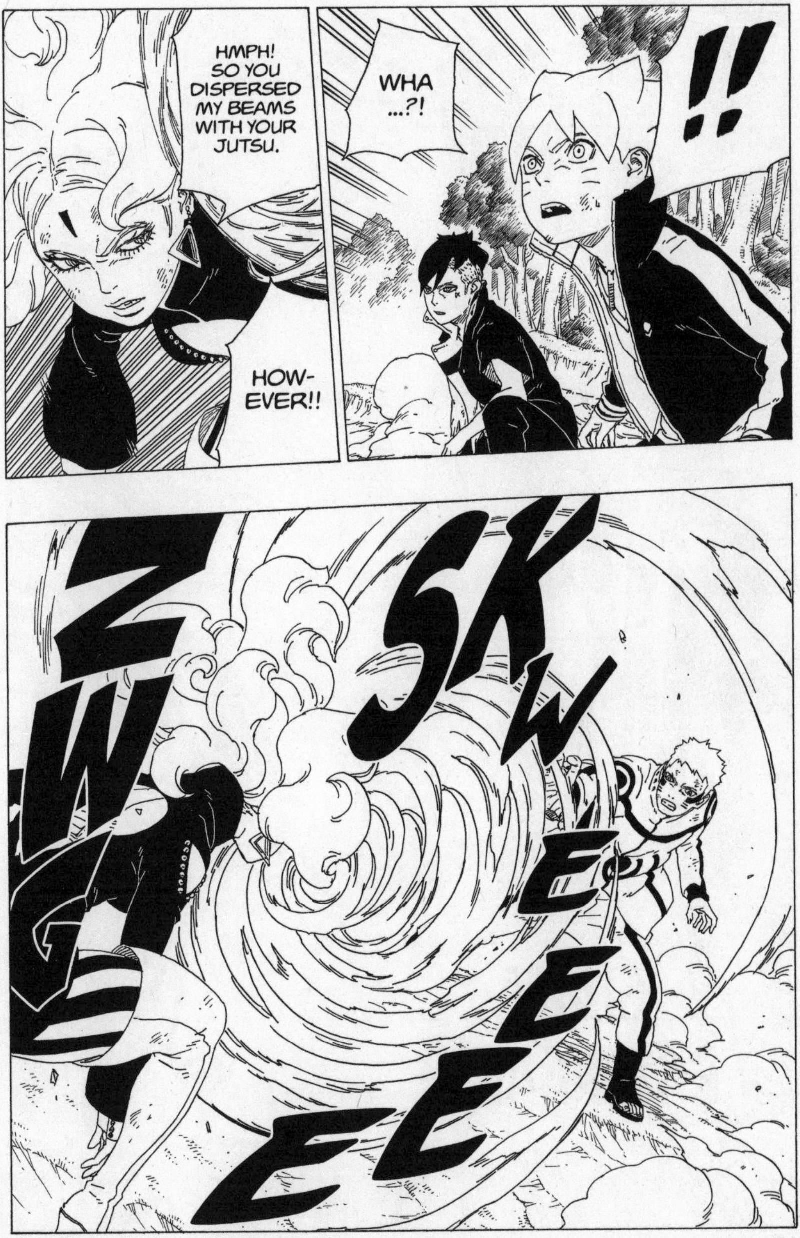

WHA ...?!
!!
HMPH! SO YOU DISPERSED MY BEAMS WITH YOUR JUTSU.
HOW-EVER!!
SKWEEEEE
ZWG

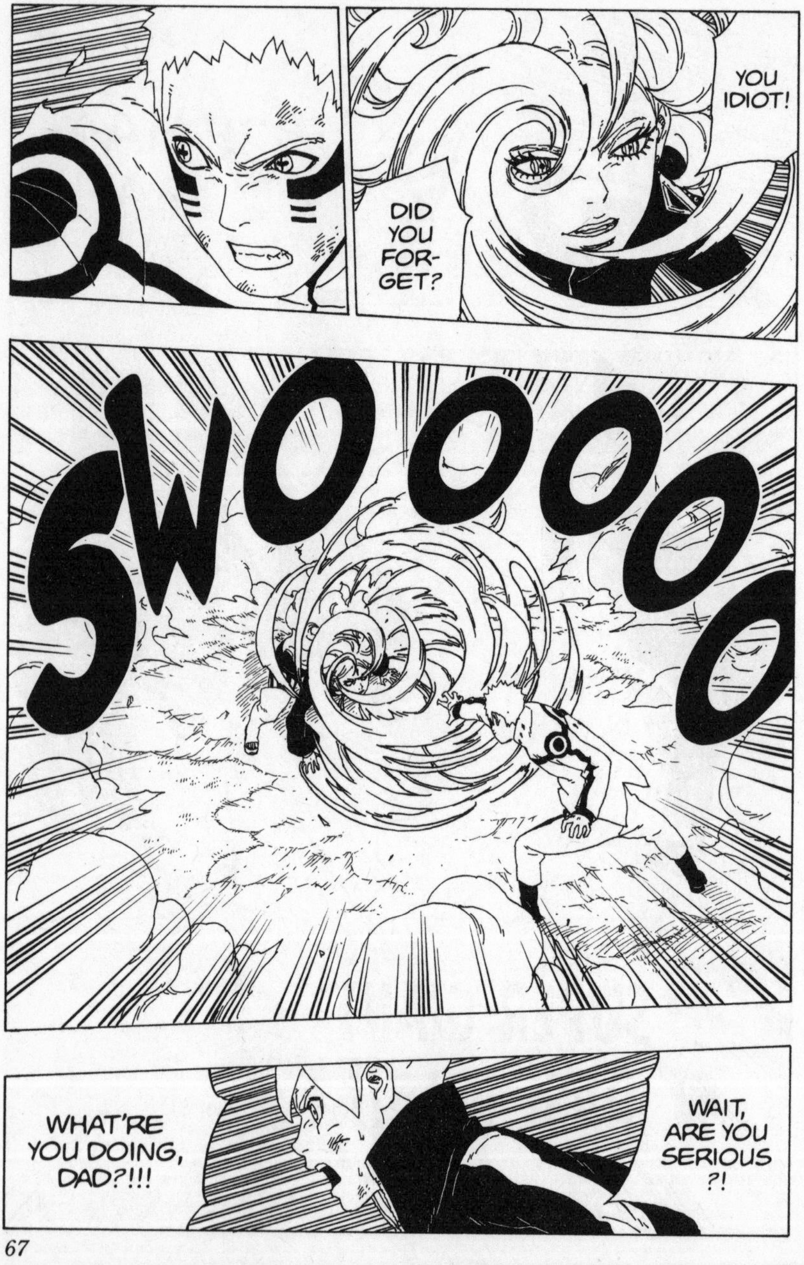
YOU IDIOT!
DID YOU FOR-GET?
SWOOOOO
WAIT, ARE YOU SERIOUS ?!
WHAT'RE YOU DOING, DAD?!!!

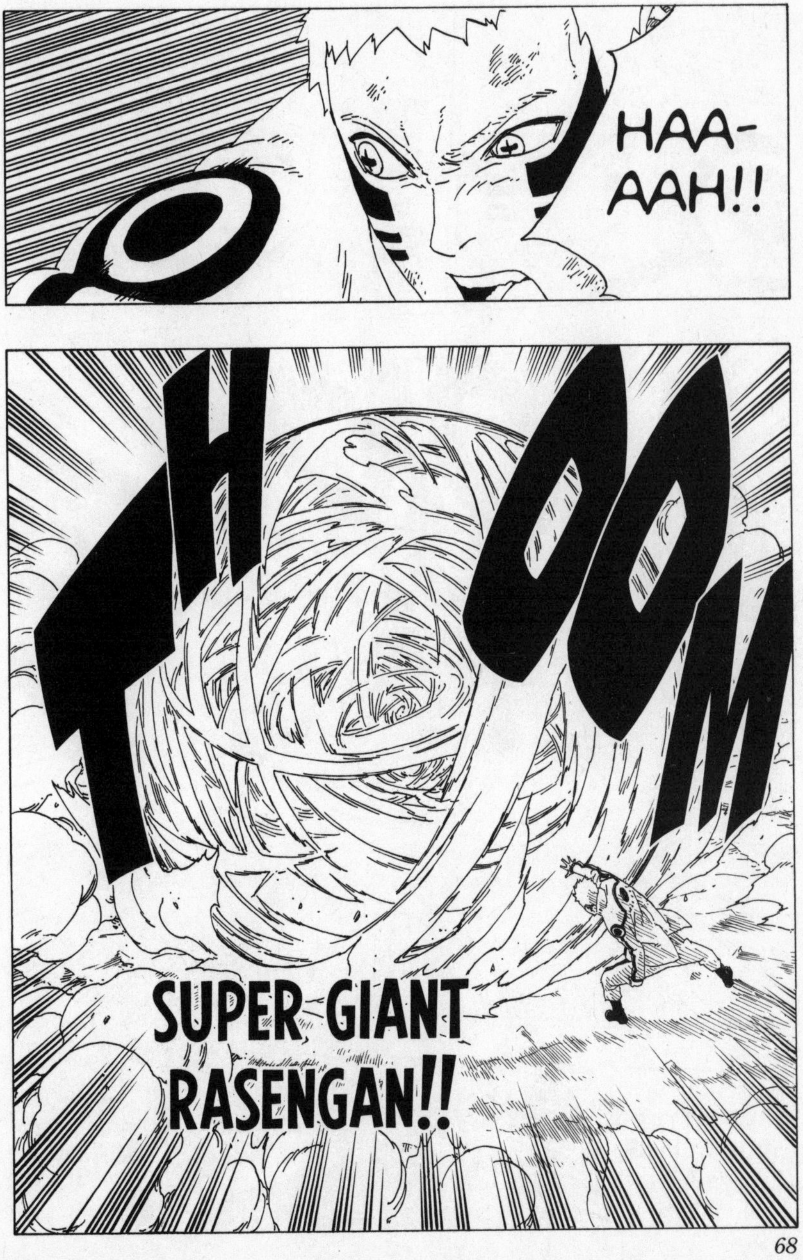
HAA-AAH!!
THOOM
SUPER-GIANT RASENGAN!!

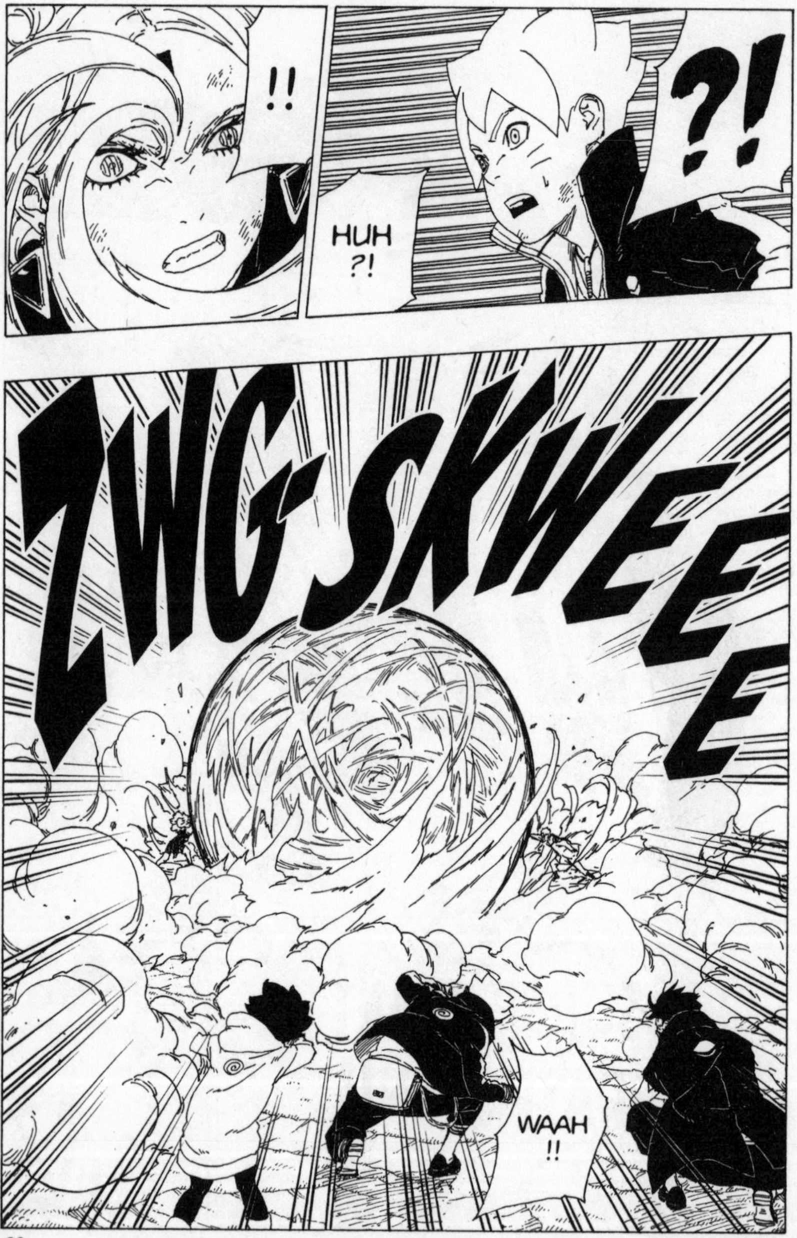
?!
HUH ?!
!!
ZWG-SKWEEE
WAAH !!

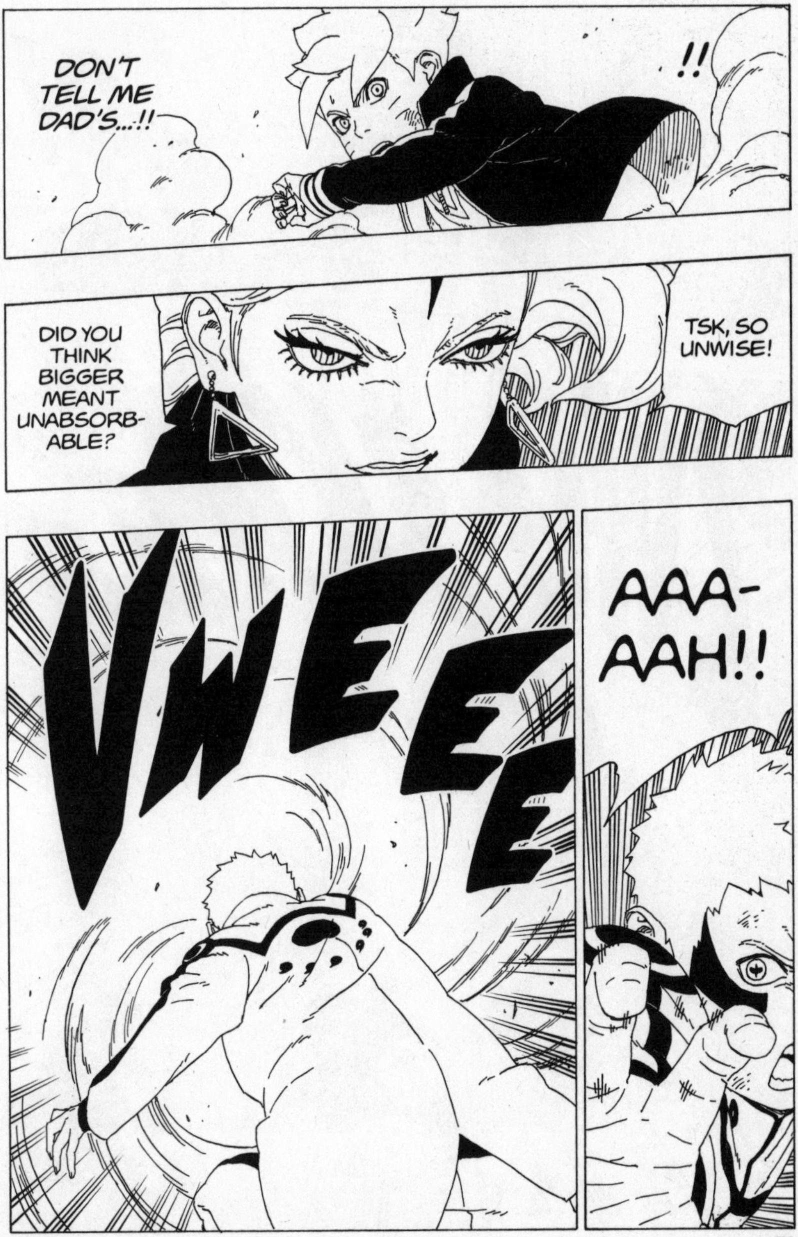
!!
DON'T TELL ME DAD'S...!!
TSK, SO UNWISE!
DID YOU THINK BIGGER MEANT UNABSORB-ABLE?
AAA-AAH!!
VWEEE

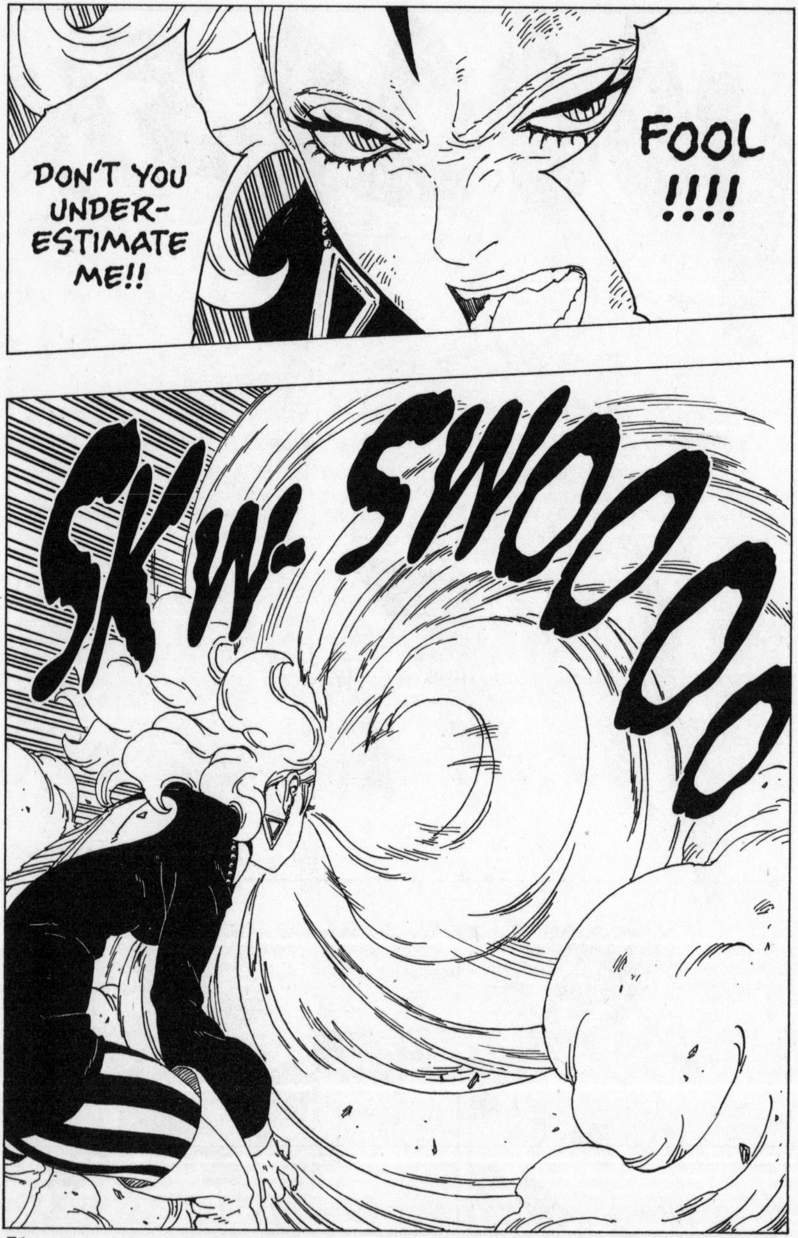
FOOL !!!!
DON'T YOU UNDER-ESTIMATE ME!!
SKW-SWOOOOO

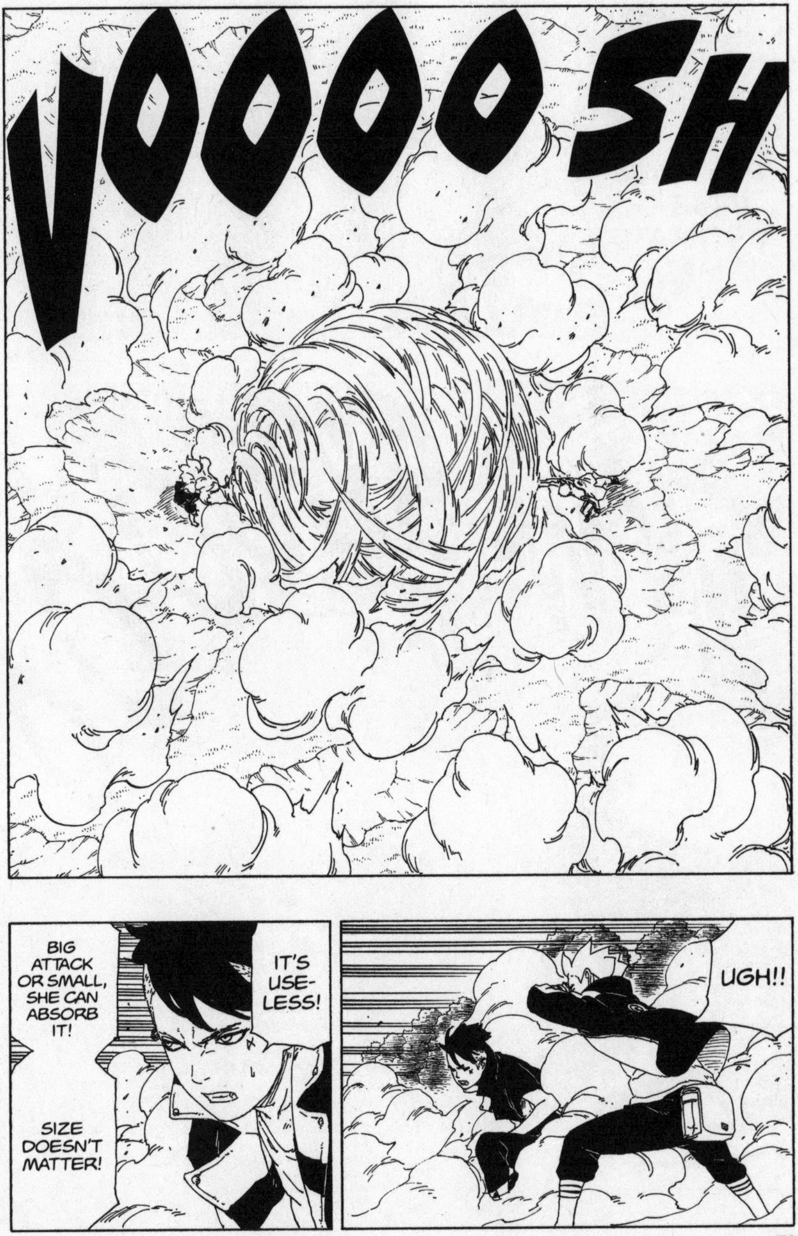
VOOOSH
UGH!!
IT'S USELESS!
BIG ATTACK OR SMALL, SHE CAN ABSORB IT!
SIZE DOESN'T MATTER!

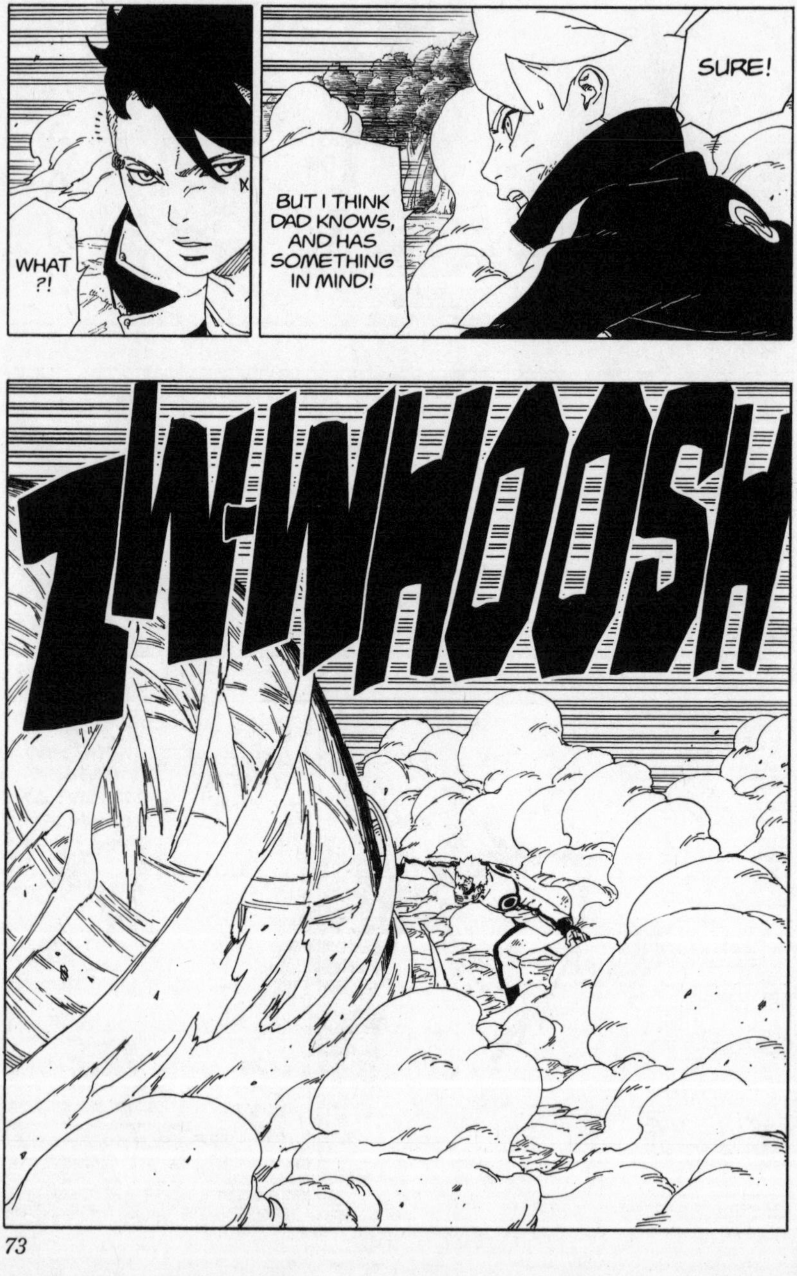
SURE!
BUT I THINK DAD KNOWS, AND HAS SOMETHING IN MIND!
WHAT ?!
TW-WHOOSH

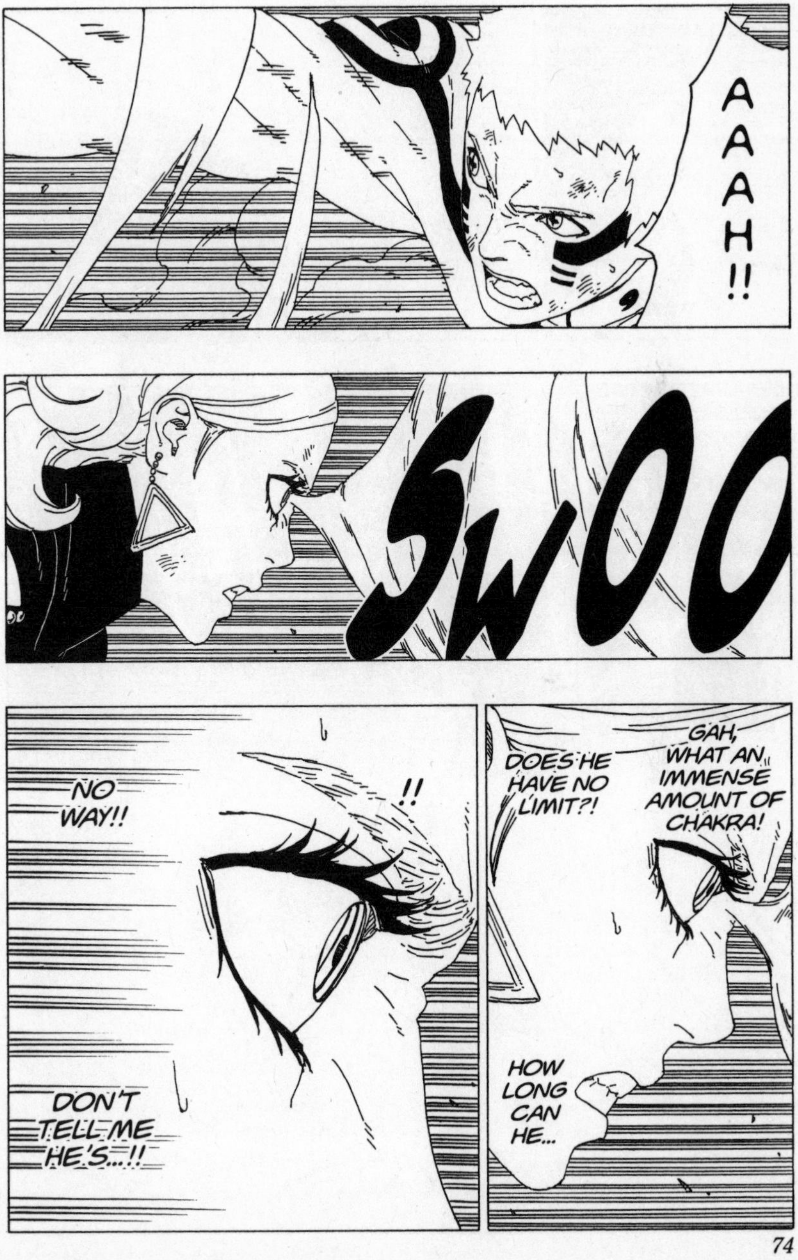
AAAH!!
SWOO
GAH, WHAT AN IMMENSE AMOUNT OF CHAKRA!
DOES HE HAVE NO LIMIT?!
HOW LONG CAN HE...
!!
NO WAY!!
DON'T TELL ME HE'S...!!

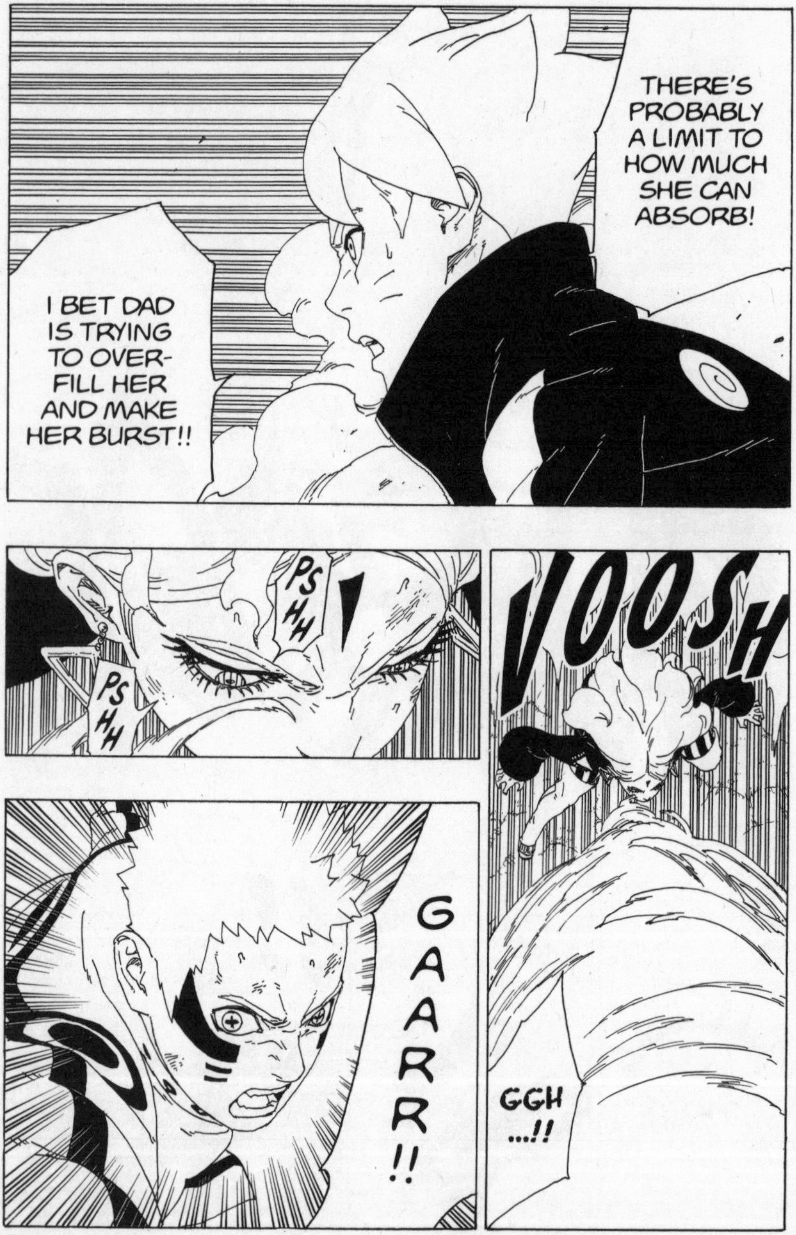
THERE'S PROBABLY A LIMIT TO HOW MUCH SHE CAN ABSORB!
I BET DAD IS TRYING TO OVER-FILL HER AND MAKE HER BURST!!
VOOSH
GGH ...!!
PSHH
PSHH
GAARR!!

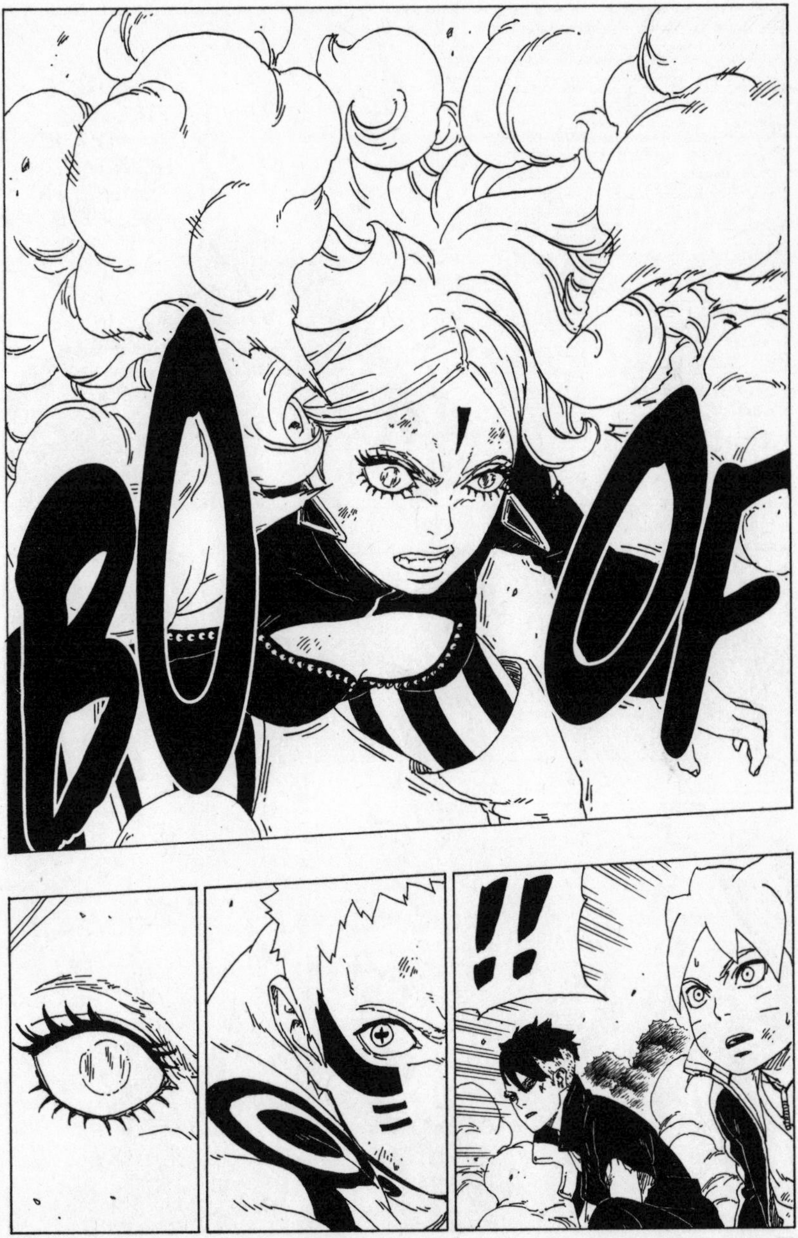
BOOF
!!

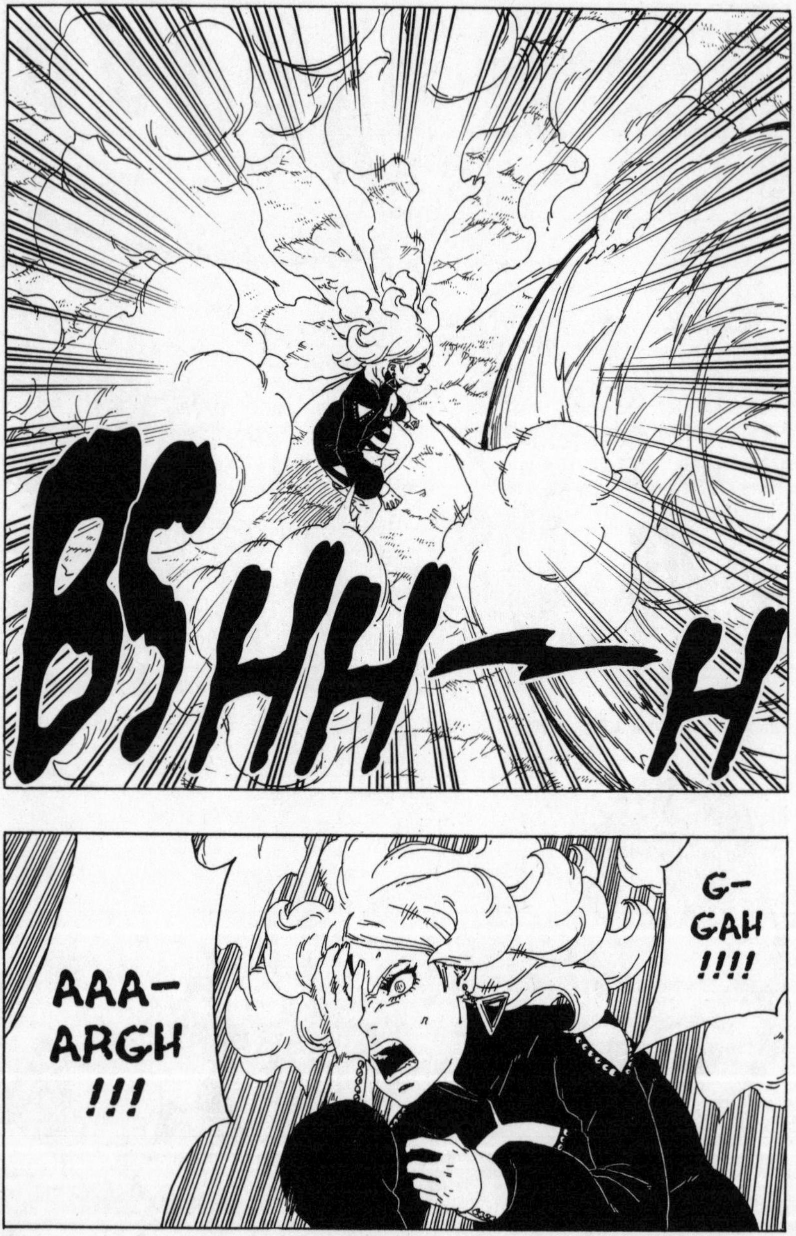
BSHH—H
G-GAH!!!!
AAA-ARGH!!!

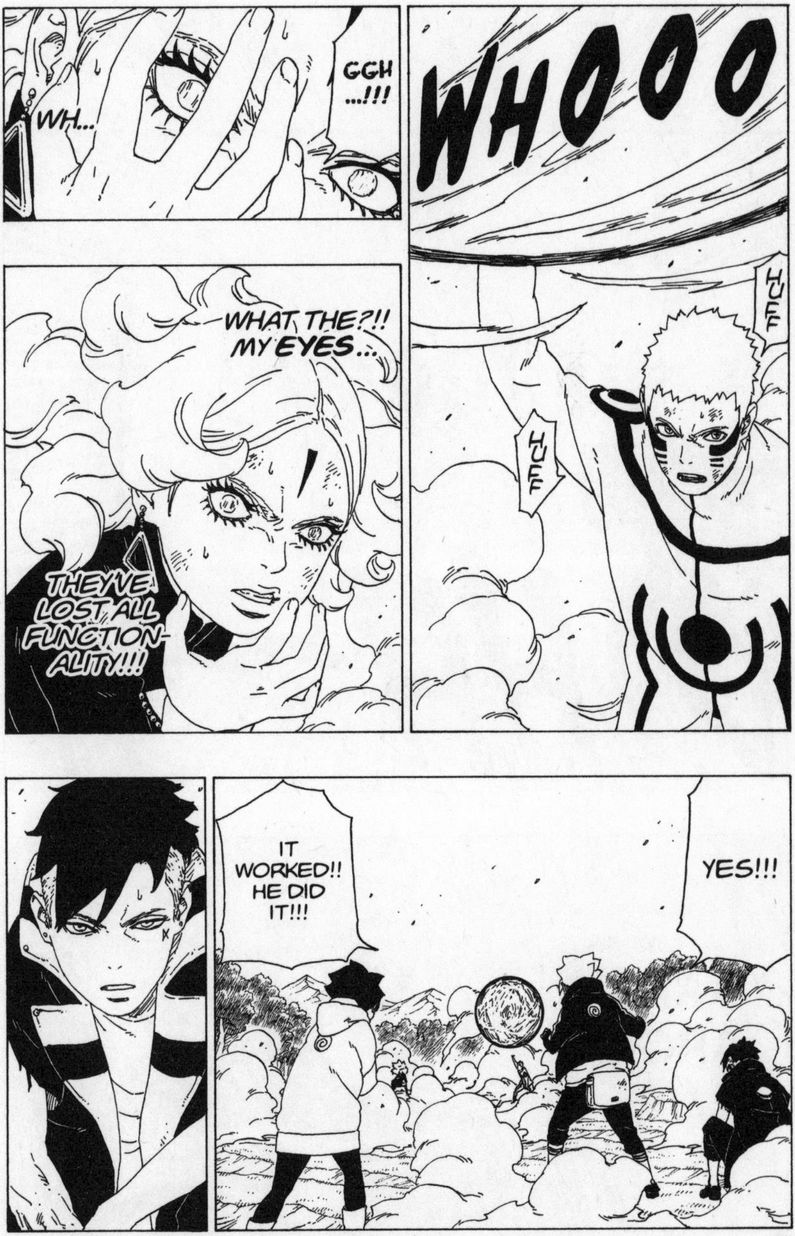
WHOOO
GGH ...!!!
WH...
HUFF
HUFF
WHAT THE?!! MY EYES...
THEY'VE LOST ALL FUNCTION-ALITY!!!
YES!!!
IT WORKED!! HE DID IT!!!

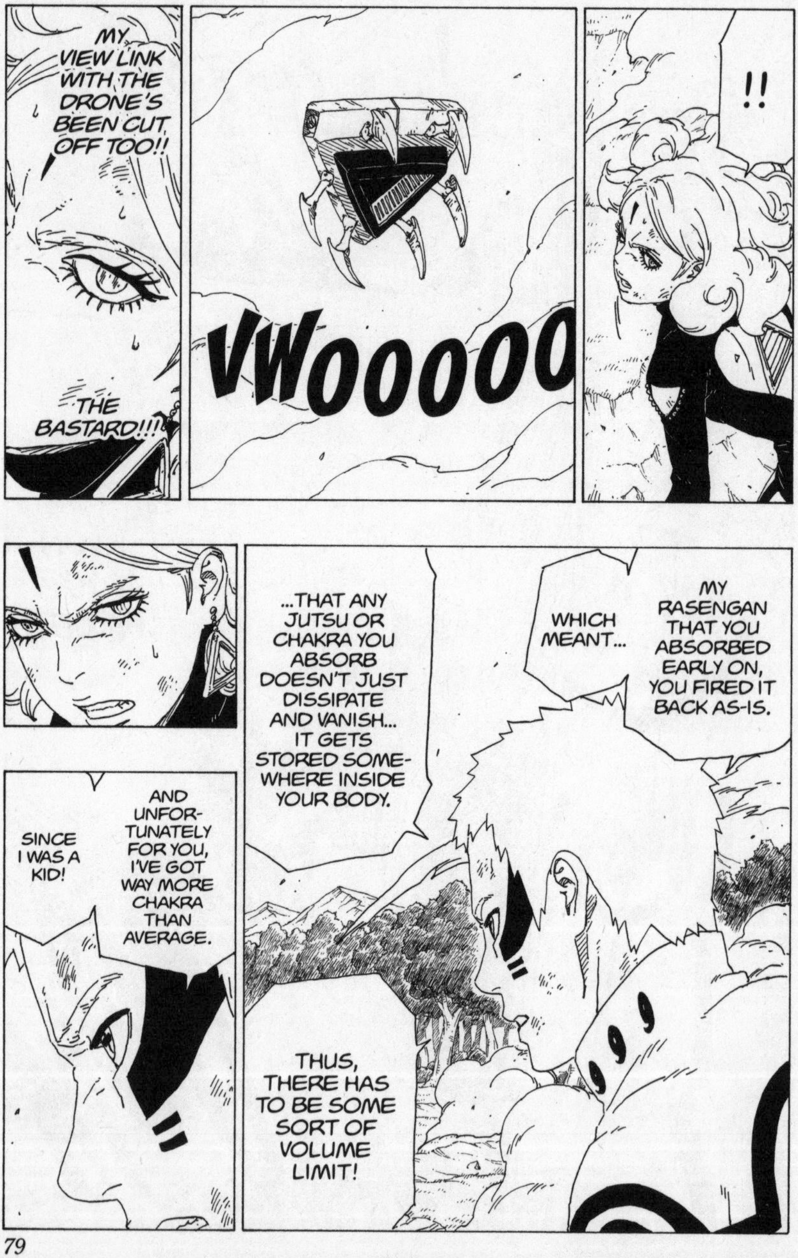
!!
VWOOOOO
MY VIEW LINK WITH THE DRONE'S BEEN CUT OFF TOO!!
THE BASTARD!!!
MY RASENGAN THAT YOU ABSORBED EARLY ON, YOU FIRED IT BACK AS-IS.
WHICH MEANT...
...THAT ANY JUTSU OR CHAKRA YOU ABSORB DOESN'T JUST DISSIPATE AND VANISH... IT GETS STORED SOME-WHERE INSIDE YOUR BODY.
THUS, THERE HAS TO BE SOME SORT OF VOLUME LIMIT!
AND UNFORTUNATELY FOR YOU, I'VE GOT WAY MORE CHAKRA THAN AVERAGE.
SINCE I WAS A KID!

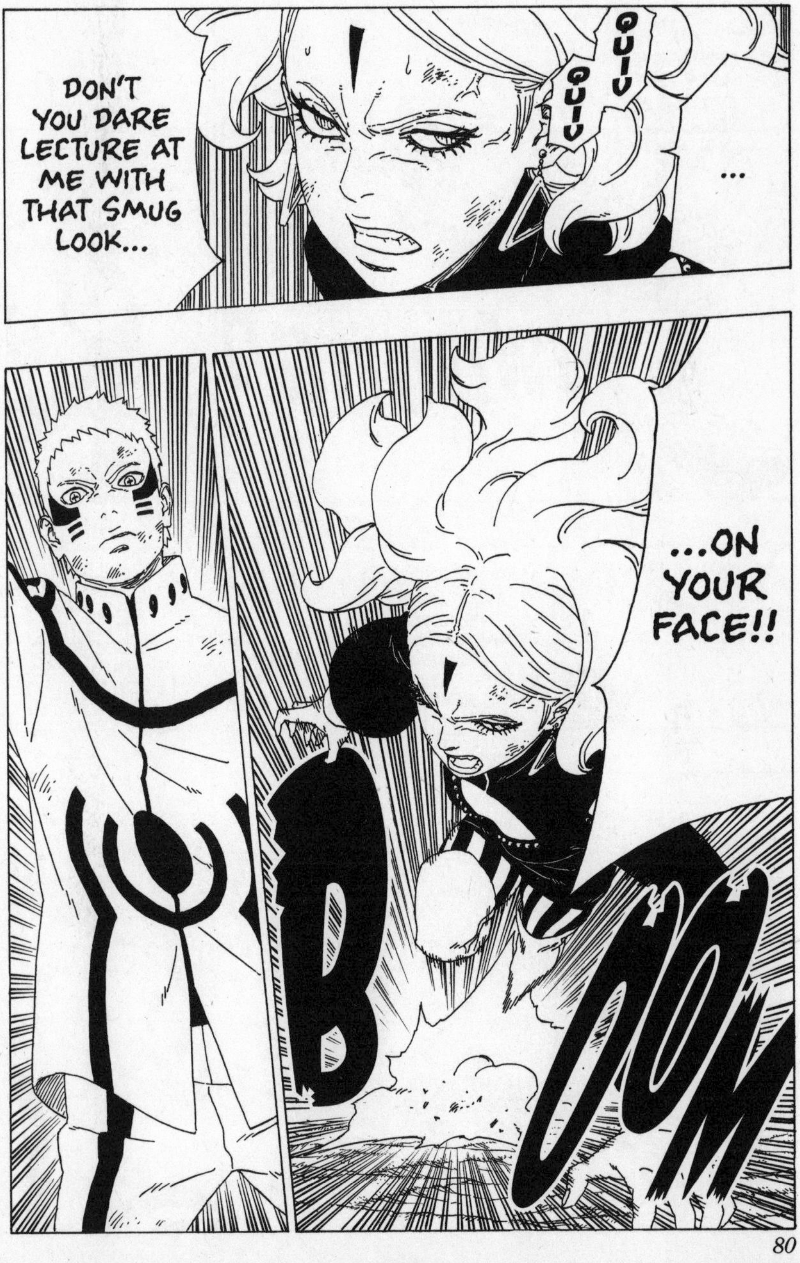
QUIV
QUIV
...
DON'T YOU DARE LECTURE AT ME WITH THAT SMUG LOOK...
...ON YOUR FACE!!
BOOM

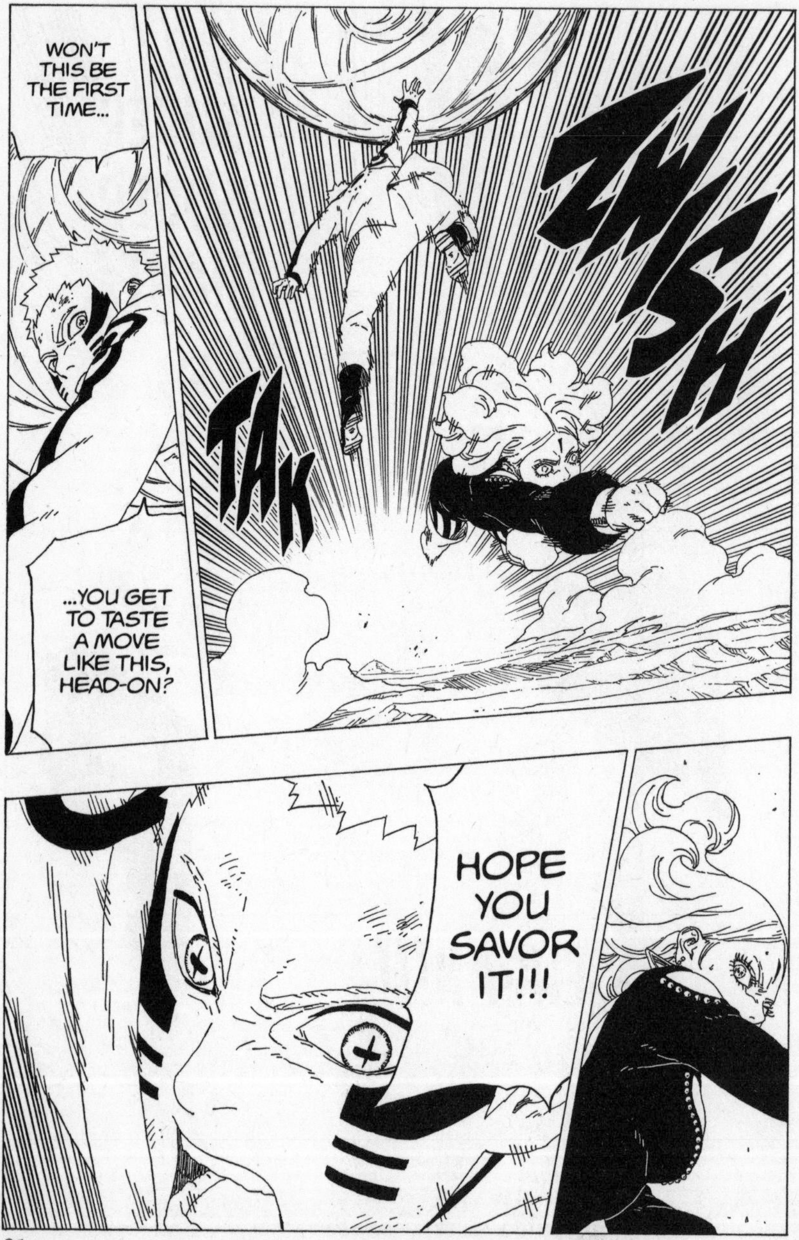
ZHSH
TAK
WON'T THIS BE THE FIRST TIME...
...YOU GET TO TASTE A MOVE LIKE THIS, HEAD-ON?
HOPE YOU SAVOR IT!!!

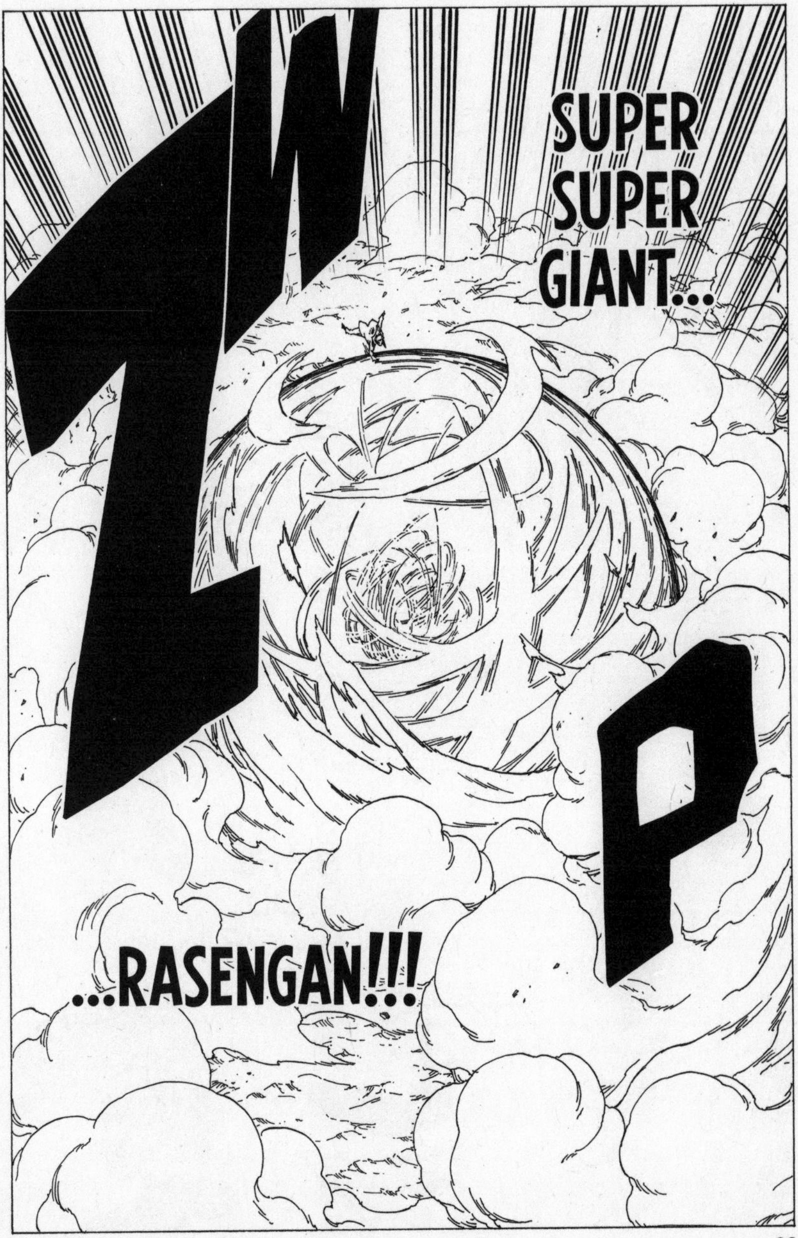
SUPER SUPER GIANT...
ZWP
...RASENGAN!!!

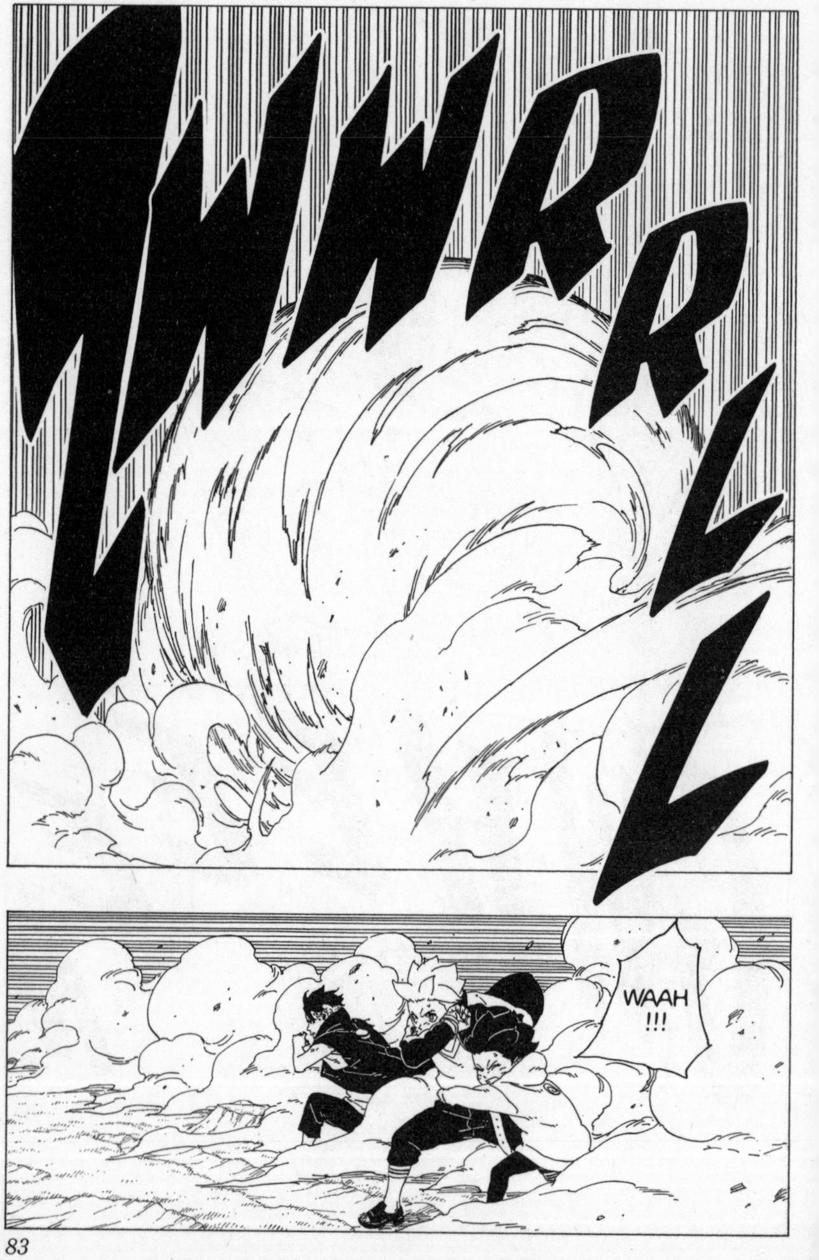
WHRRLL
WAAH !!!

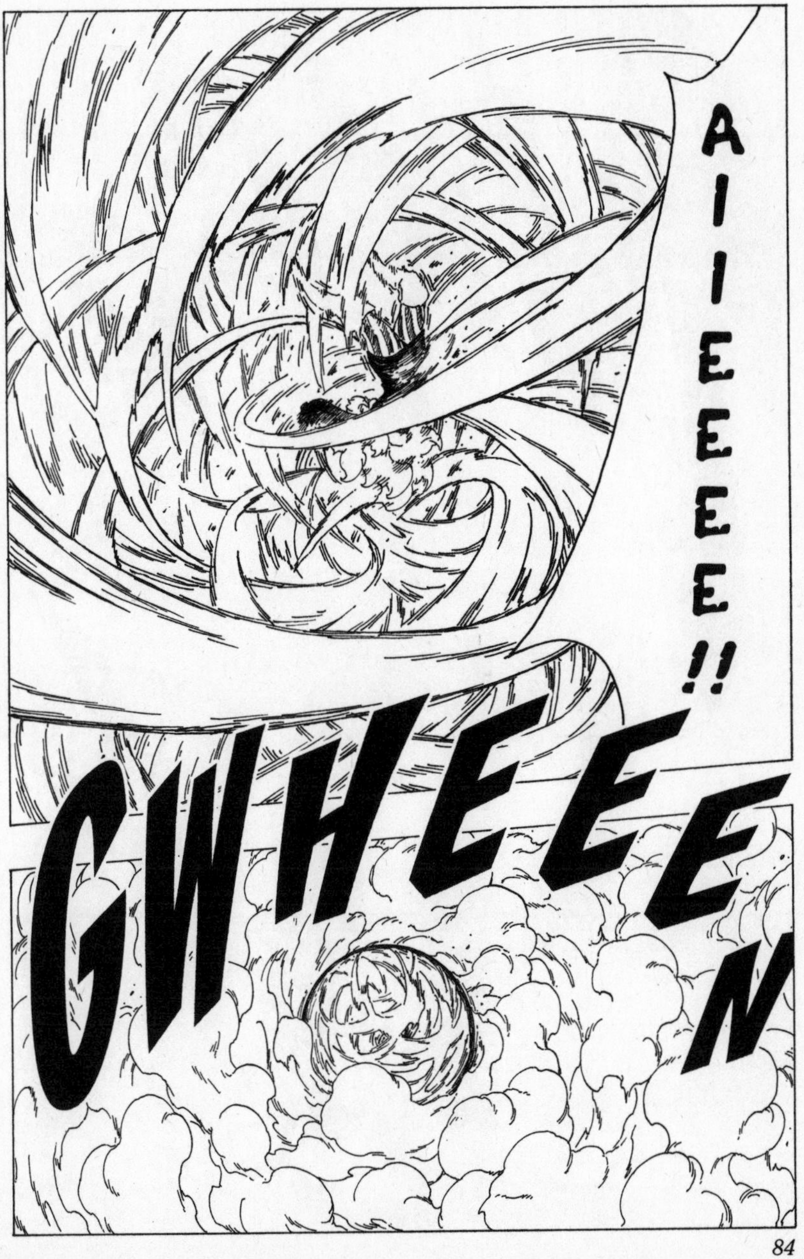
AIIEEEE!!
GWHEEEN

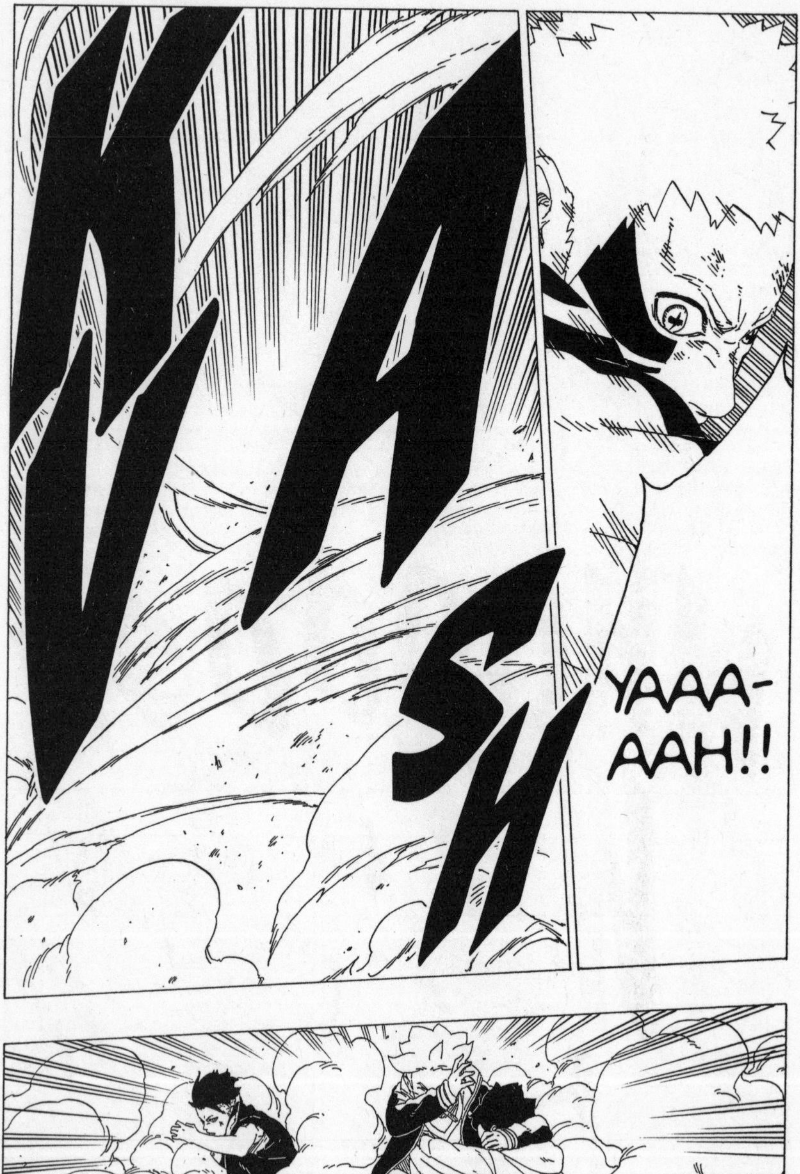
YAAA-AAH!!
WHASH

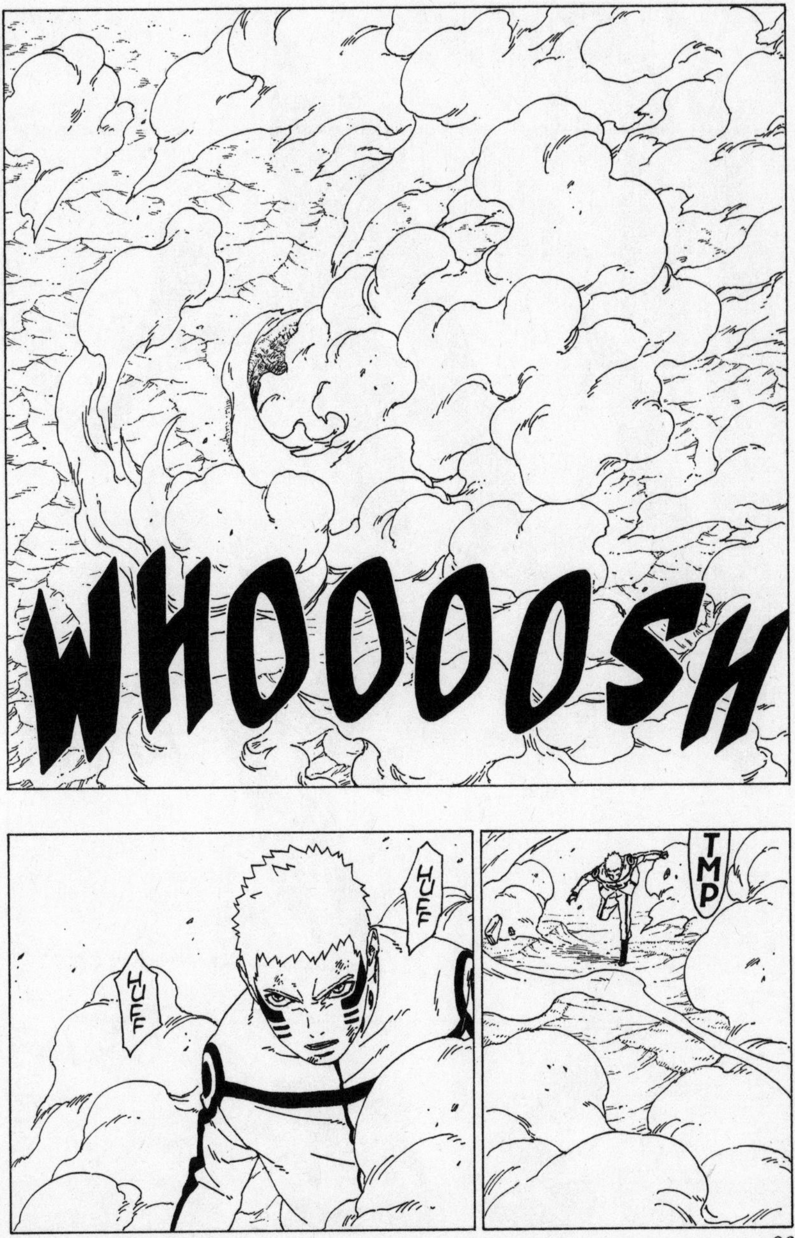
WHOOOOSH
TMP
HUFF
HUFF

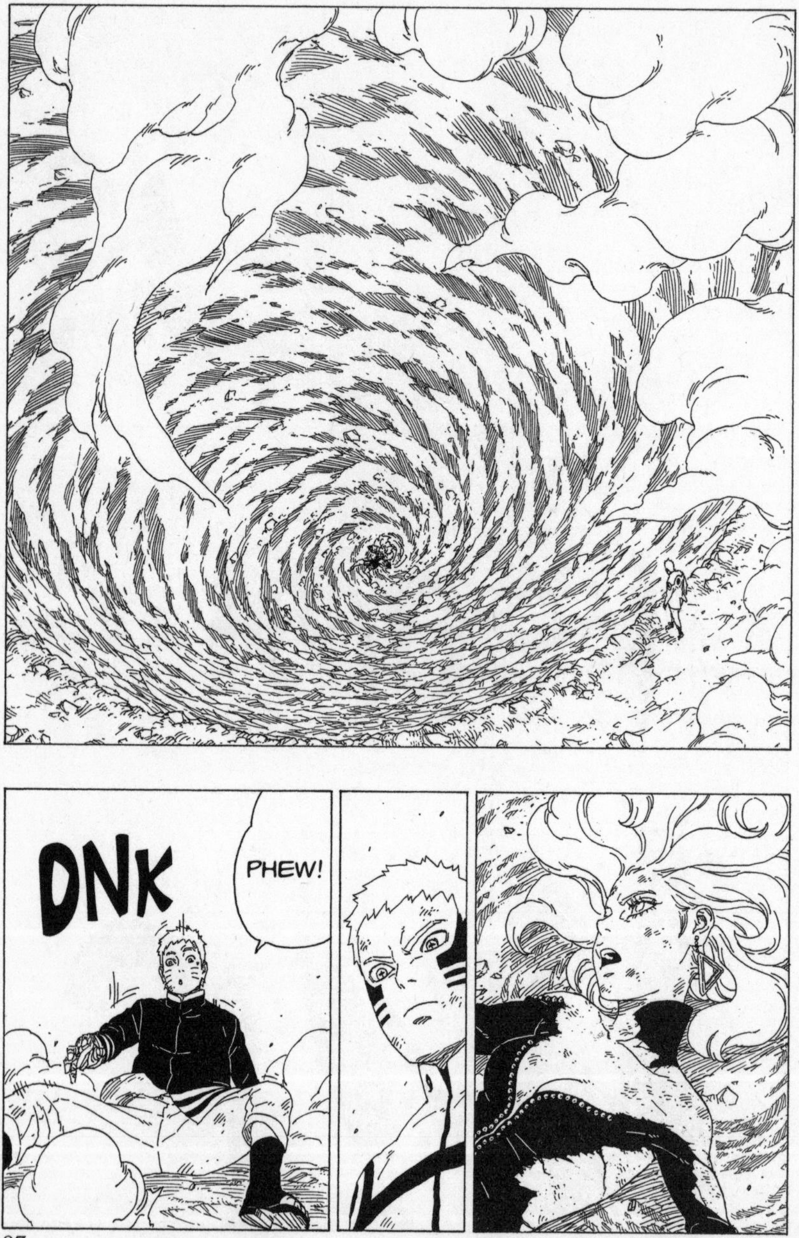
PHEW!
DNK

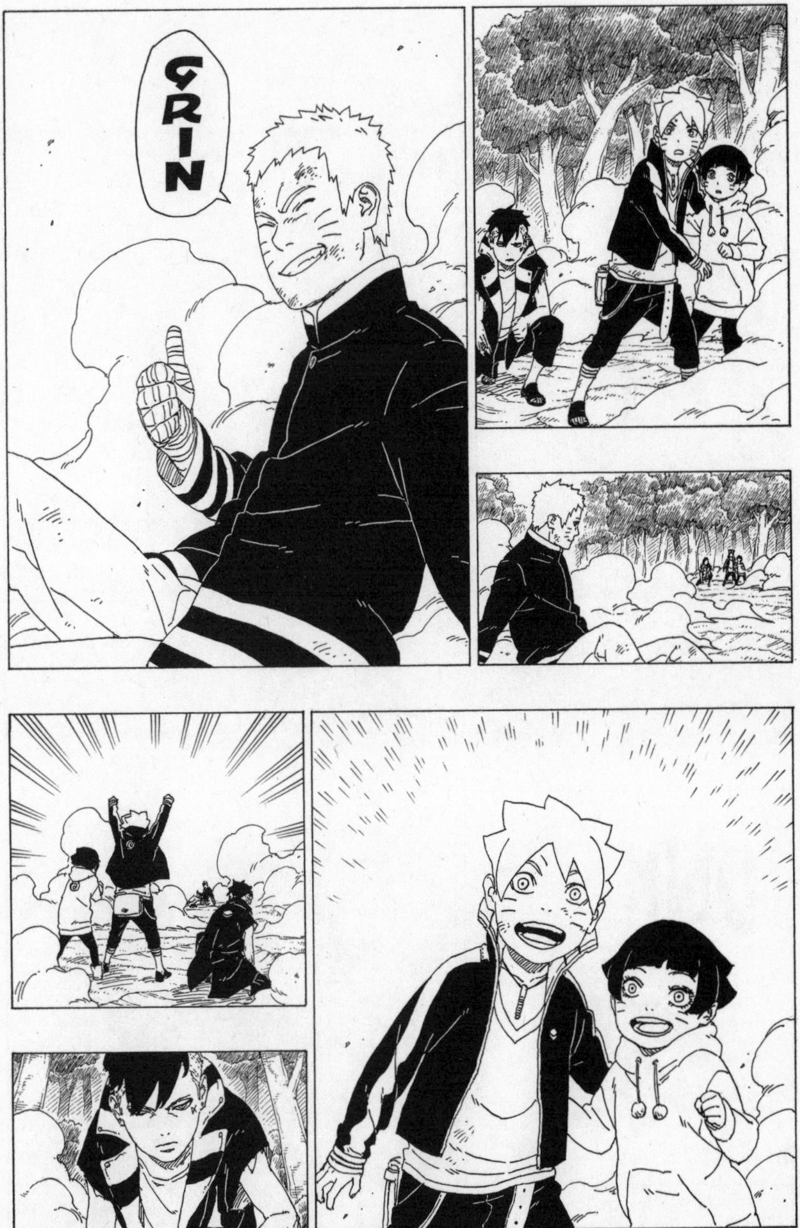
GRIN

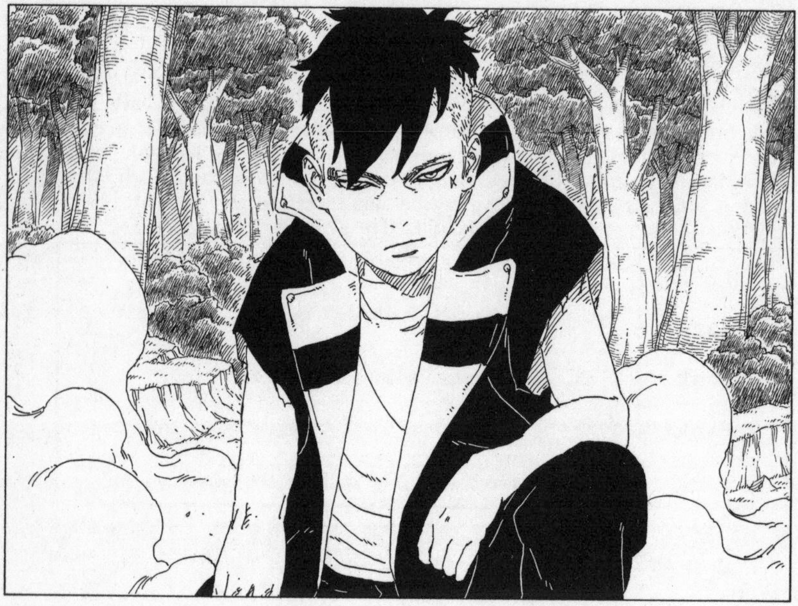
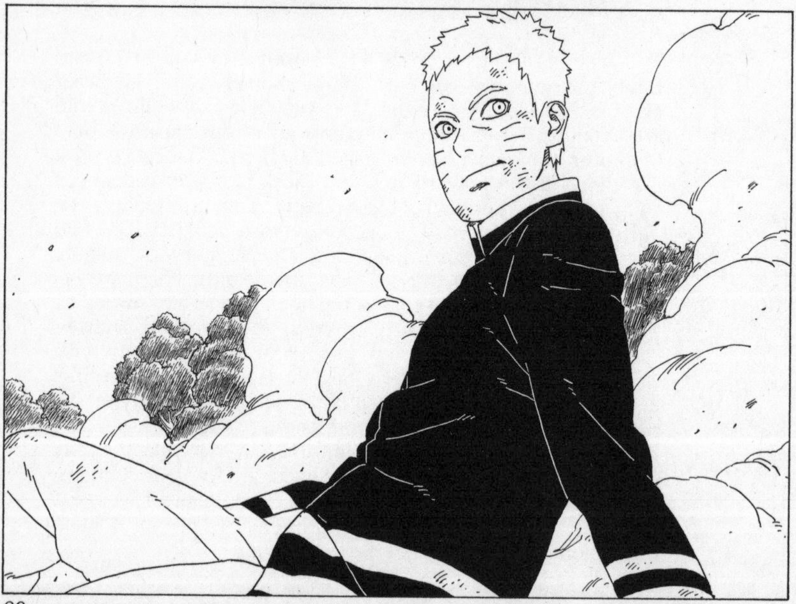

Shinobi Hiden Column 2: Shinobi and Their Missions

Shinobi are active in order to earn money. In movies or television dramas, shinobi gloriously battle evils that threaten the world, or hidden villages shrouded in mystery, every day. Not that this impression is totally mistaken, but it is also not the entire picture. Shinobi undertake missions, and receive money in return. Clients pay money to a Village on a per-mission basis, and then the Village deducts a commission and disburses the remainder to each respective shinobi. However, there are also many Villages (including Konoha) that guarantee a minimum fixed salary, because otherwise shinobi who stop getting assigned missions would not be able to eat. At the present time, a uniform mission ranking system is utilized by the Five Great Villages.

D rank	**Odd jobs** (such as finding cats, babysitting, errands, digging for sweet potatoes)
C rank	**Regular missions** (such as intelligence gathering, eradicating bandits, medical treatments)
B rank	**VS. ninja missions** (combat against genin anticipated)
A rank	**Military missions** (combat against one or more squads of ninja which include chunin)
S rank	**VS. jonin missions** (combat against jonin and Gokage-class ninja)

As a general rule, genin are only supposed to be assigned D and C rank missions, but due to workforce shortages after the Great Ninja War, there are more than a few genin in every Village who are assigned B and A rank missions. (of whom Boruto is one) Moreover, shinobi who are engaged in chronic, invariable work like those in the Police Force and Black Ops are paid wages comparable to missions of equivalent rank ordered by the Village. As shinobi society becomes more sophisticated and missions increase correspondingly, the number of shinobi receiving such "fixed salaries" has also grown. For instance, Katasuke and Sumire are contracted by the laboratory owned by Konoha Village to perform research as their mission, and are shinobi who are restricted to do just research (incidentally, their work corresponds to A rank, so their pay is better than Boruto's). External commissions are doled out based on suitability by the two chunin in charge of commissions, "Explanation Lady" Kannonji Suika and "Miss Receptionist" Mishiro Fuyuki. If A rank or higher, they consult Naruto and Shikamaru for their opinions, but otherwise, the chunin in charge of commissions have great authority, and are regarded with both fear and awe for holding the shinobi's purse strings in their grasp.

Number 34: Training!!

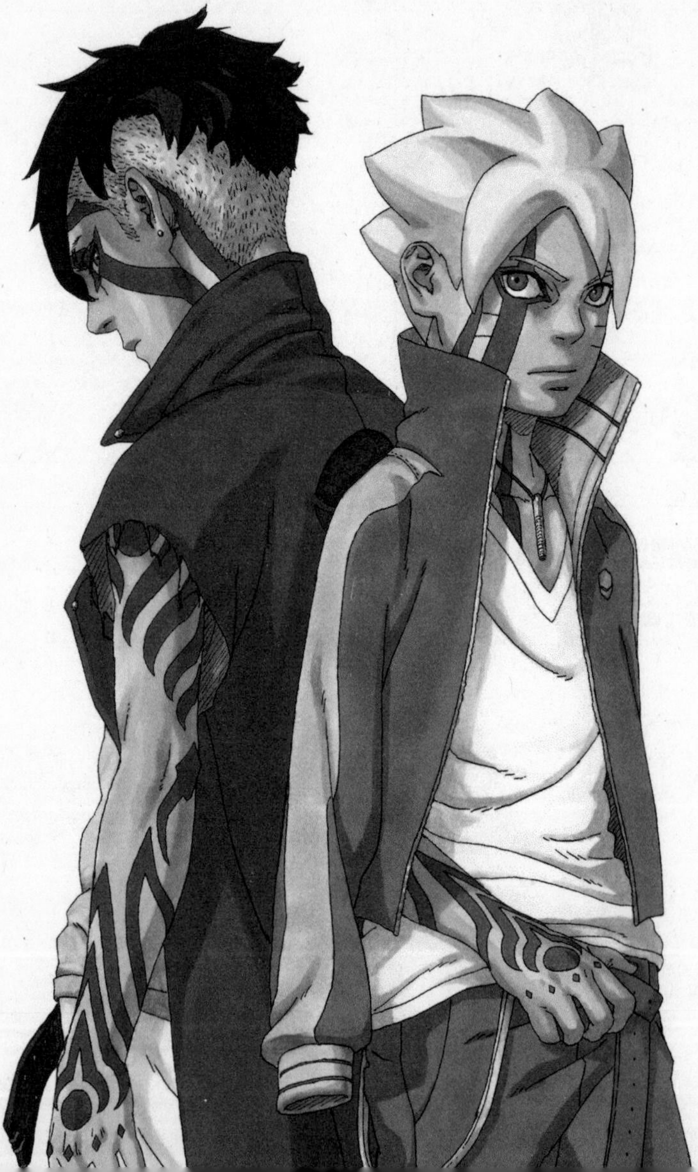

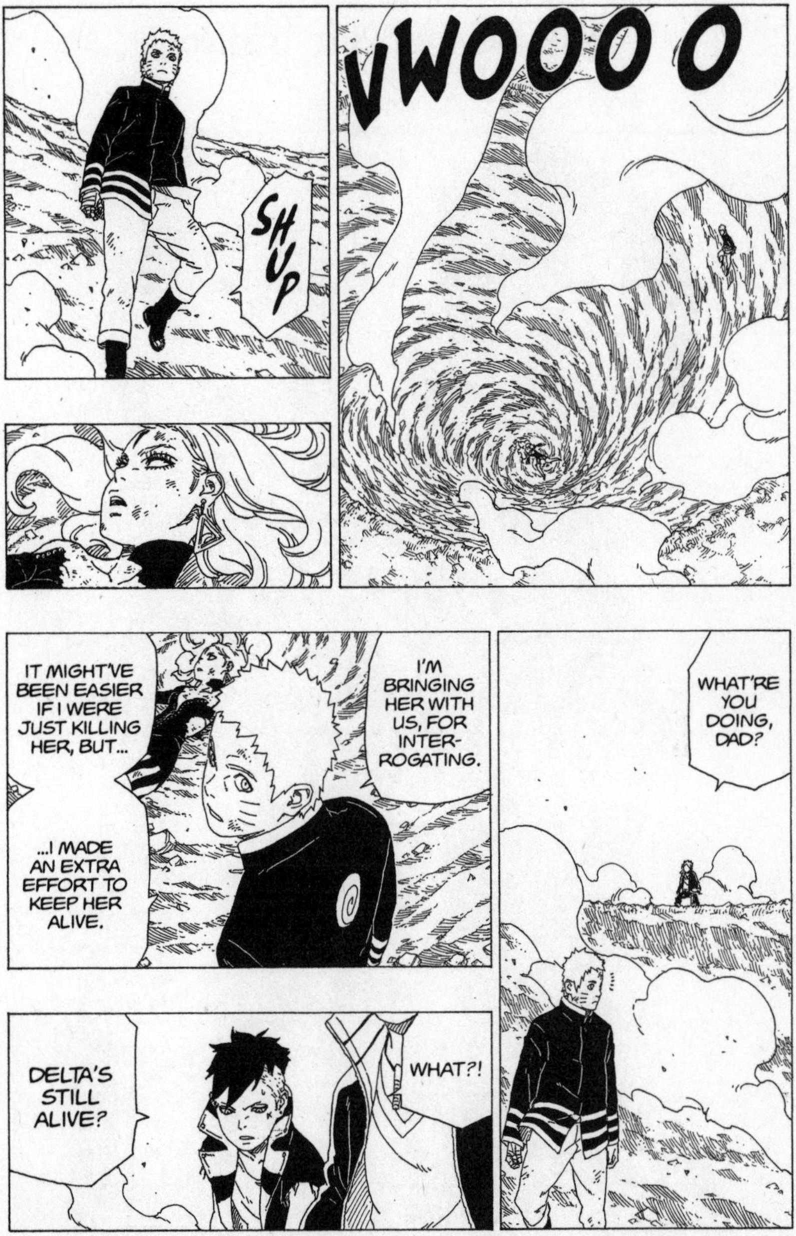
VWOOO O
SHUP
WHAT'RE YOU DOING, DAD?
I'M BRINGING HER WITH US, FOR INTER-ROGATING.
IT MIGHT'VE BEEN EASIER IF I WERE JUST KILLING HER, BUT...
...I MADE AN EXTRA EFFORT TO KEEP HER ALIVE.
WHAT?!
DELTA'S STILL ALIVE?

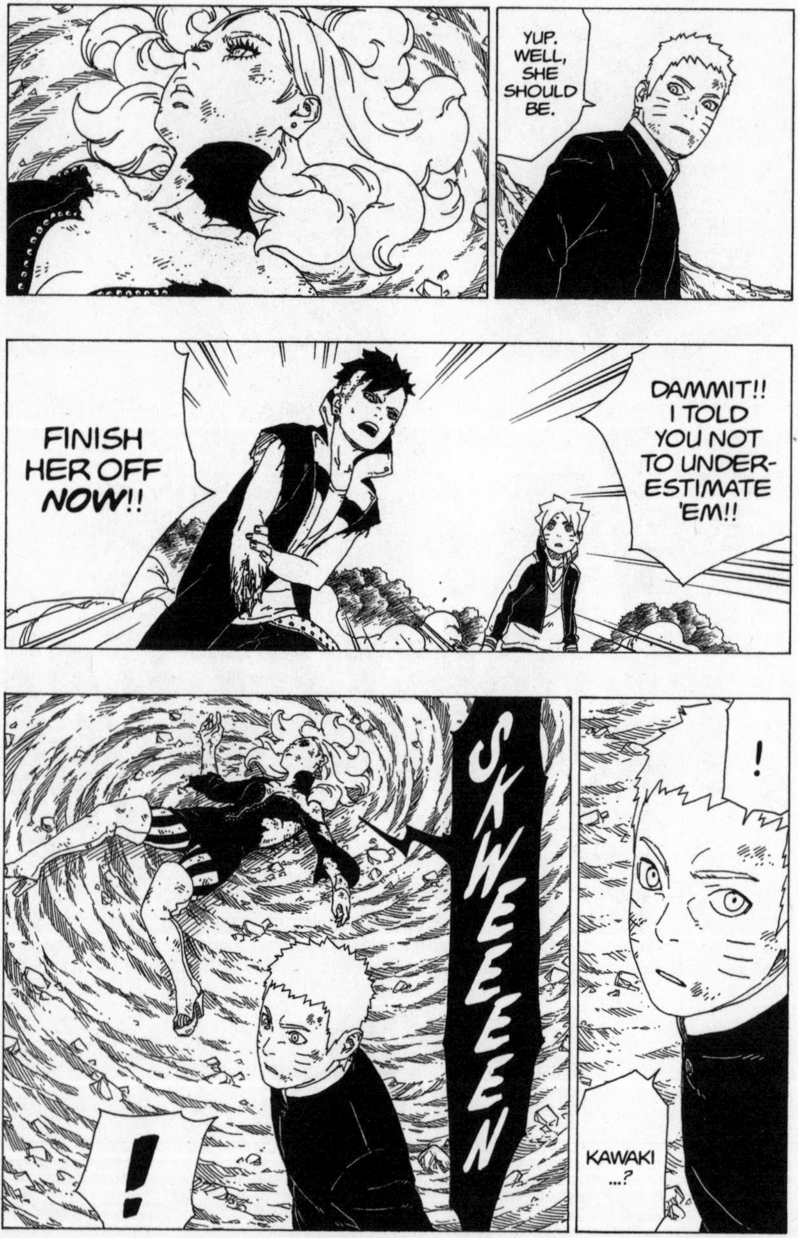
YUP. WELL, SHE SHOULD BE.
DAMMIT!! I TOLD YOU NOT TO UNDER-ESTIMATE 'EM!!
FINISH HER OFF NOW!!
!
KAWAKI ...?
SKWEEEEN
!

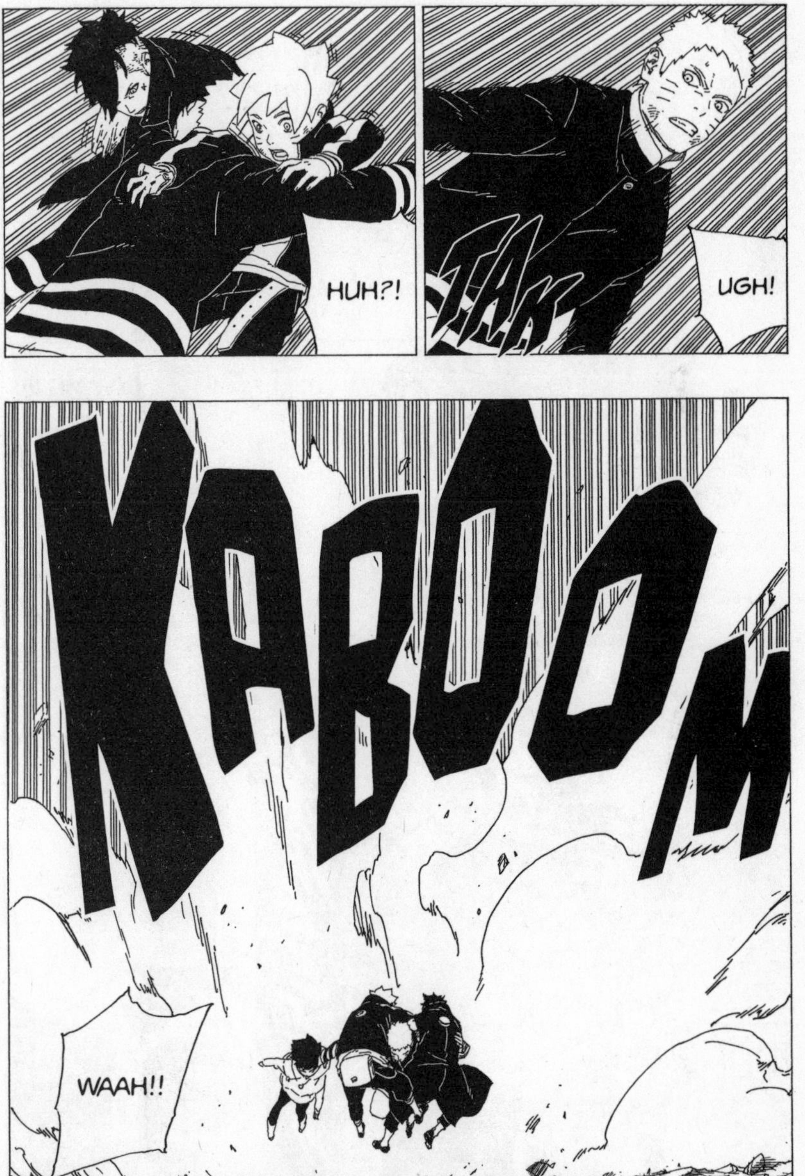
UGH!
TAK
HUH?!
KABOOM
WAAH!!

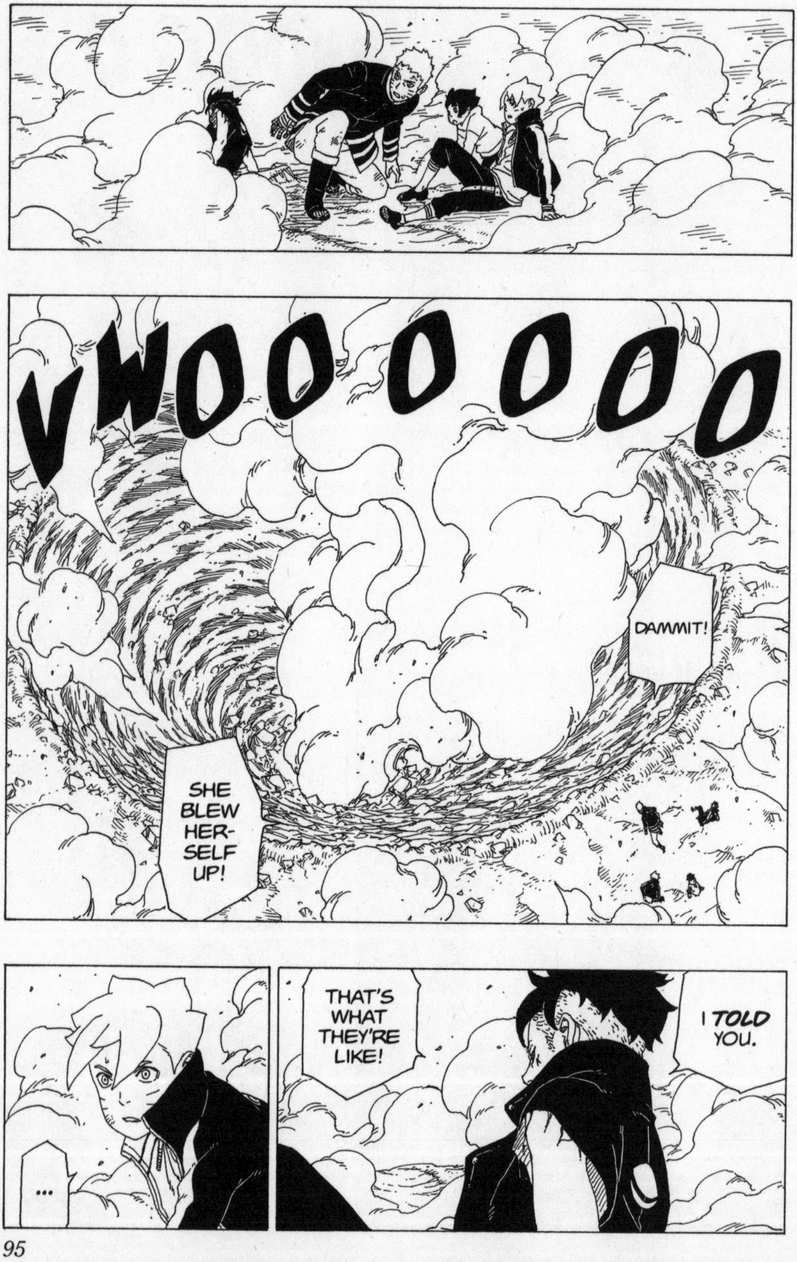
VWOOOOOO
DAMMIT!
SHE BLEW HER-SELF UP!
I TOLD YOU.
THAT'S WHAT THEY'RE LIKE!
...

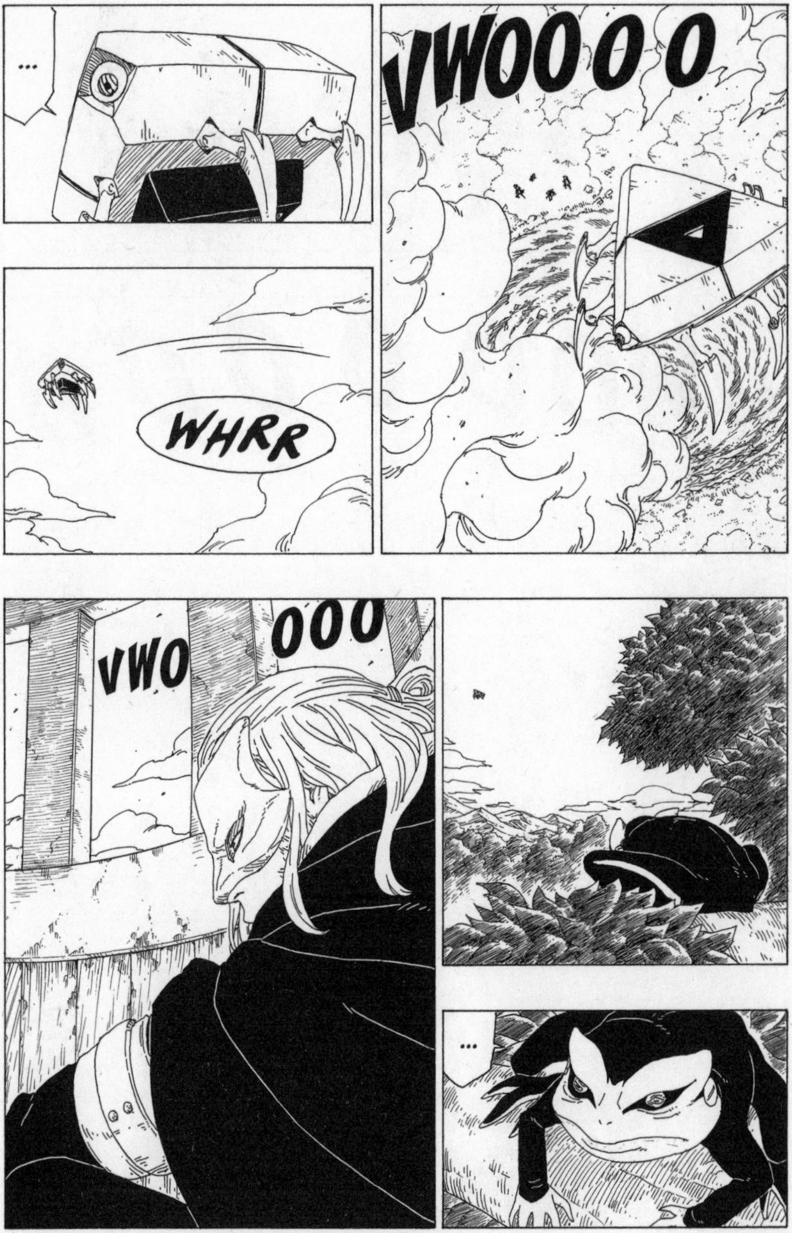
VWOO O O
...
WHRR
...
VWO OOO

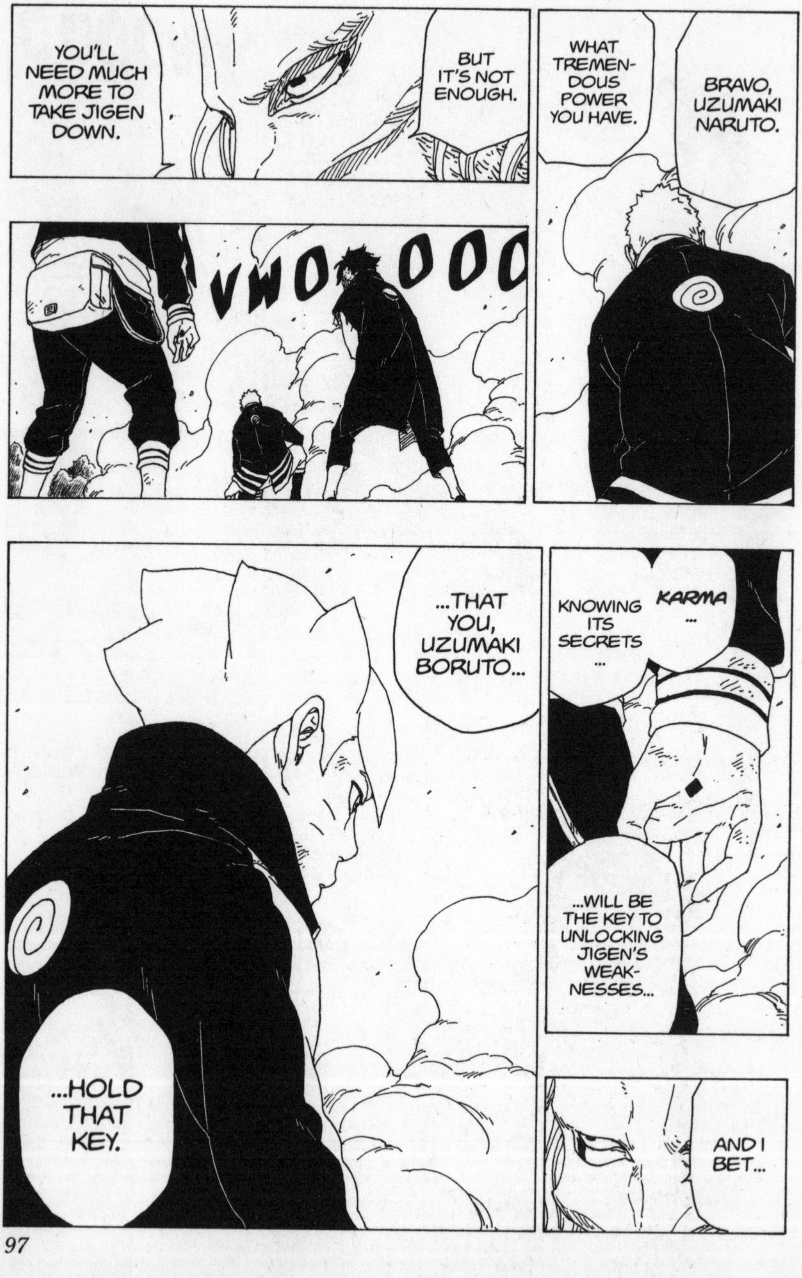
BRAVO, UZUMAKI NARUTO.
WHAT TREMEN-DOUS POWER YOU HAVE.
BUT IT'S NOT ENOUGH.
YOU'LL NEED MUCH MORE TO TAKE JIGEN DOWN.
VWOOOO
KARMA...
KNOWING ITS SECRETS...
...WILL BE THE KEY TO UNLOCKING JIGEN'S WEAK-NESSES...
AND I BET...
...THAT YOU, UZUMAKI BORUTO...
...HOLD THAT KEY.

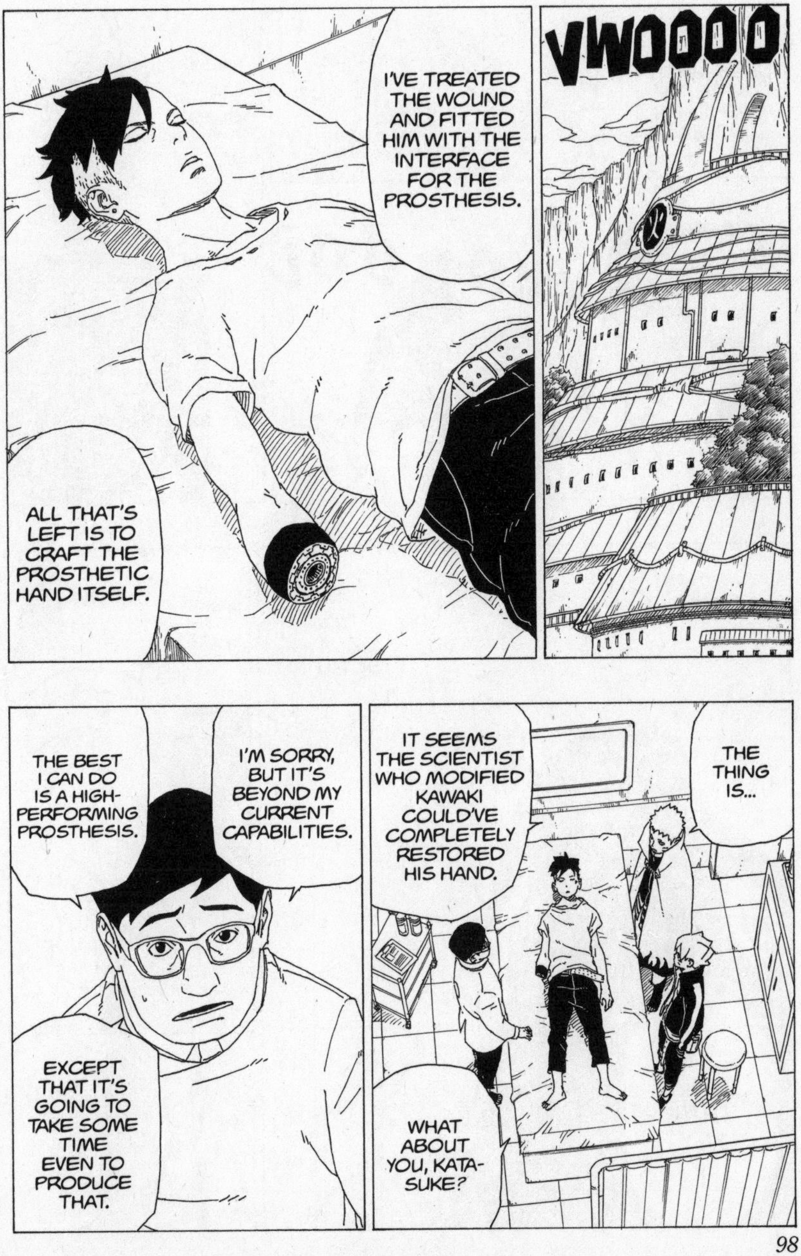
VWOOOO
I'VE TREATED THE WOUND AND FITTED HIM WITH THE INTERFACE FOR THE PROSTHESIS.
ALL THAT'S LEFT IS TO CRAFT THE PROSTHETIC HAND ITSELF.
THE THING IS...
IT SEEMS THE SCIENTIST WHO MODIFIED KAWAKI COULD'VE COMPLETELY RESTORED HIS HAND.
WHAT ABOUT YOU, KATA-SUKE?
I'M SORRY, BUT IT'S BEYOND MY CURRENT CAPABILITIES.
THE BEST I CAN DO IS A HIGH-PERFORMING PROSTHESIS.
EXCEPT THAT IT'S GOING TO TAKE SOME TIME EVEN TO PRODUCE THAT.

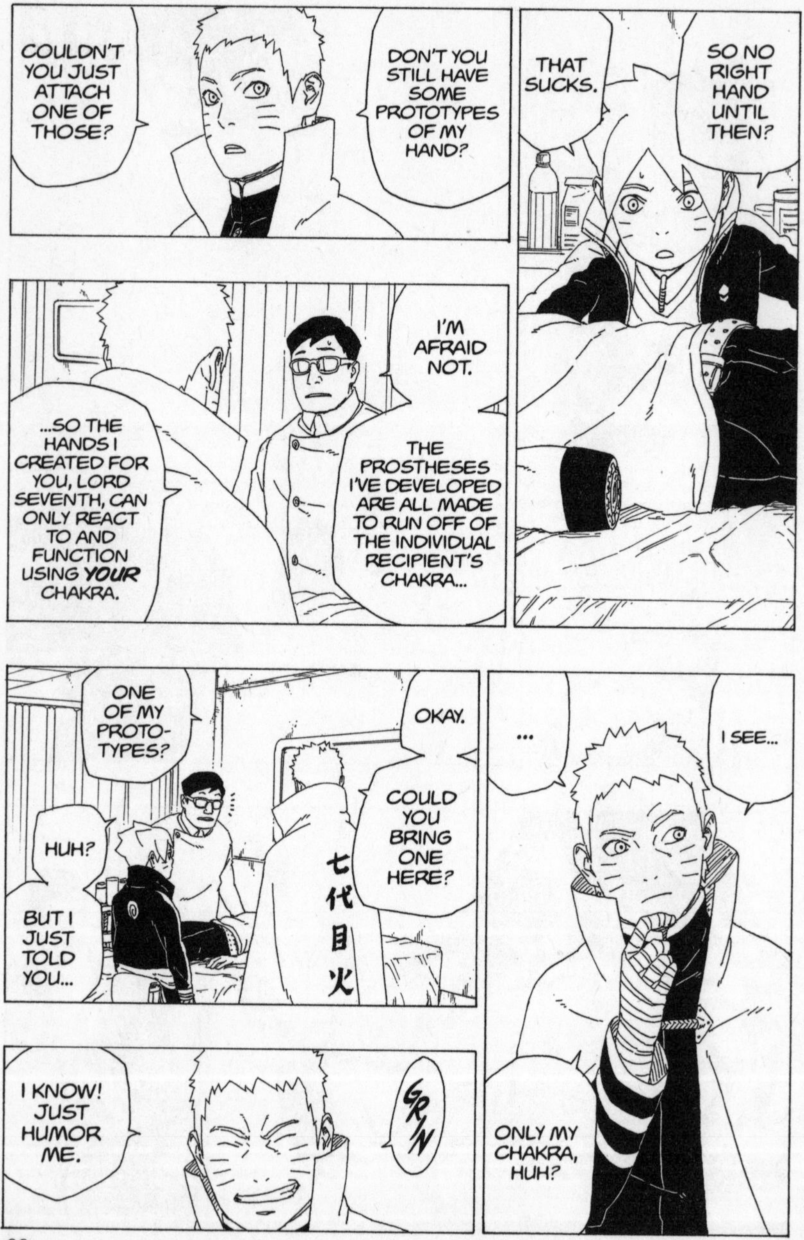
SO NO RIGHT HAND UNTIL THEN?
THAT SUCKS.
DON'T YOU STILL HAVE SOME PROTOTYPES OF MY HAND?
COULDN'T YOU JUST ATTACH ONE OF THOSE?
I'M AFRAID NOT.
THE PROSTHESES I'VE DEVELOPED ARE ALL MADE TO RUN OFF OF THE INDIVIDUAL RECIPIENT'S CHAKRA...
...SO THE HANDS I CREATED FOR YOU, LORD SEVENTH, CAN ONLY REACT TO AND FUNCTION USING **YOUR** CHAKRA.
I SEE...
...
ONLY MY CHAKRA, HUH?
OKAY.
COULD YOU BRING ONE HERE?
七代目火
ONE OF MY PROTO-TYPES?
HUH?
BUT I JUST TOLD YOU...
GRIN
I KNOW! JUST HUMOR ME.

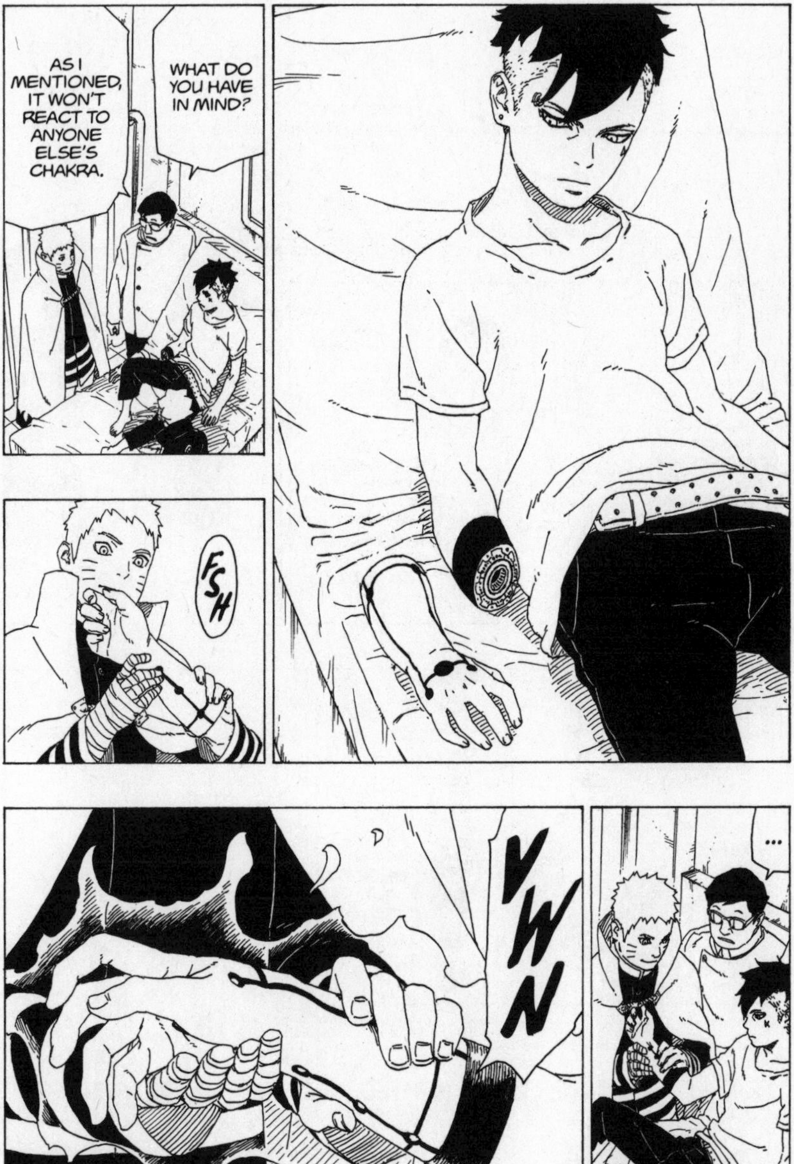
WHAT DO YOU HAVE IN MIND?
AS I MENTIONED, IT WON'T REACT TO ANYONE ELSE'S CHAKRA.
FSH
...
VWN

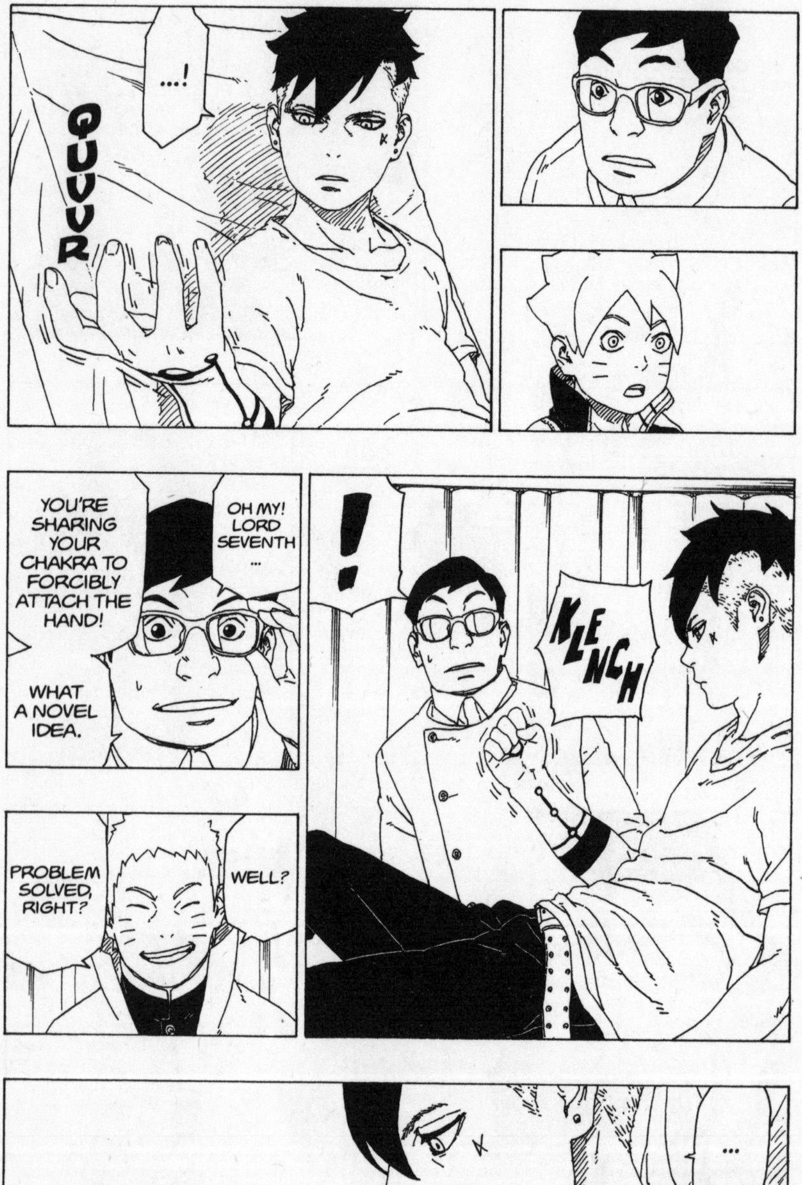
...!
QUVVR
!
KLENCH
OH MY! LORD SEVENTH ...
YOU'RE SHARING YOUR CHAKRA TO FORCIBLY ATTACH THE HAND!
WHAT A NOVEL IDEA.
WELL?
PROBLEM SOLVED, RIGHT?
...

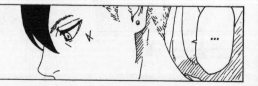

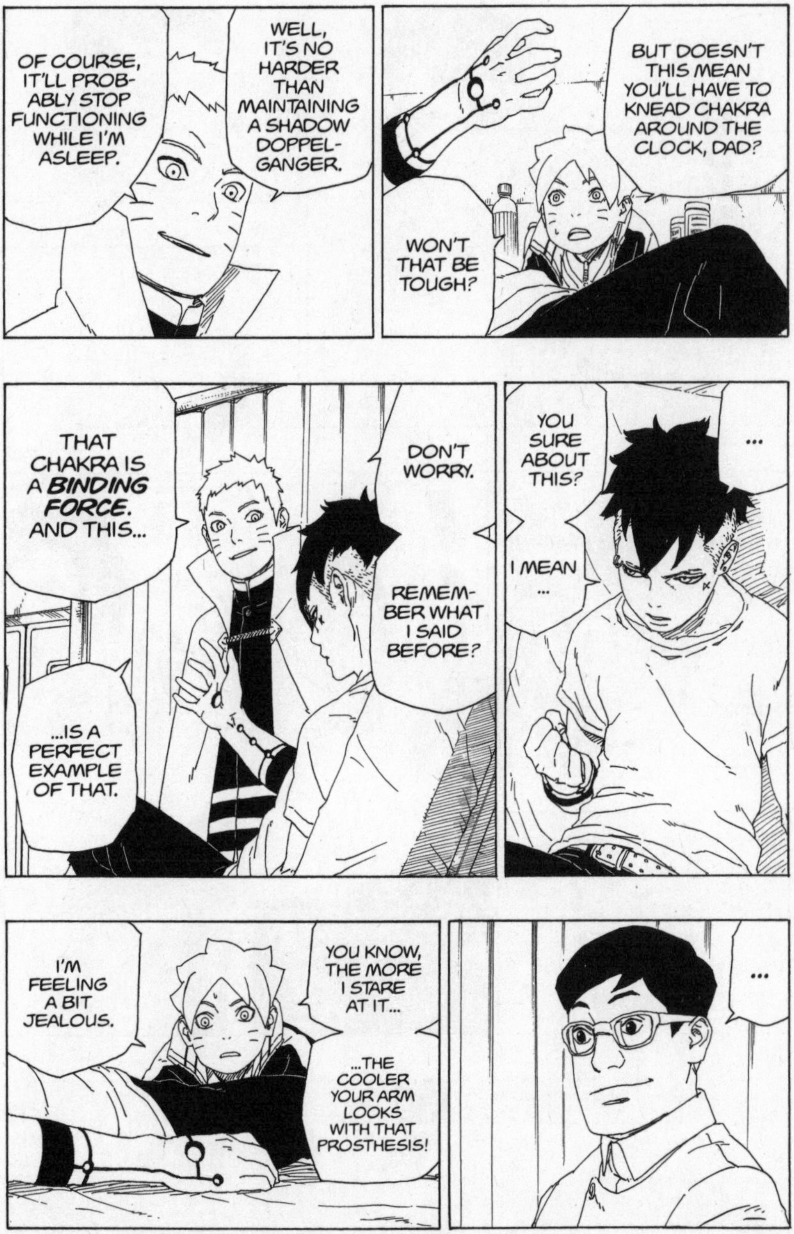
BUT DOESN'T THIS MEAN YOU'LL HAVE TO KNEAD CHAKRA AROUND THE CLOCK, DAD?
WON'T THAT BE TOUGH?
WELL, IT'S NO HARDER THAN MAINTAINING A SHADOW DOPPEL-GANGER.
OF COURSE, IT'LL PROB-ABLY STOP FUNCTIONING WHILE I'M ASLEEP.
...
YOU SURE ABOUT THIS?
I MEAN ...
DON'T WORRY.
REMEM-BER WHAT I SAID BEFORE?
THAT CHAKRA IS A ***BINDING FORCE***. AND THIS...
...IS A PERFECT EXAMPLE OF THAT.
...
YOU KNOW, THE MORE I STARE AT IT...
...THE COOLER YOUR ARM LOOKS WITH THAT PROSTHESIS!
I'M FEELING A BIT JEALOUS.

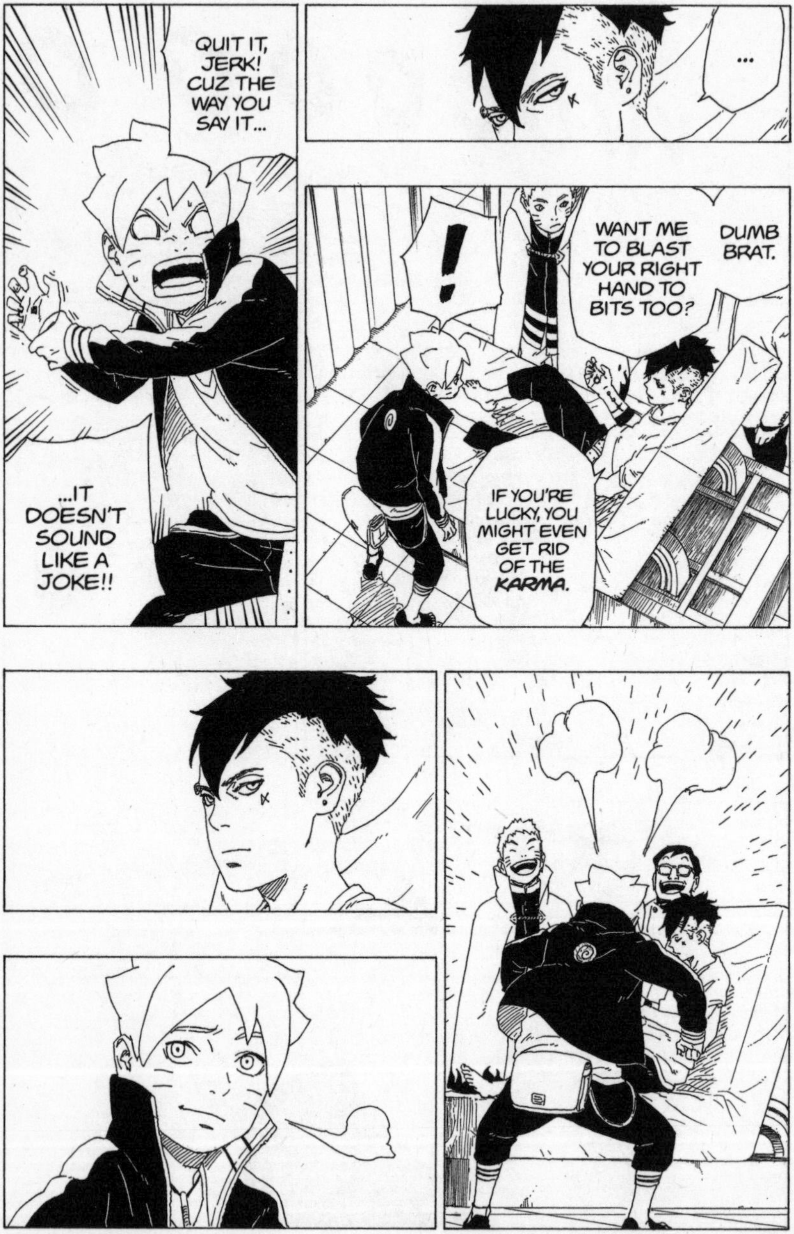
...
DUMB BRAT.
WANT ME TO BLAST YOUR RIGHT HAND TO BITS TOO?
!
IF YOU'RE LUCKY, YOU MIGHT EVEN GET RID OF THE *KARMA*.
QUIT IT, JERK! CUZ THE WAY YOU SAY IT...
...IT DOESN'T SOUND LIKE A JOKE!!

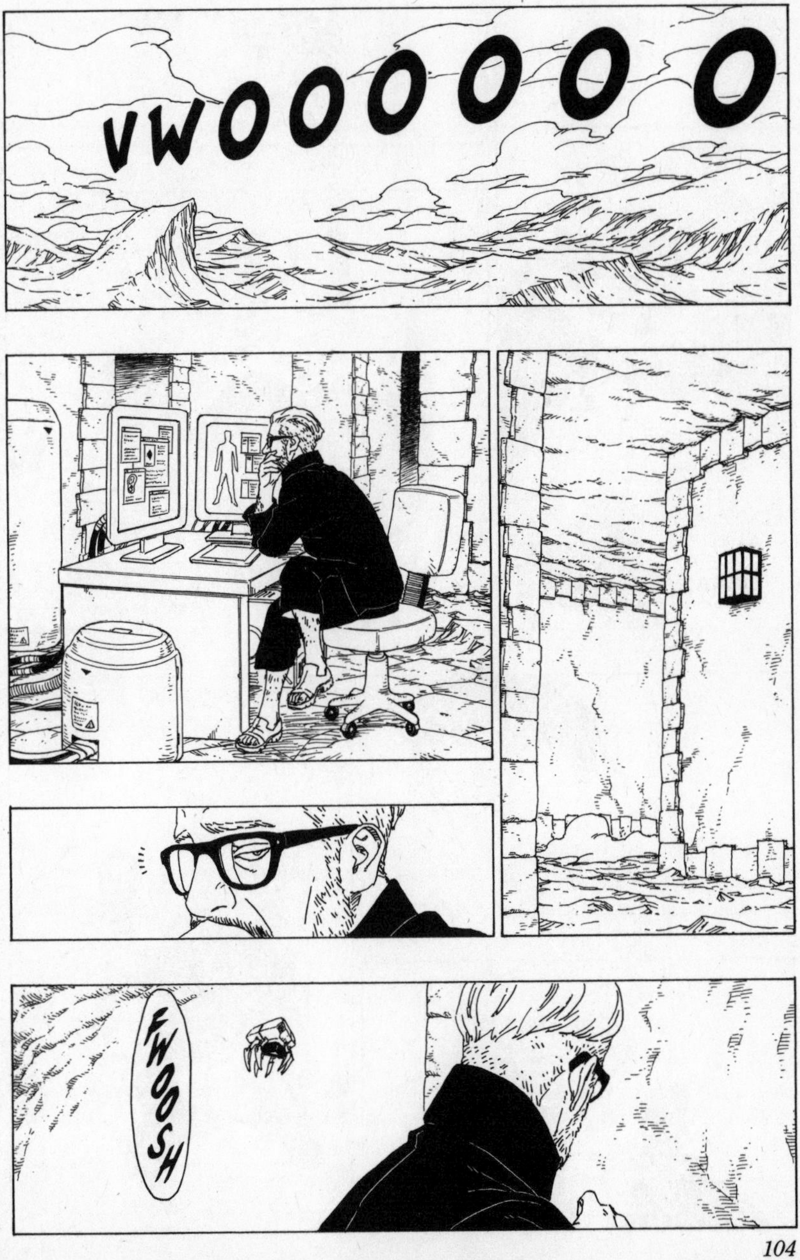
VWOOOOOO
FWOOSH

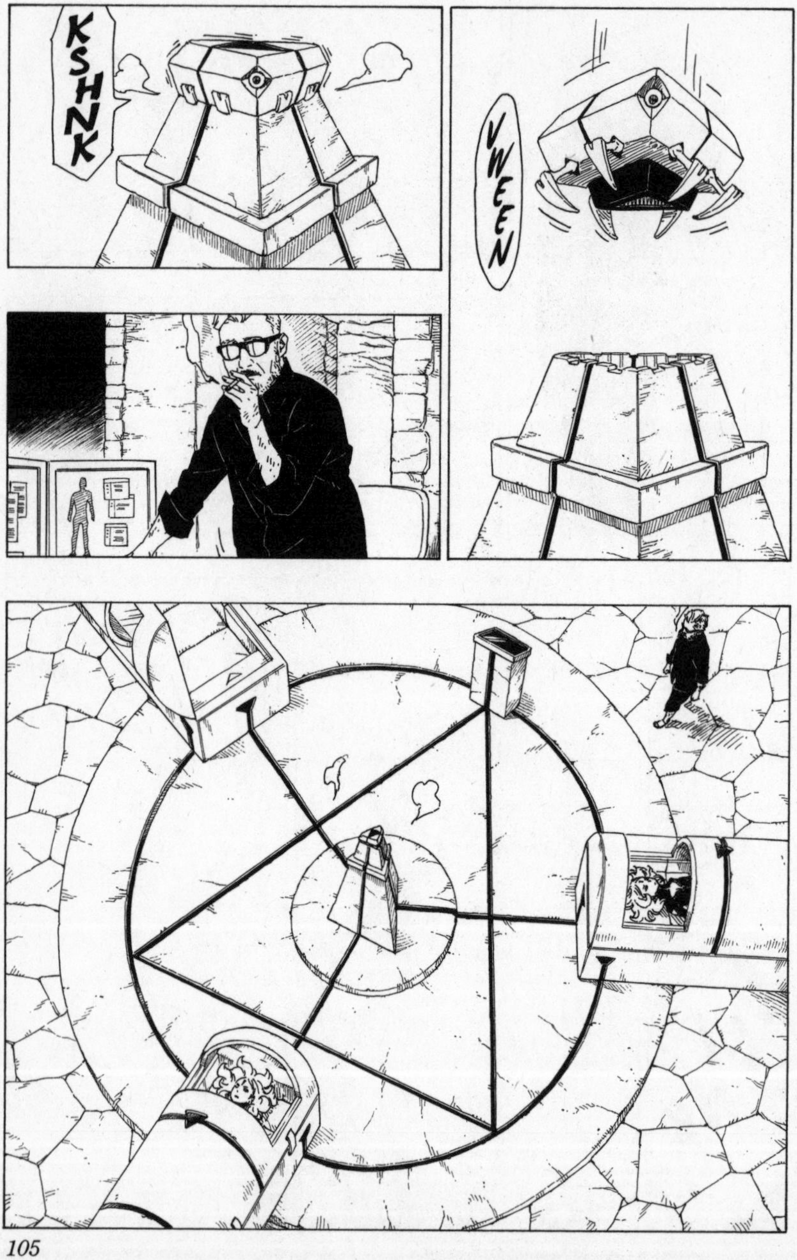
VWEEN
KSHNK

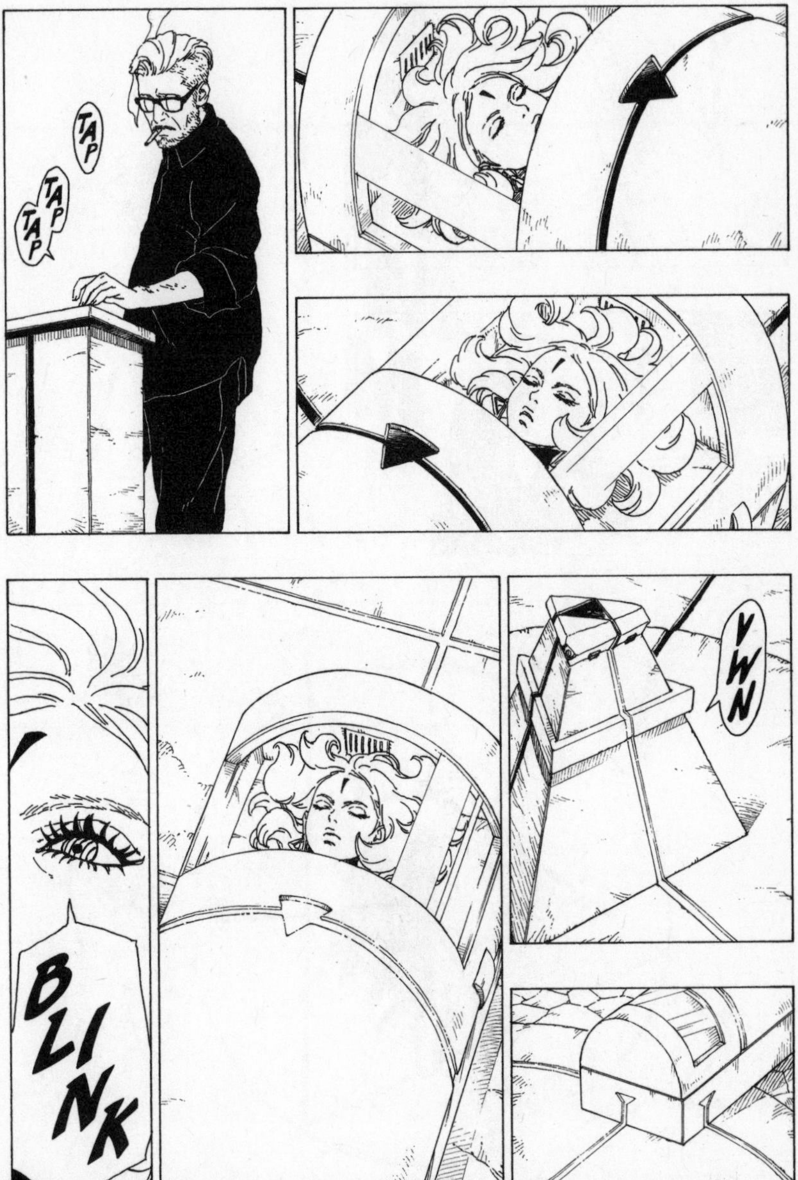
TAP
TAP TAP
VWN
BLINK

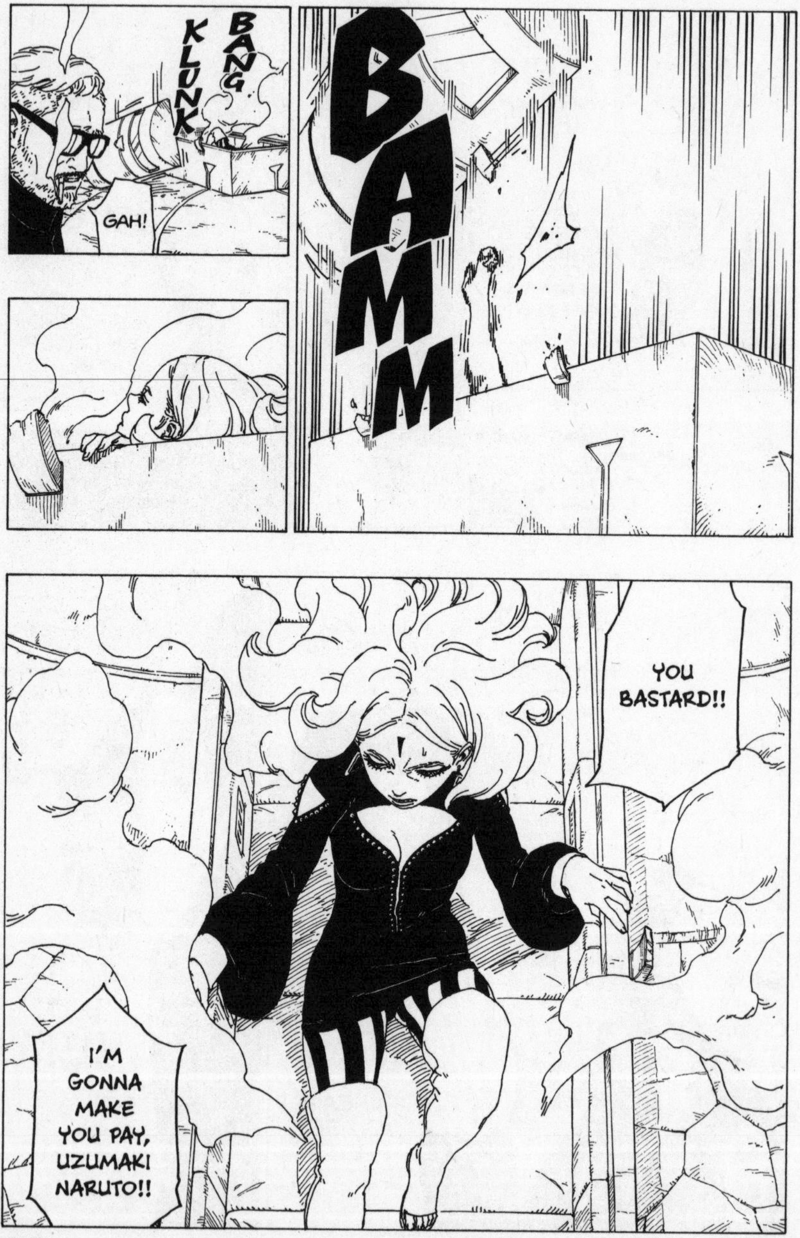
BAMM
BANG
KLUNK
GAH!
YOU BASTARD!!
I'M GONNA MAKE YOU PAY, UZUMAKI NARUTO!!

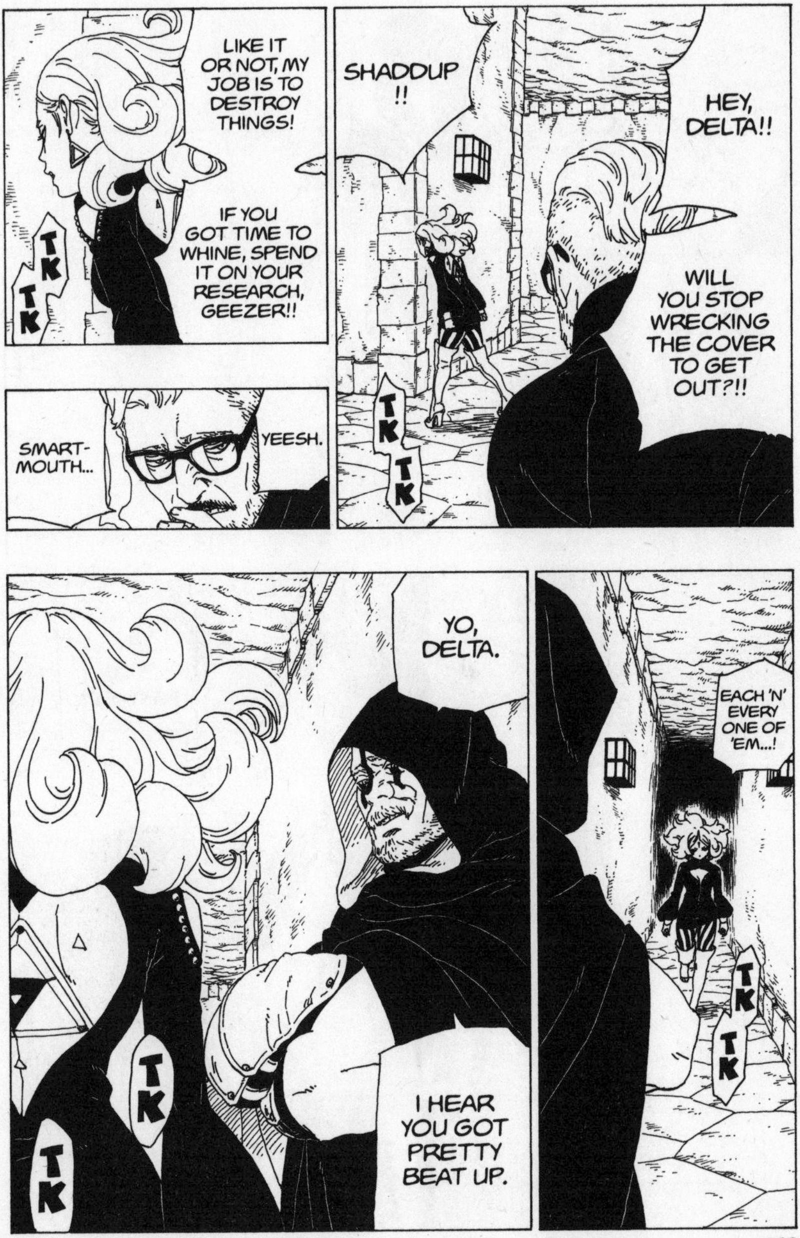
HEY, DELTA!!
WILL YOU STOP WRECKING THE COVER TO GET OUT?!!
SHADDUP !!
TK TK TK
LIKE IT OR NOT, MY JOB IS TO DESTROY THINGS!
IF YOU GOT TIME TO WHINE, SPEND IT ON YOUR RESEARCH, GEEZER!!
TK TK TK
YEESH.
SMART-MOUTH...
EACH 'N' EVERY ONE OF 'EM...!
TK TK TK
YO, DELTA.
I HEAR YOU GOT PRETTY BEAT UP.
TK TK TK

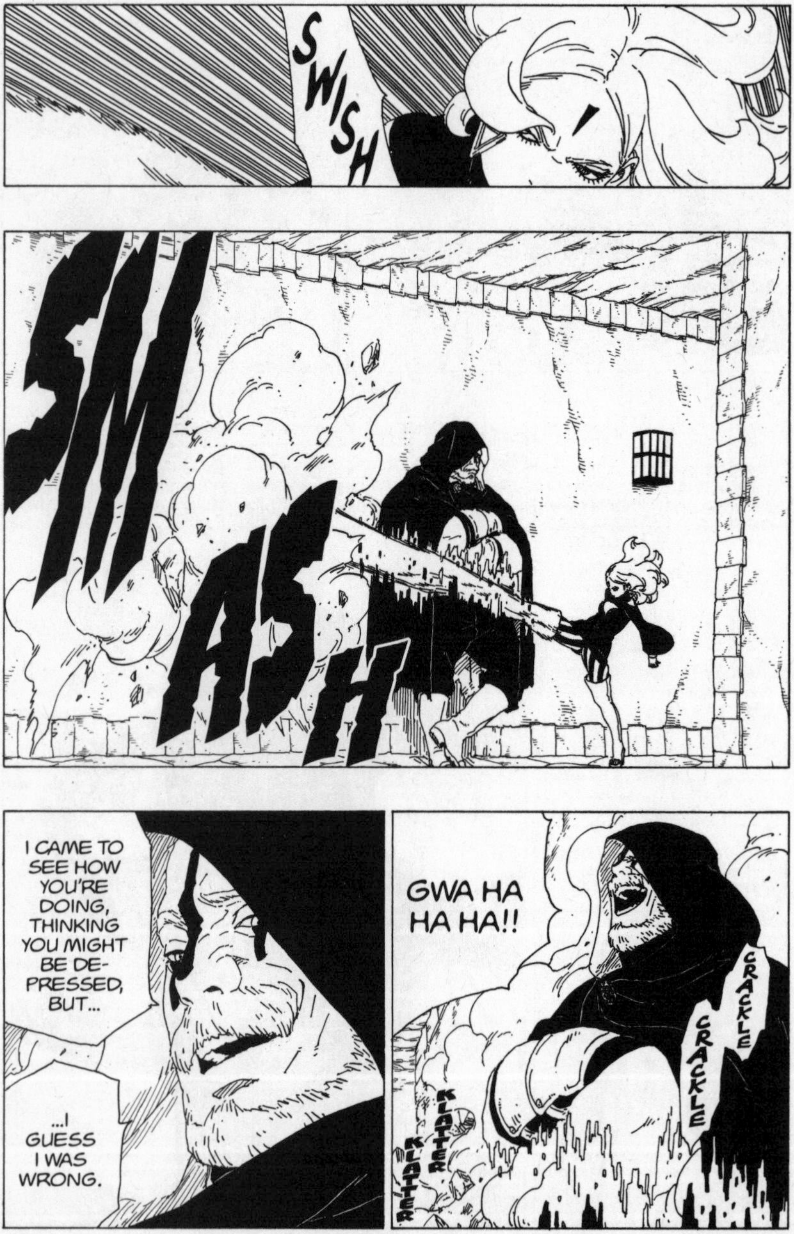
SWISH
SMASH
GWA HA HA HA!!
CRACKLE
CRACKLE
KLATTER
KLATTER
I CAME TO SEE HOW YOU'RE DOING, THINKING YOU MIGHT BE DE-PRESSED, BUT...
...I GUESS I WAS WRONG.

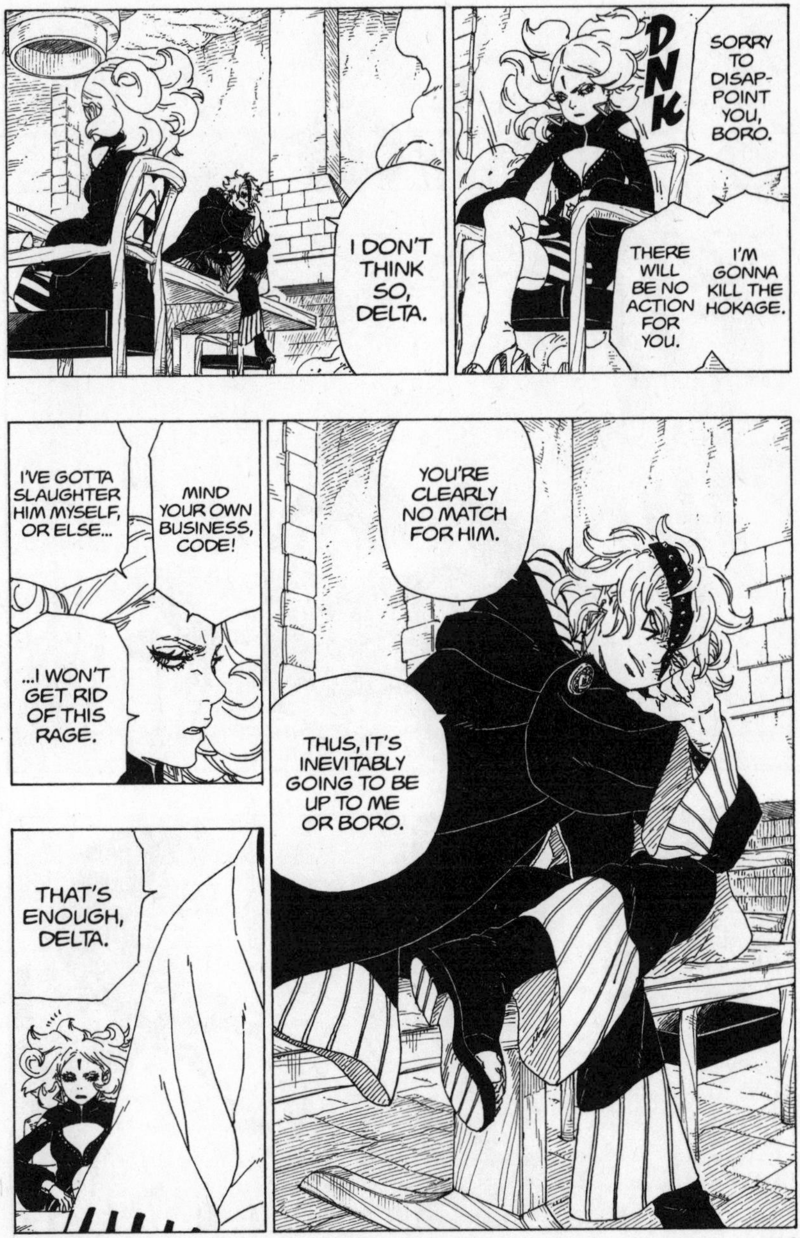
DNK
SORRY TO DISAP-POINT YOU, BORO.
I'M GONNA KILL THE HOKAGE.
THERE WILL BE NO ACTION FOR YOU.
I DON'T THINK SO, DELTA.
YOU'RE CLEARLY NO MATCH FOR HIM.
THUS, IT'S INEVITABLY GOING TO BE UP TO ME OR BORO.
MIND YOUR OWN BUSINESS, CODE!
I'VE GOTTA SLAUGHTER HIM MYSELF, OR ELSE...
...I WON'T GET RID OF THIS RAGE.
THAT'S ENOUGH, DELTA.

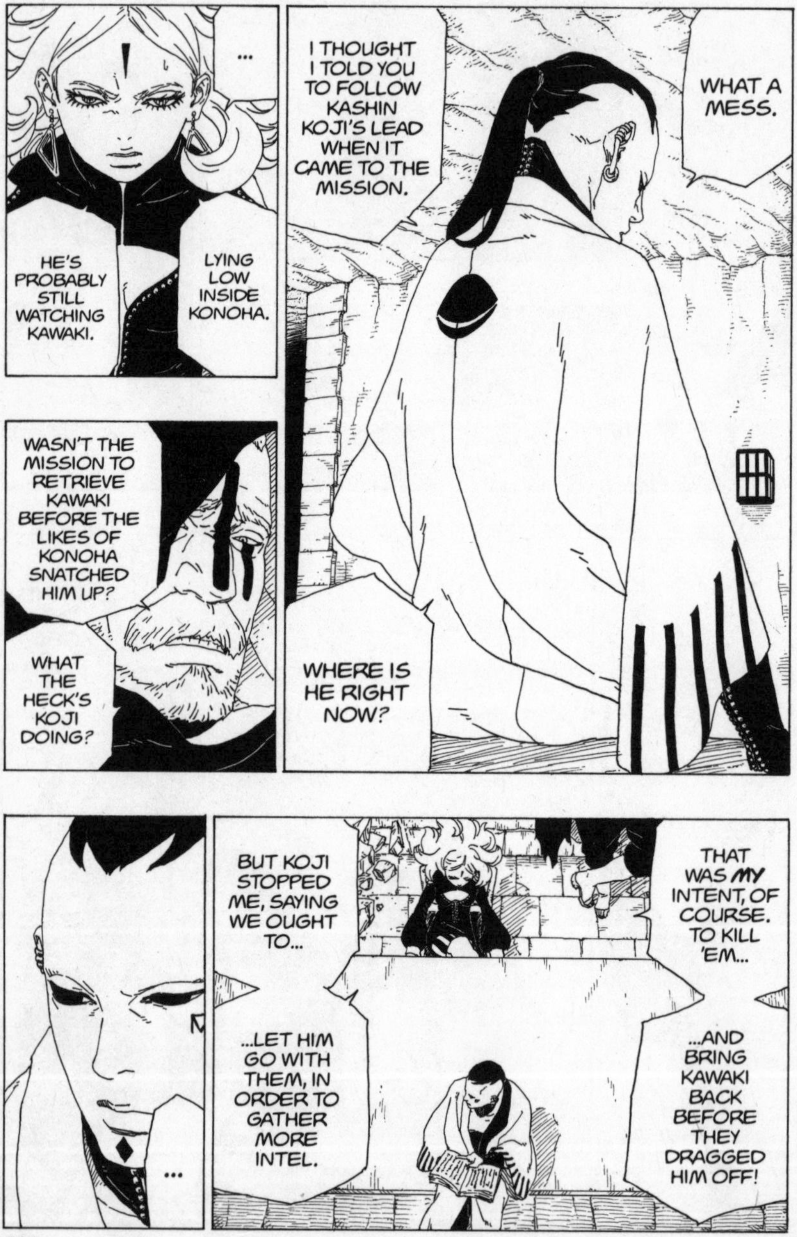
WHAT A MESS.
I THOUGHT I TOLD YOU TO FOLLOW KASHIN KOJI'S LEAD WHEN IT CAME TO THE MISSION.
WHERE IS HE RIGHT NOW?
...
LYING LOW INSIDE KONOHA.
HE'S PROBABLY STILL WATCHING KAWAKI.
WASN'T THE MISSION TO RETRIEVE KAWAKI BEFORE THE LIKES OF KONOHA SNATCHED HIM UP?
WHAT THE HECK'S KOJI DOING?
THAT WAS *MY* INTENT, OF COURSE. TO KILL 'EM...
...AND BRING KAWAKI BACK BEFORE THEY DRAGGED HIM OFF!
BUT KOJI STOPPED ME, SAYING WE OUGHT TO...
...LET HIM GO WITH THEM, IN ORDER TO GATHER MORE INTEL.
...

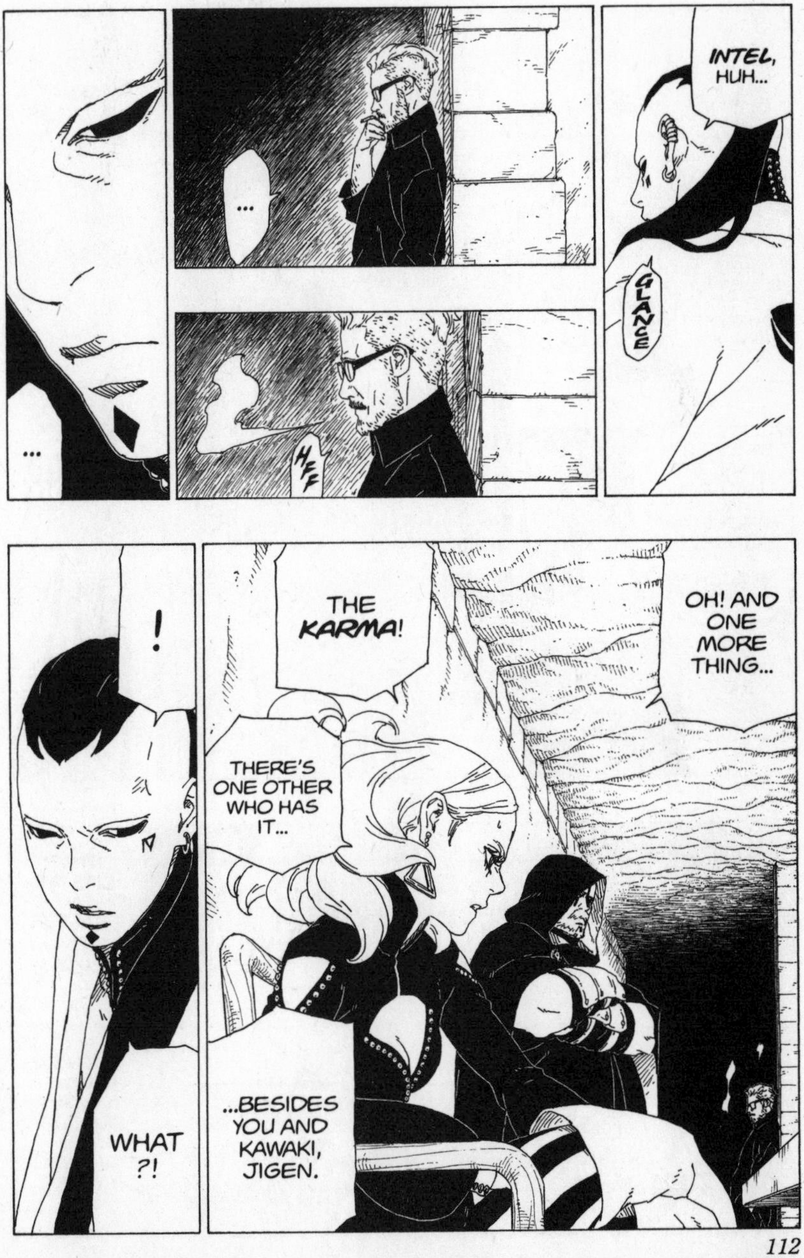
INTEL, HUH...
GLANCE
...
HFF
...
OH! AND ONE MORE THING...
THE KARMA!
THERE'S ONE OTHER WHO HAS IT...
...BESIDES YOU AND KAWAKI, JIGEN.
!
WHAT?!

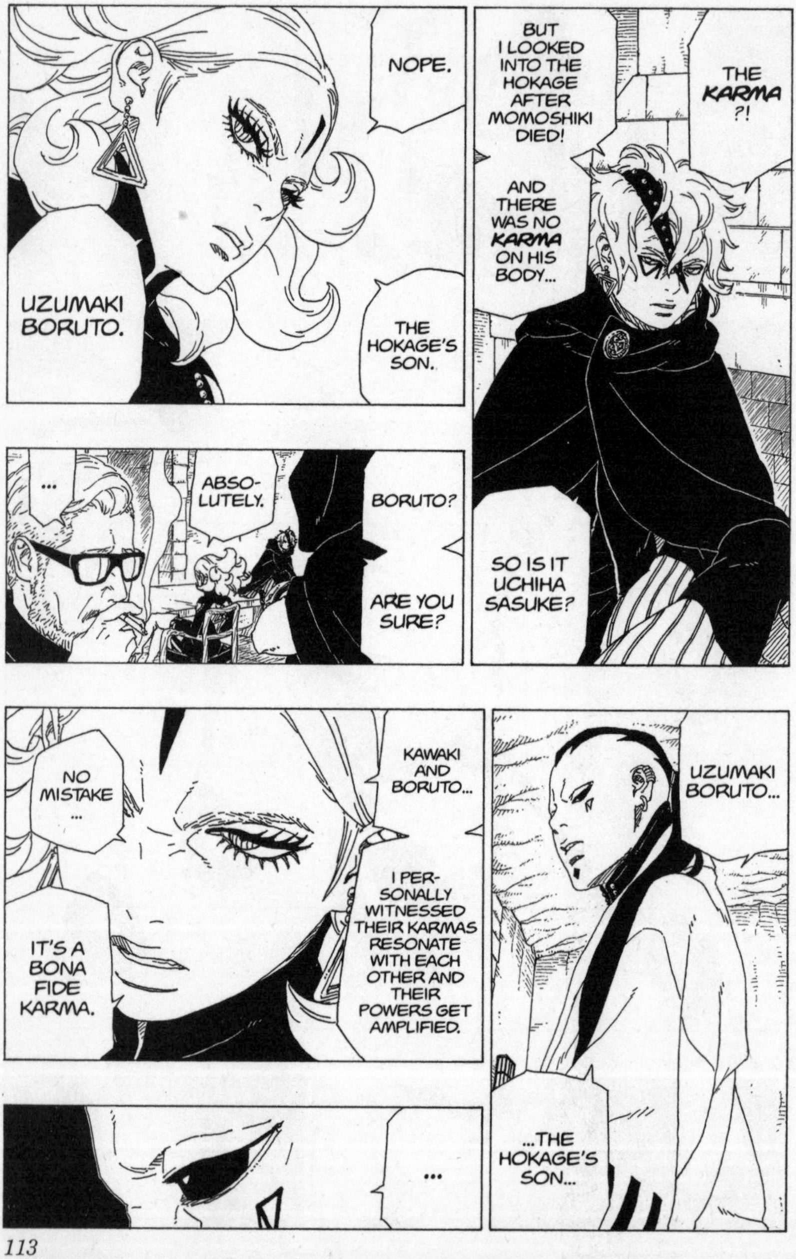
THE KARMA ?!
BUT I LOOKED INTO THE HOKAGE AFTER MOMOSHIKI DIED!
AND THERE WAS NO KARMA ON HIS BODY...
SO IS IT UCHIHA SASUKE?
NOPE.
UZUMAKI BORUTO.
THE HOKAGE'S SON.
BORUTO?
ARE YOU SURE?
ABSO-LUTELY.
...
UZUMAKI BORUTO...
...THE HOKAGE'S SON...
KAWAKI AND BORUTO...
I PER-SONALLY WITNESSED THEIR KARMAS RESONATE WITH EACH OTHER AND THEIR POWERS GET AMPLIFIED.
NO MISTAKE ...
IT'S A BONA FIDE KARMA.
...

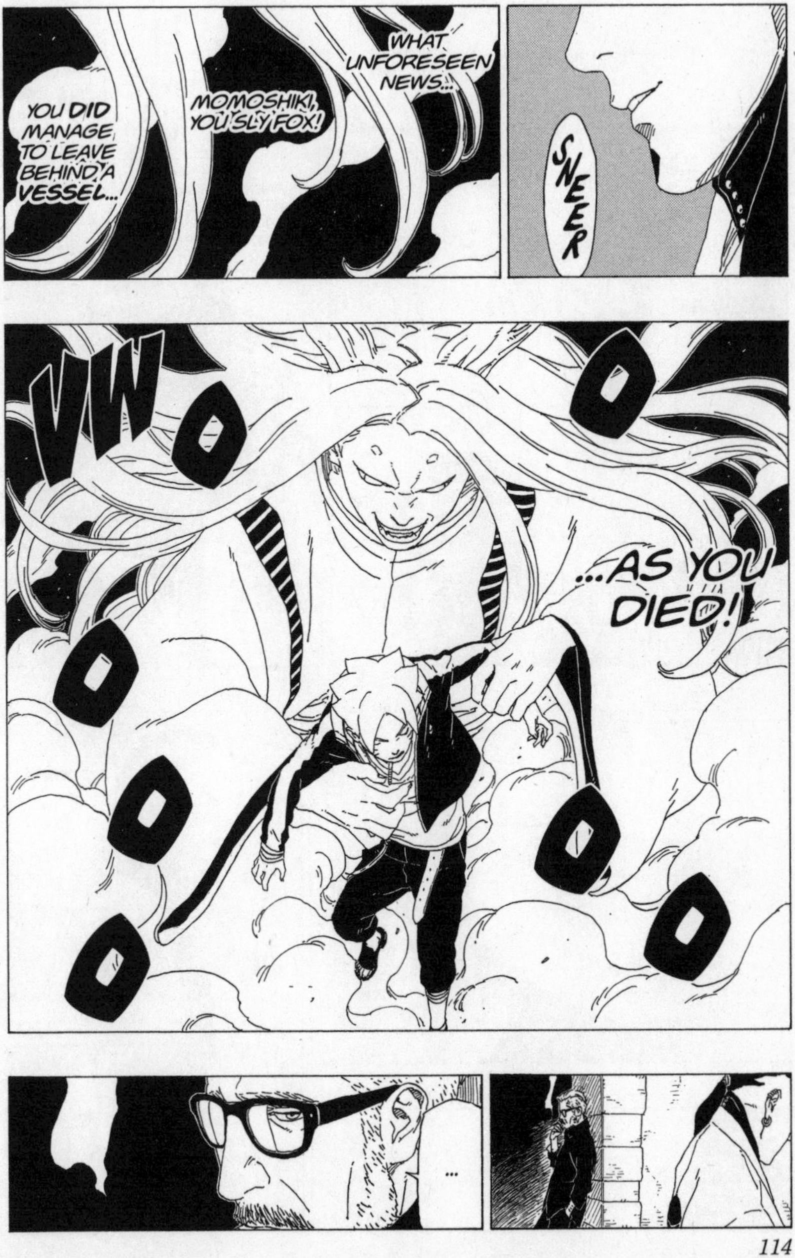
SNEER
WHAT UNFORESEEN NEWS...
MOMOSHIKI, YOU SLY FOX!
YOU DID MANAGE TO LEAVE BEHIND A VESSEL...
...AS YOU DIED!
VWOOOOOOO
...

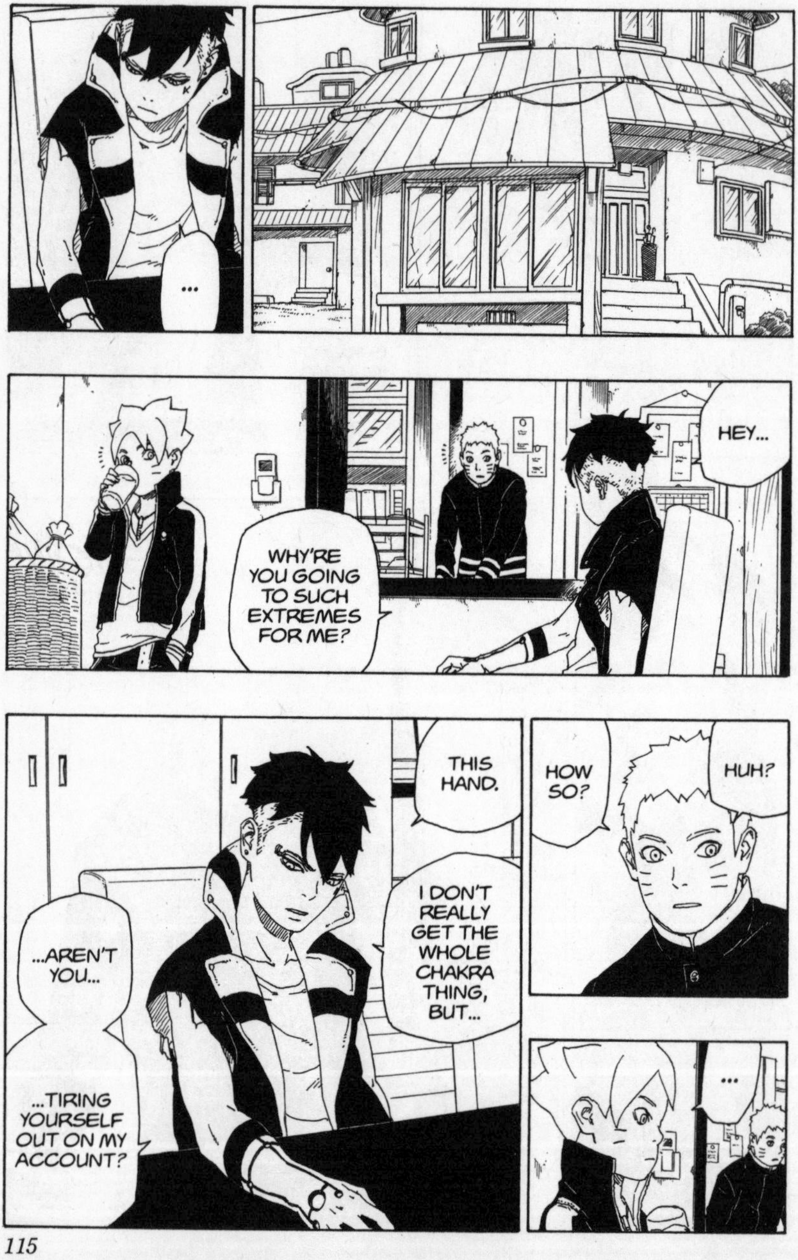
...
HEY...
WHY'RE YOU GOING TO SUCH EXTREMES FOR ME?
HUH?
HOW SO?
...
THIS HAND.
I DON'T REALLY GET THE WHOLE CHAKRA THING, BUT...
...AREN'T YOU...
...TIRING YOURSELF OUT ON MY ACCOUNT?

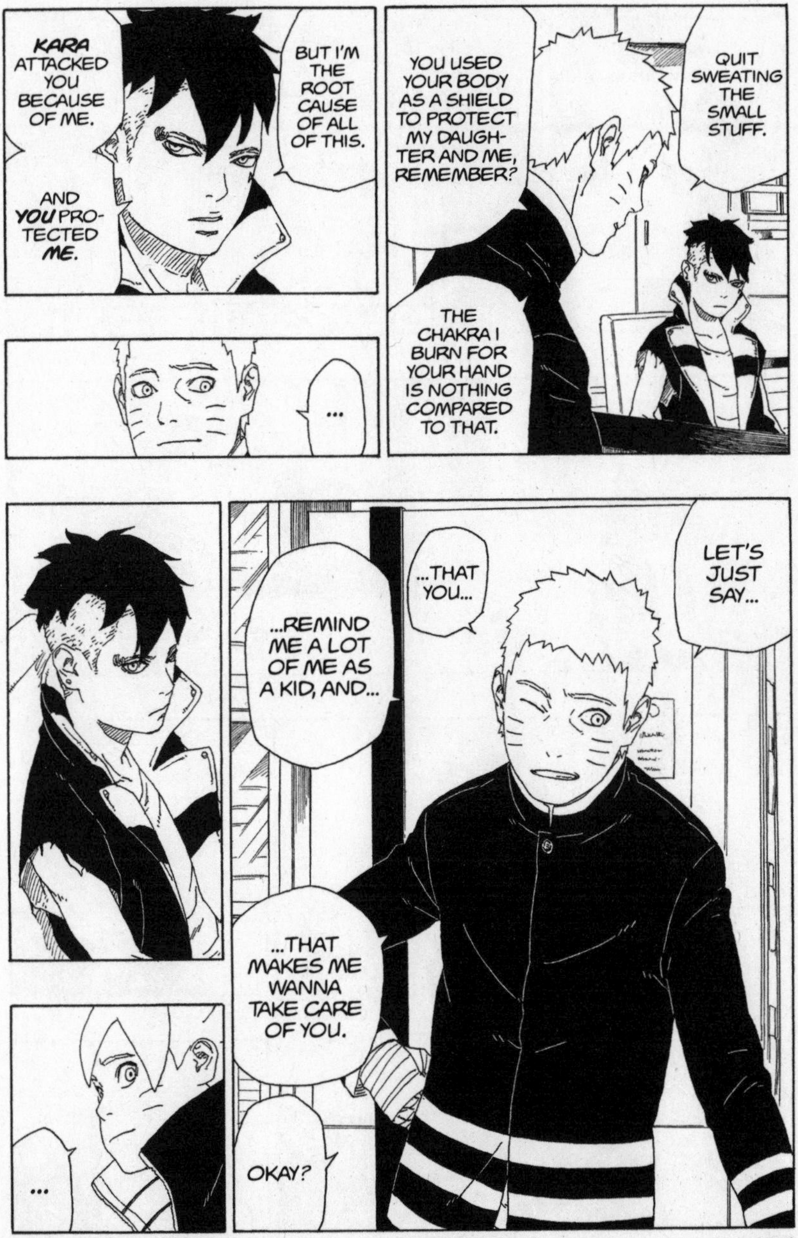
QUIT SWEATING THE SMALL STUFF.
YOU USED YOUR BODY AS A SHIELD TO PROTECT MY DAUGHTER AND ME, REMEMBER?
THE CHAKRA I BURN FOR YOUR HAND IS NOTHING COMPARED TO THAT.
BUT I'M THE ROOT CAUSE OF ALL OF THIS.
KARA ATTACKED YOU BECAUSE OF ME.
AND *YOU* PROTECTED *ME*.
...
LET'S JUST SAY...
...THAT YOU...
...REMIND ME A LOT OF ME AS A KID, AND...
...THAT MAKES ME WANNA TAKE CARE OF YOU.
OKAY?
...

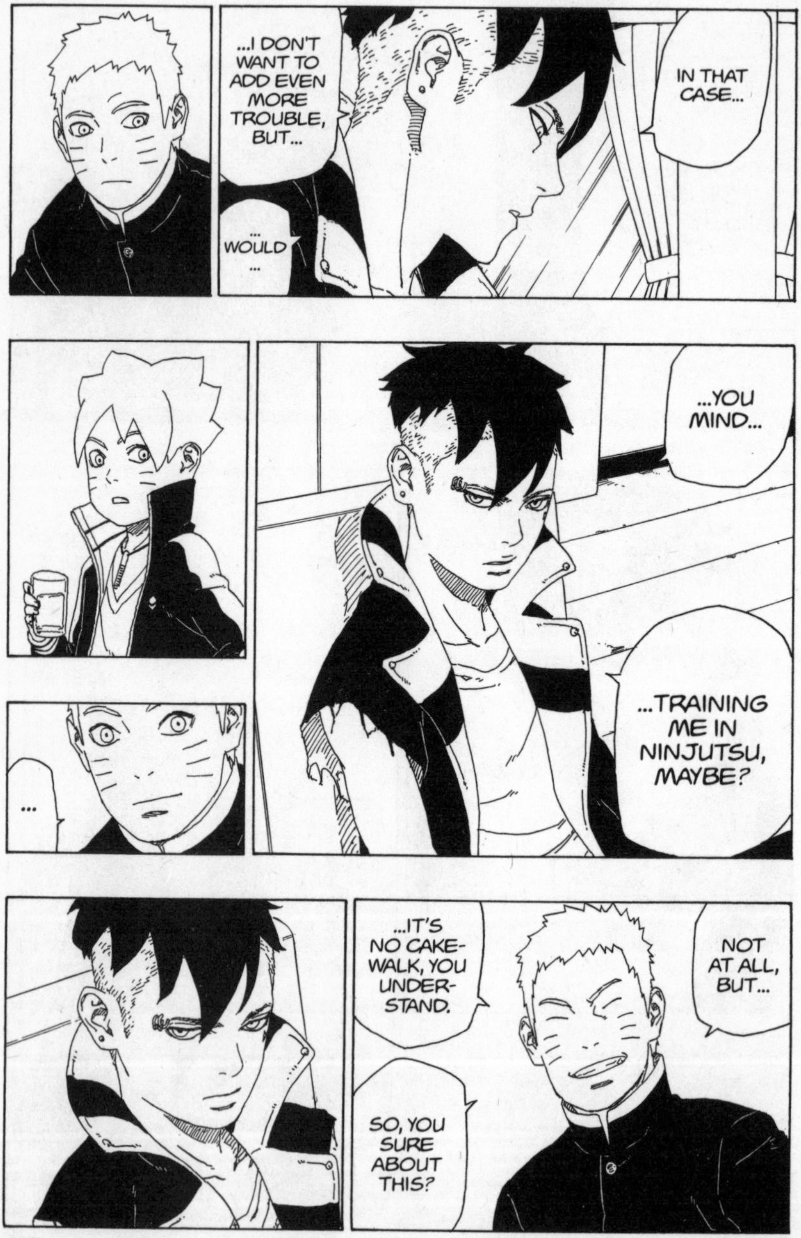
IN THAT CASE...
...I DON'T WANT TO ADD EVEN MORE TROUBLE, BUT...
...WOULD...
...YOU MIND...
...TRAINING ME IN NINJUTSU, MAYBE?
...
NOT AT ALL, BUT...
...IT'S NO CAKEWALK, YOU UNDERSTAND.
SO, YOU SURE ABOUT THIS?

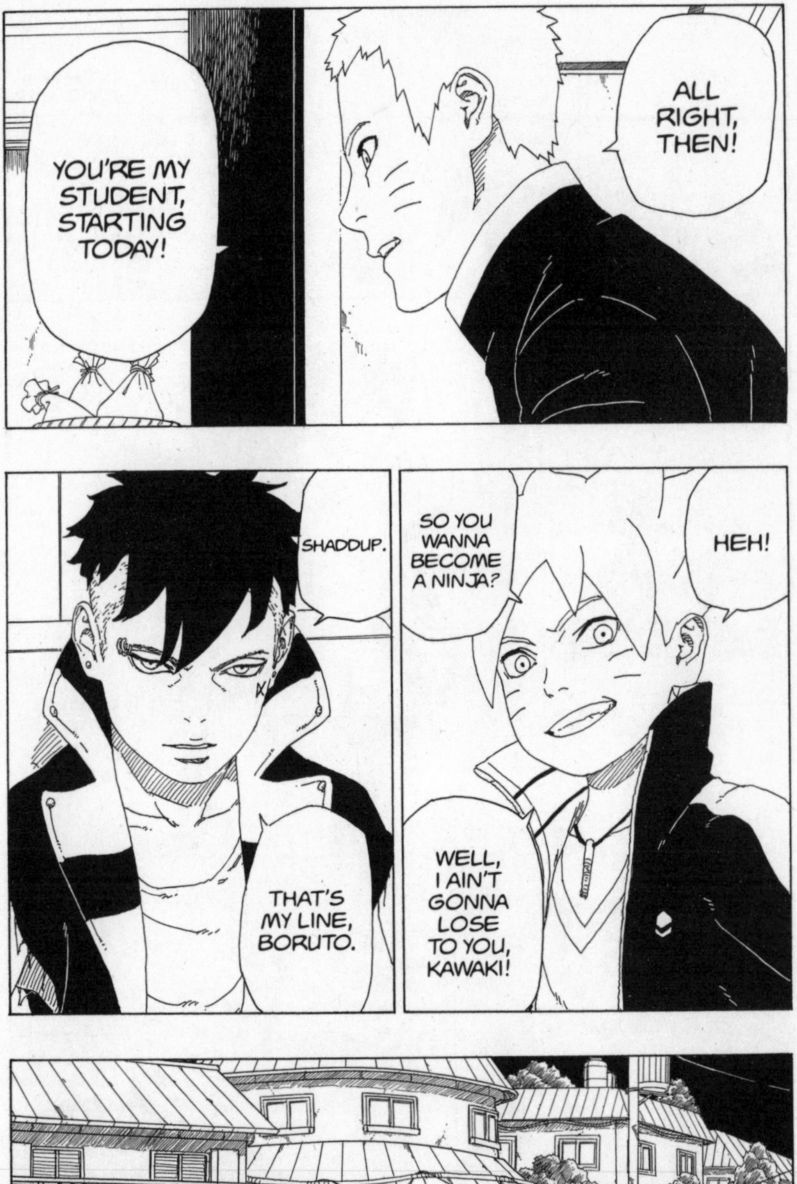
ALL RIGHT, THEN!
YOU'RE MY STUDENT, STARTING TODAY!
HEH!
SO YOU WANNA BECOME A NINJA?
WELL, I AIN'T GONNA LOSE TO YOU, KAWAKI!
SHADDUP.
THAT'S MY LINE, BORUTO.

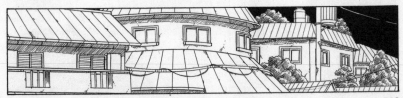

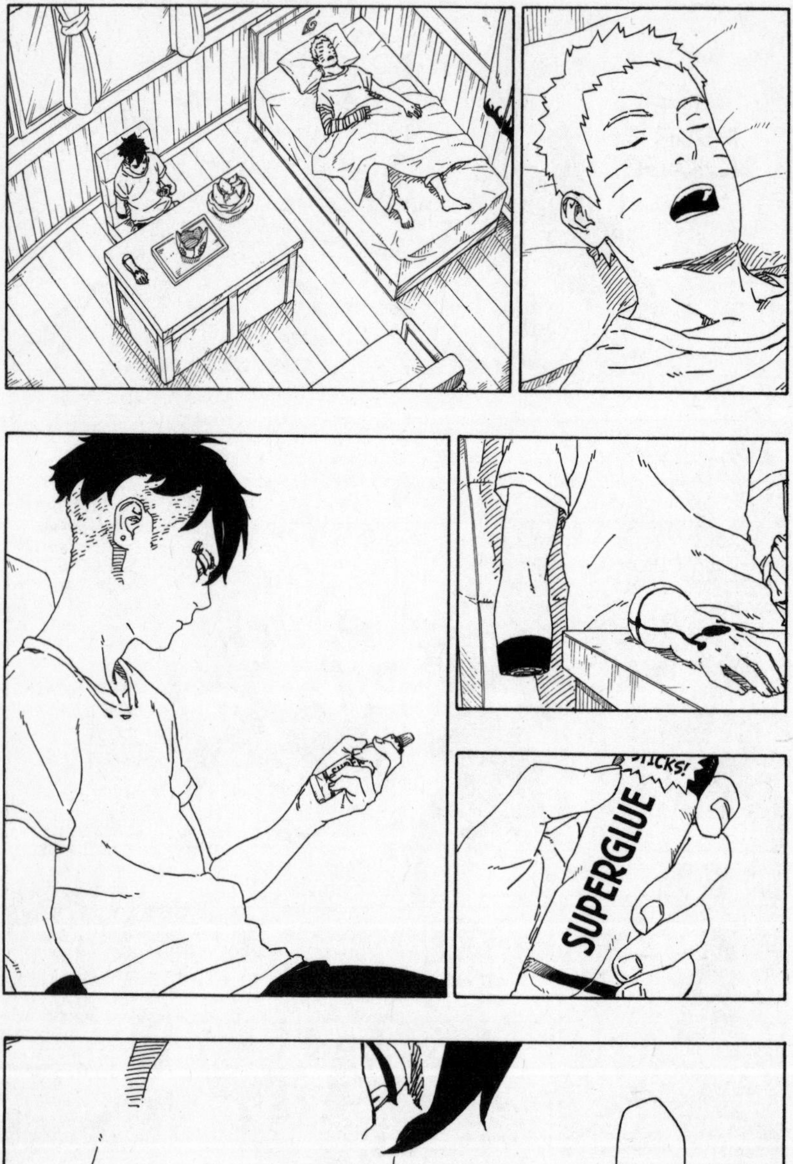
SUPERGLUE
STICKS!
...

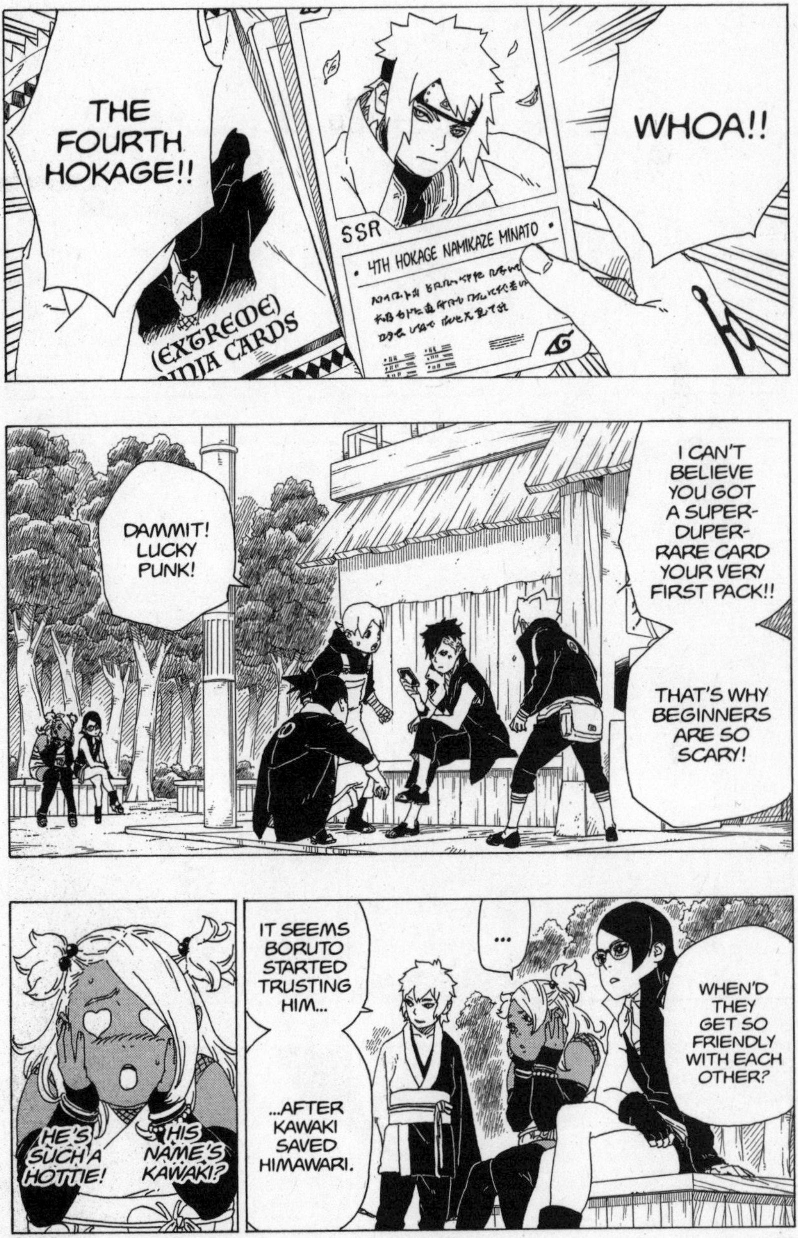
WHOA!!
SSR
4TH HOKAGE NAMIKAZE MINATO
THE FOURTH HOKAGE!!
(EXTREME)
I CAN'T BELIEVE YOU GOT A SUPER-DUPER-RARE CARD YOUR VERY FIRST PACK!!
THAT'S WHY BEGINNERS ARE SO SCARY!
DAMMIT! LUCKY PUNK!
WHEN'D THEY GET SO FRIENDLY WITH EACH OTHER?
...
IT SEEMS BORUTO STARTED TRUSTING HIM...
...AFTER KAWAKI SAVED HIMAWARI.
HIS NAME'S KAWAKI?
HE'S SUCH A HOTTIE!

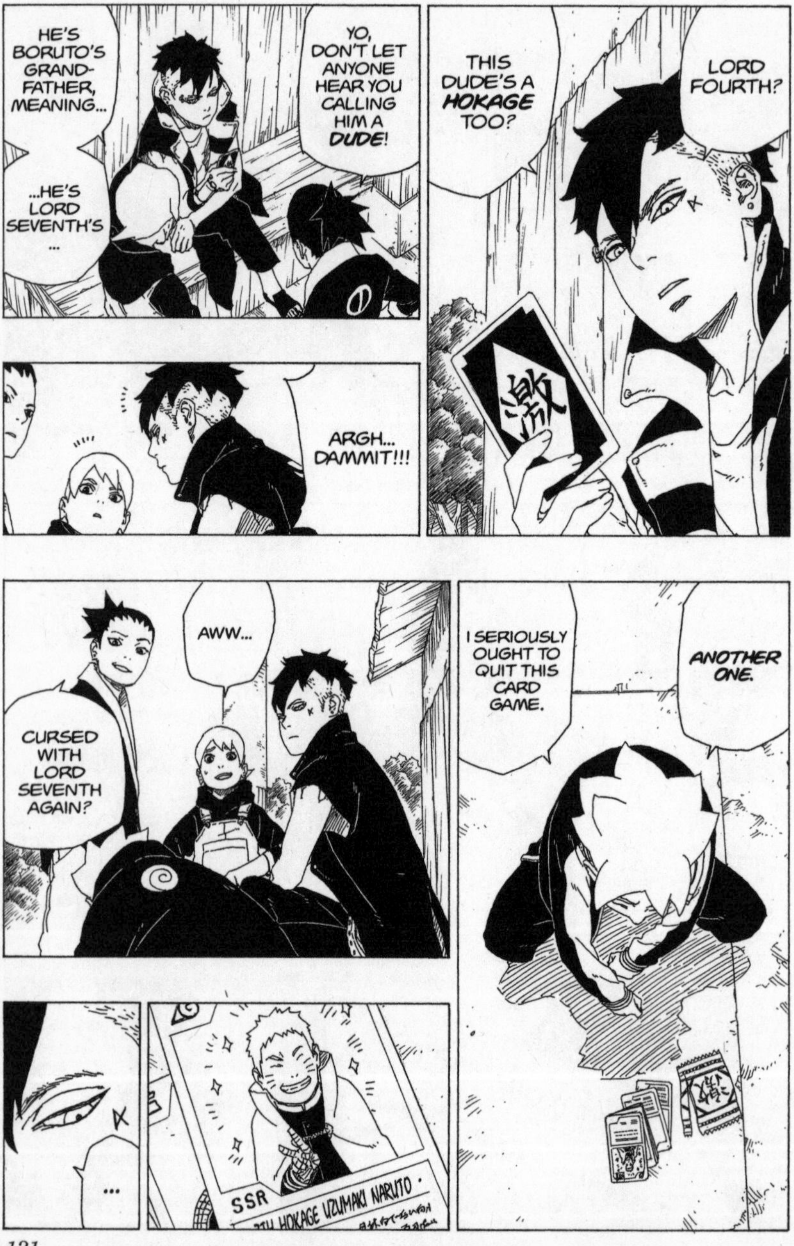
LORD FOURTH?
THIS DUDE'S A **HOKAGE** TOO?
YO, DON'T LET ANYONE HEAR YOU CALLING HIM A **DUDE**!
HE'S BORUTO'S GRAND-FATHER, MEANING...
...HE'S LORD SEVENTH'S ...
ARGH... DAMMIT!!!
ANOTHER ONE.
I SERIOUSLY OUGHT TO QUIT THIS CARD GAME.
AWW...
CURSED WITH LORD SEVENTH AGAIN?
SSR
7TH HOKAGE UZUMAKI NARUTO
...

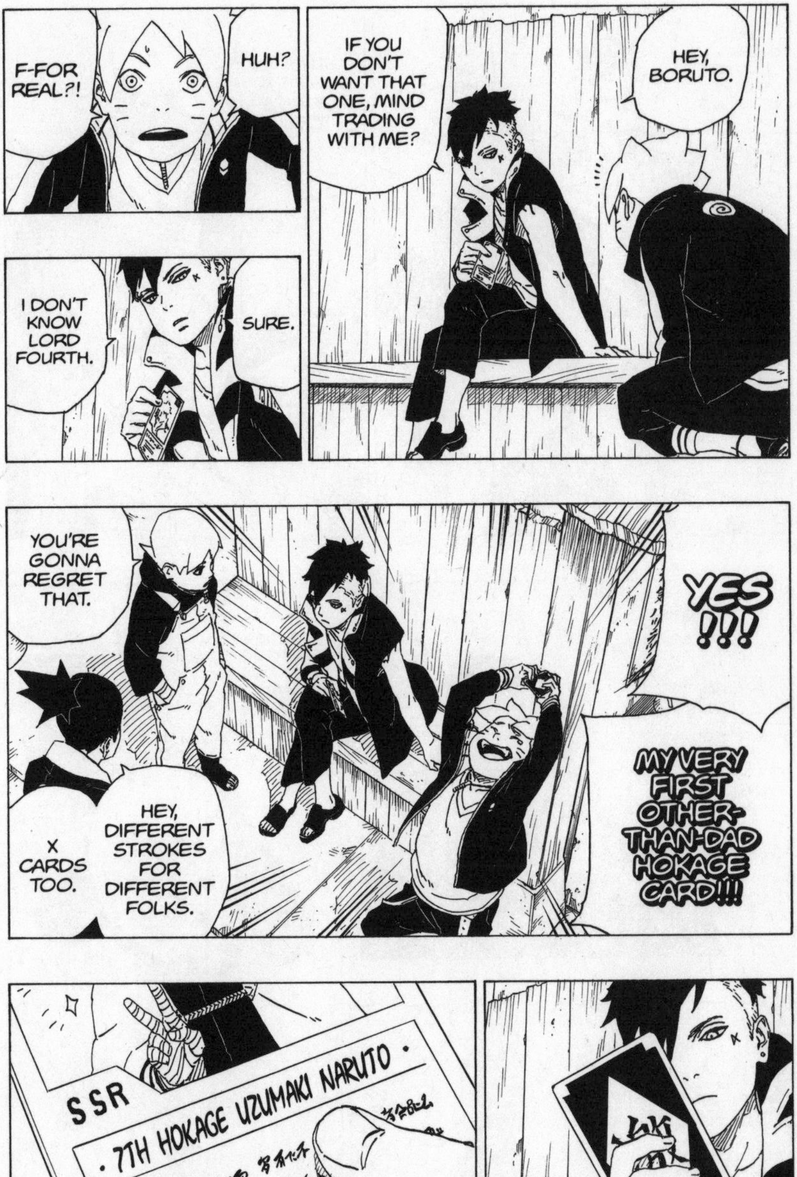
HEY, BORUTO.
IF YOU DON'T WANT THAT ONE, MIND TRADING WITH ME?
HUH?
F-FOR REAL?!
SURE.
I DON'T KNOW LORD FOURTH.
YES!!!
MY VERY FIRST OTHER-THAN-DAD HOKAGE CARD!!!
YOU'RE GONNA REGRET THAT.
HEY, DIFFERENT STROKES FOR DIFFERENT FOLKS.
X CARDS TOO.
SSR
· 7TH HOKAGE UZUMAKI NARUTO ·

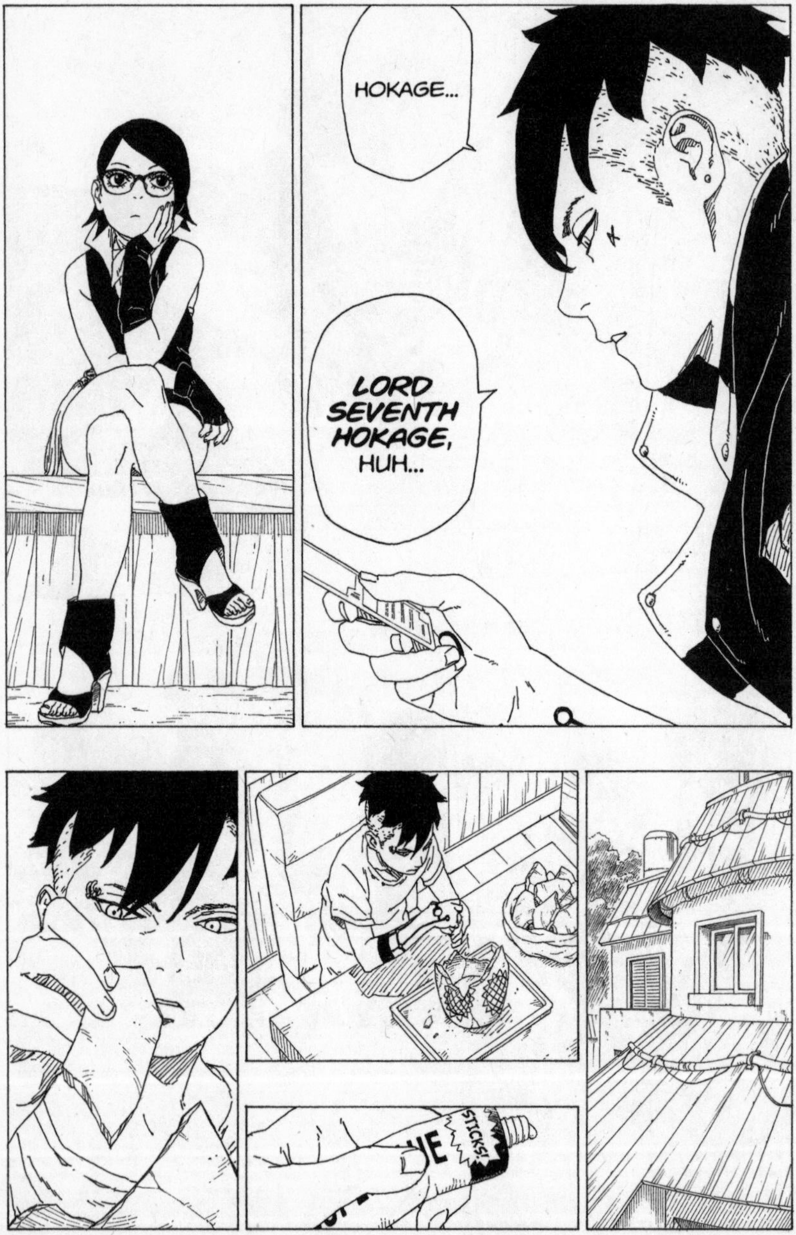
HOKAGE...
LORD SEVENTH HOKAGE, HUH...
STICKS!

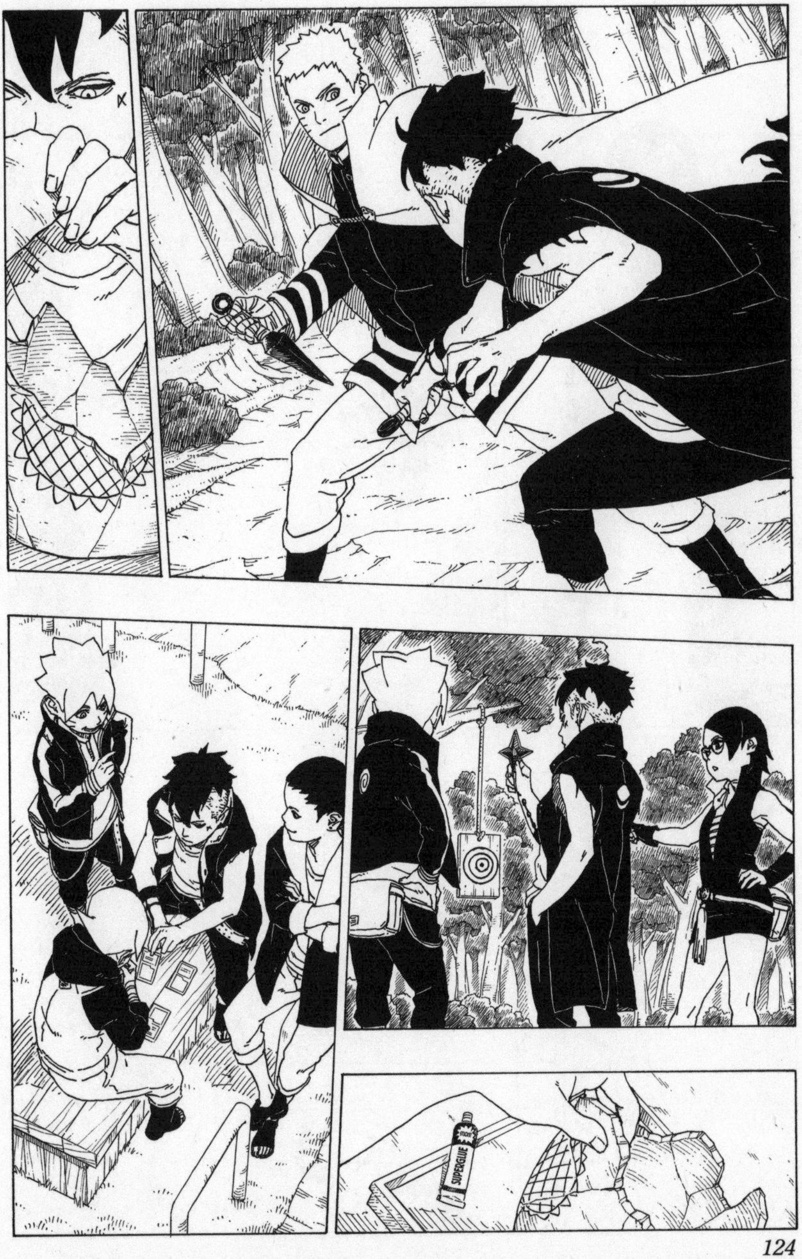
SUPERGLUE

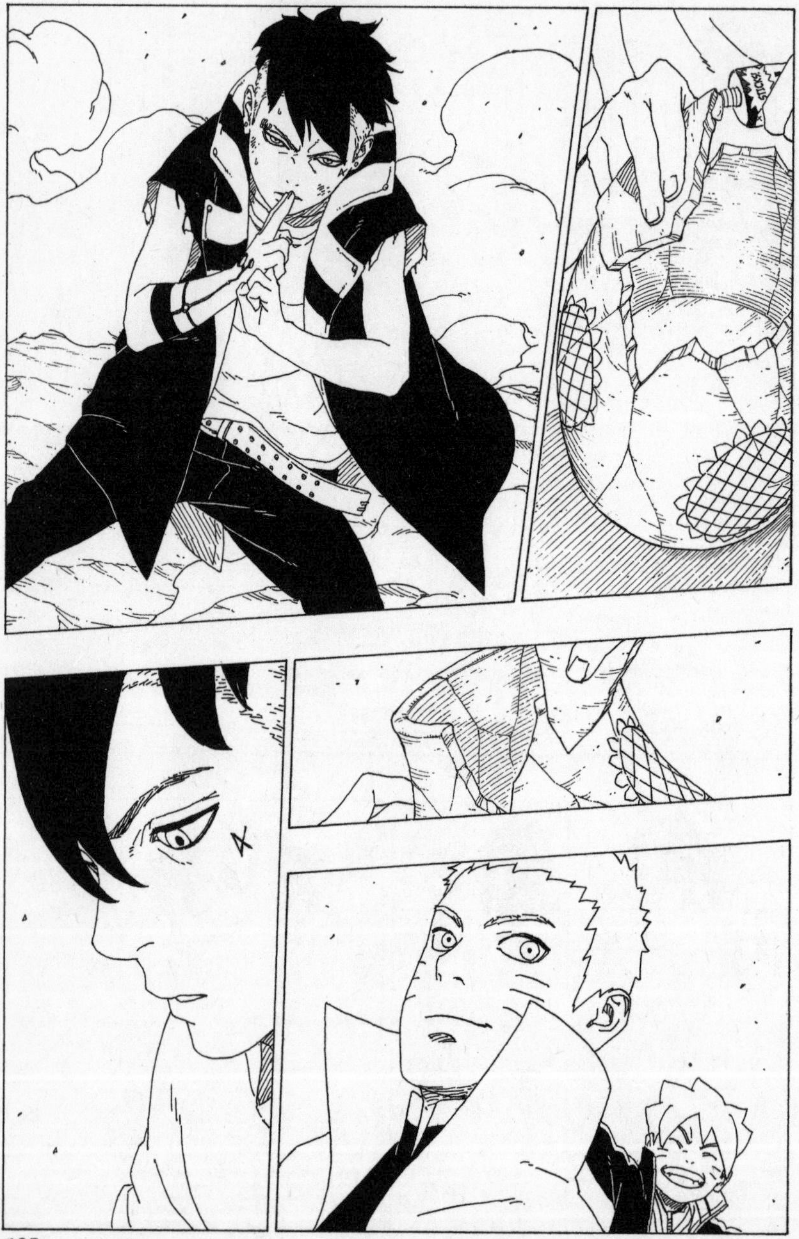
STICKS!

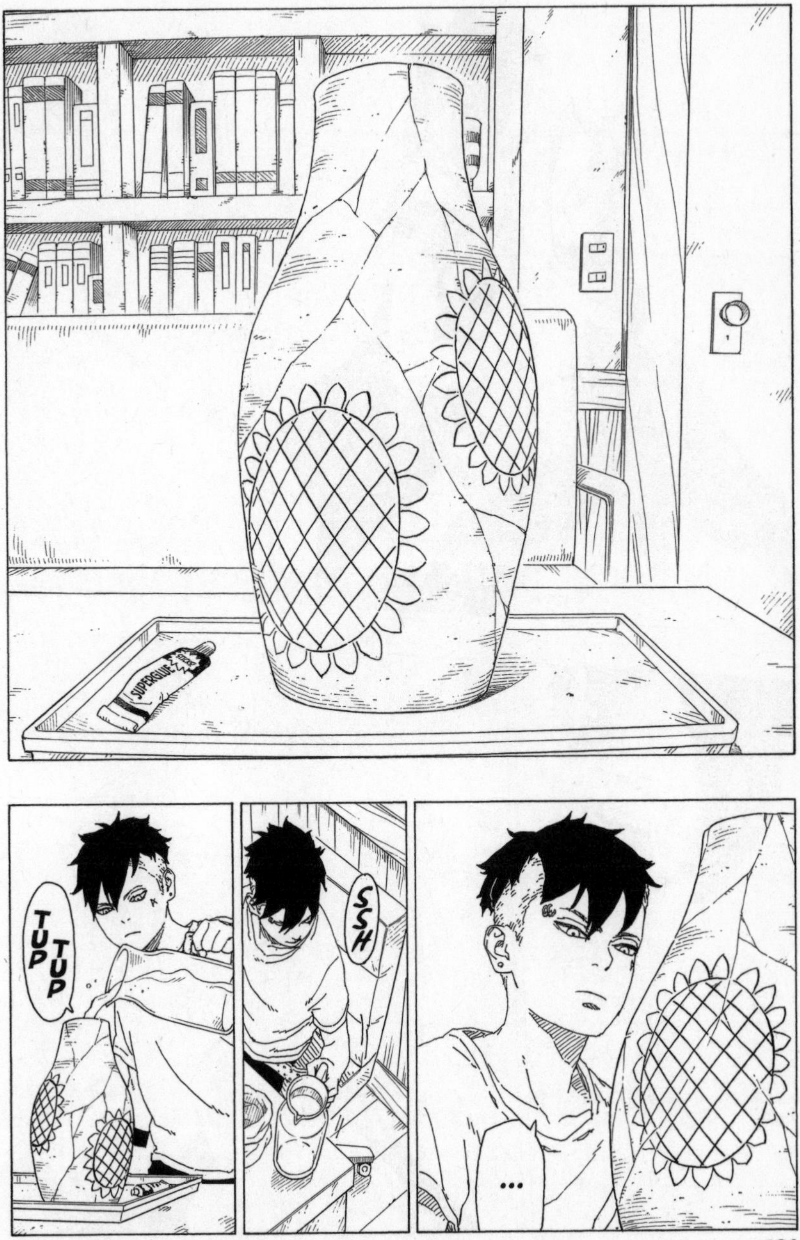
SUPERGLUE
...
SSH
TUP TUP

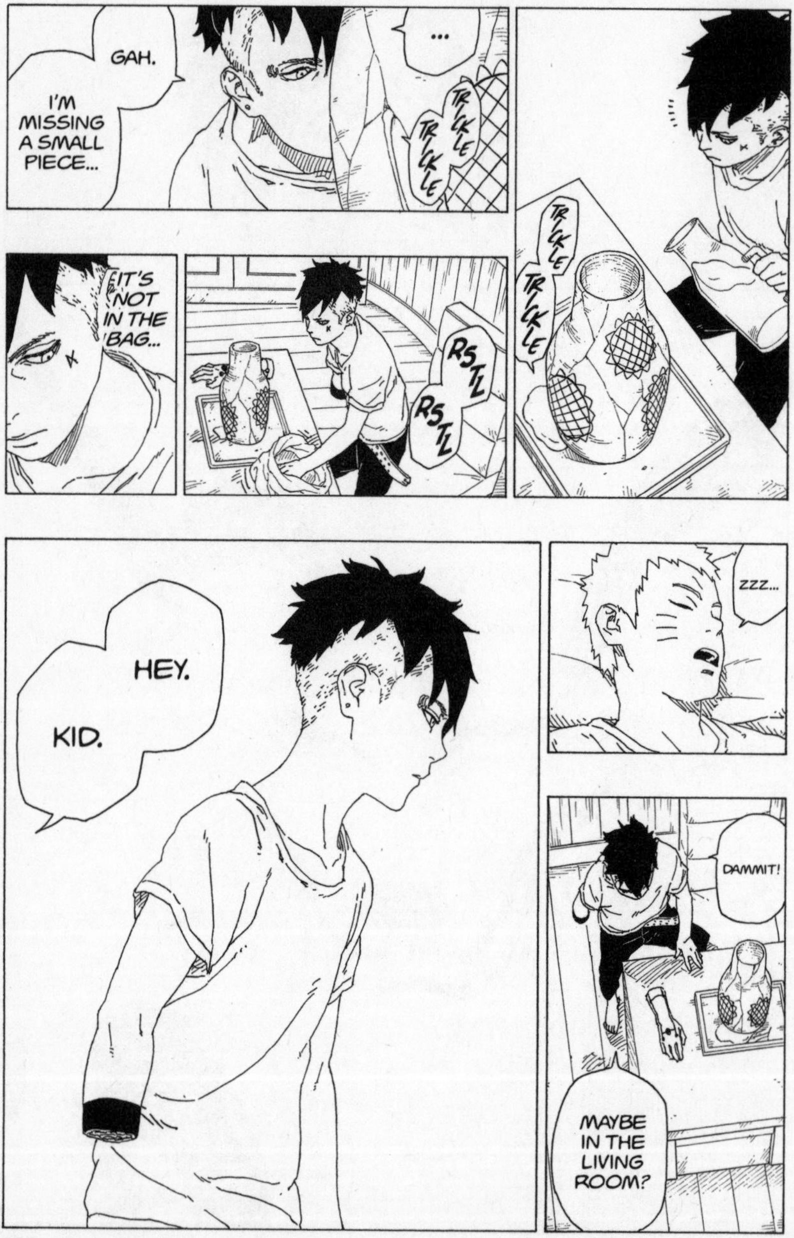
TRICKLE
TRICKLE
...
TRICKLE
TRICKLE
GAH.
I'M MISSING A SMALL PIECE...
RSTL
RSTL
IT'S NOT IN THE BAG...
ZZZ...
DAMMIT!
MAYBE IN THE LIVING ROOM?
HEY.
KID.

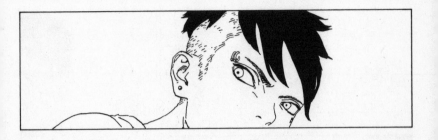

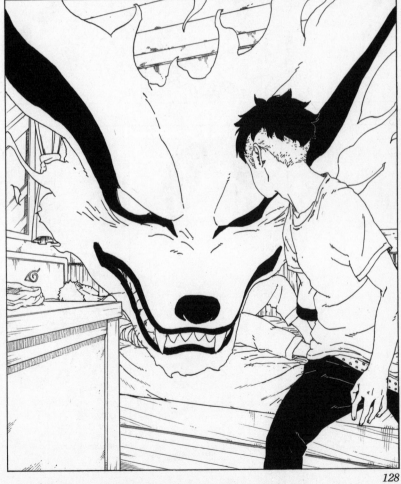

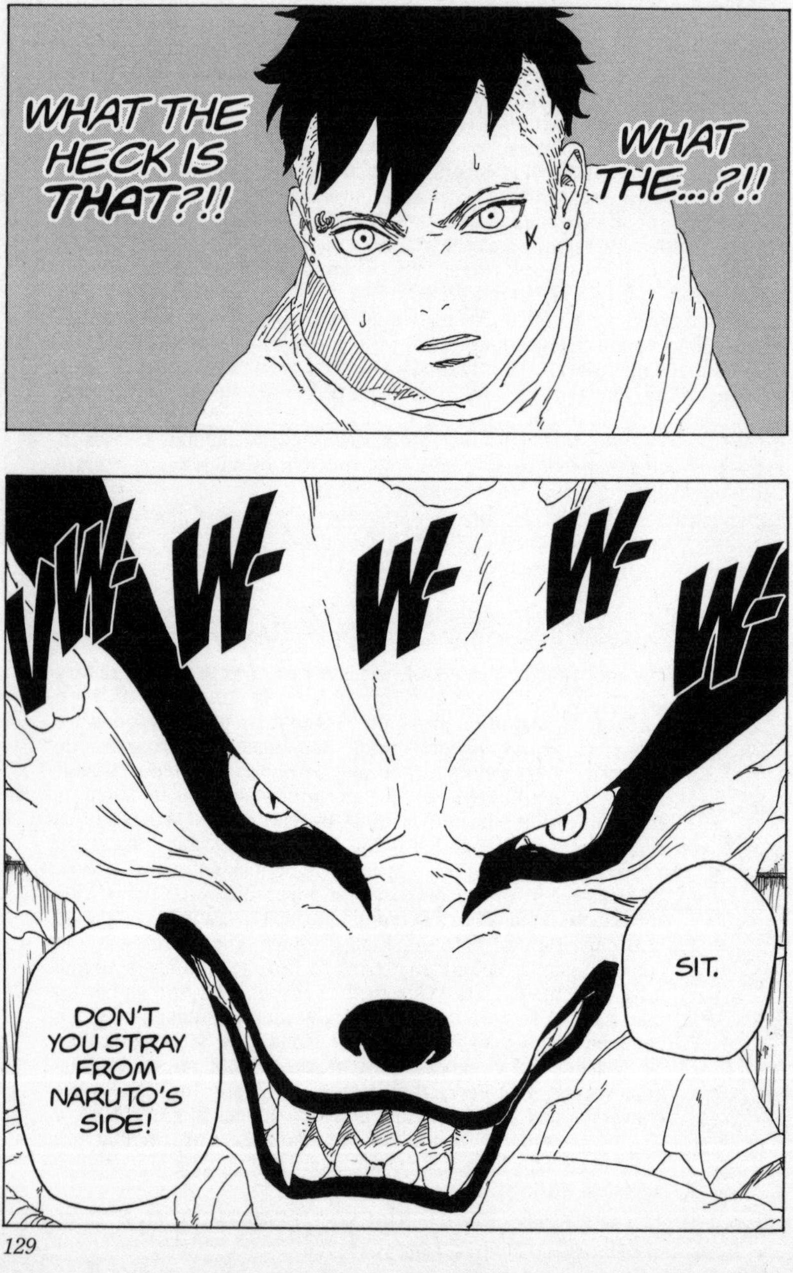
WHAT THE...?!!
WHAT THE HECK IS THAT?!!
W- W- W- W- W-
SIT.
DON'T YOU STRAY FROM NARUTO'S SIDE!

Shinobi Hiden Column 3: Shinobi and How They Are Organized

The smallest unit of shinobi is a three-member squad (Three-Man Cell). This is because three is the most appropriate number of people to cover each other's blind spots, while not placing excessive restrictions on each other's movements. A unit consisting of a Three-Man Cell plus a commanding officer (Sergeant) has the designation "Team." Team is family, Team is siblings. However, the Three-Man Cell is not a golden rule. Super high-level shinobi, such as Naruto, tend more to solo action, and Sarutobi Konohamaru, renowned as a Konoha genius, favors paired movement (Two-Man Cell) with his partner. Having said that, other than a few exceptions such as these and so long as it is not a special mission, the "Team" unit incorporating a Three-Man Cell should be regarded as the standard. Of course, depending on the details of the mission, the individual composition of the assigned Three-Man Cell might be altered. Furthermore, in the case of a large-scale mission, a six-member battle unit (Combat Squad) would be formed by combining two Teams. There would be one commanding officer in this instance too, resulting in 1 commanding officer + 6 battle unit = 7 shinobi, working in concert. Such a battle unit is almost at the limit in terms of personnel number for tactical operations; it is exceedingly rare to be able to effectively manage more individuals in a closely packed state. This is because many ninjutsu possess an extremely wide range of attack, and thus the risk of allies inadvertently becoming collateral casualties becomes too great.

The unit that is formed ad hoc in times of large-scale military campaigns is the platoon. One platoon is composed of three battle units, and is led by a high-ranked jonin ninja. Platoons are able to carry out advanced battle jutsu such as surround-and-annihilate, dam sabotage, and multi-front simultaneous assault and it is commonplace to incorporate specialists such as communication ninja, medic ninja, cyber ninja and sensory ninja to be able to independently handle every possible stratagem. There are also cases of companies being formed in Great Ninja War-class conflicts. Composed of three platoons, namely 67 shinobi, a company has just one single objective, such as engaging in the wielding of Katon or long-distance communication, and depending on its sphere, may rival the Gokage, or manage to pull off great feats even the Gokage are incapable of. And higher up than that exist battalions, which are each composed of three companies, but following the conclusion of the Great Ninja War, no Village really expects any further battalion-scale ninja deployment. However, the need to prepare for crises has conversely led to the training of senior officer ninja capable of serving as company and battalion commanders proceeding at a rapid pace. This is because many such commanding officer ninja were lost during the last Great War.

Number 35: Up to You

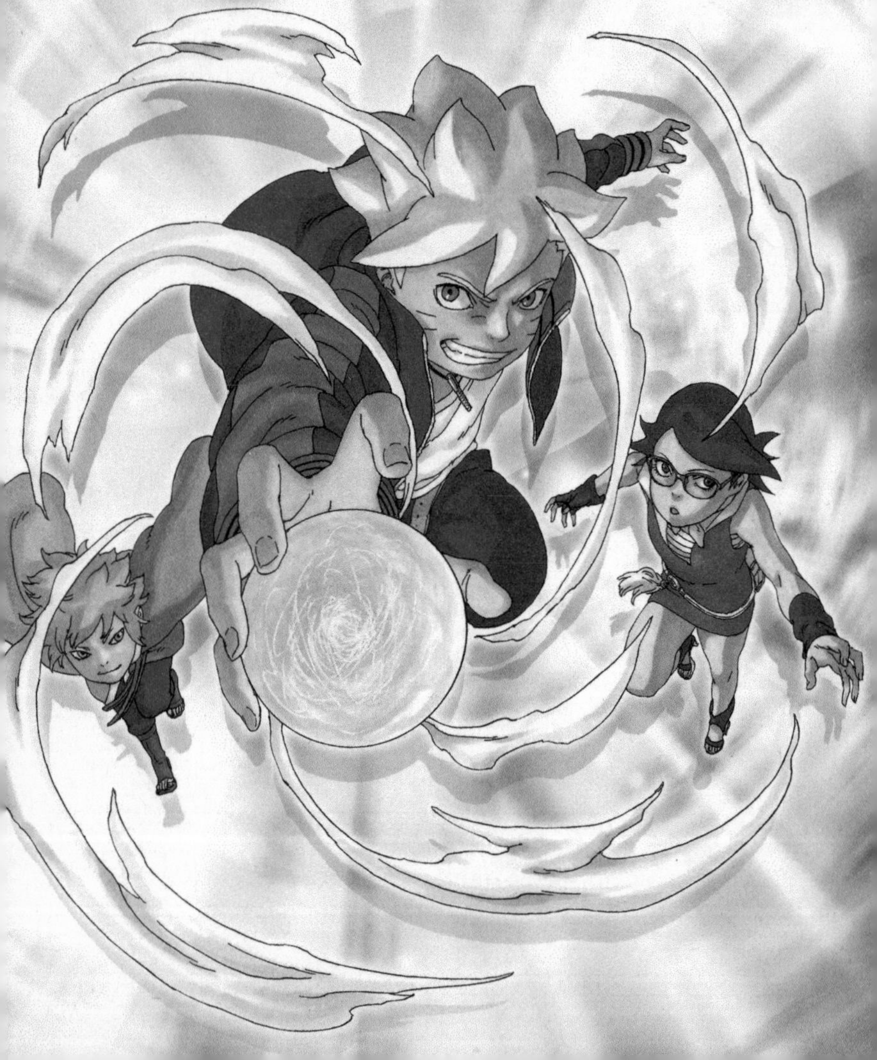

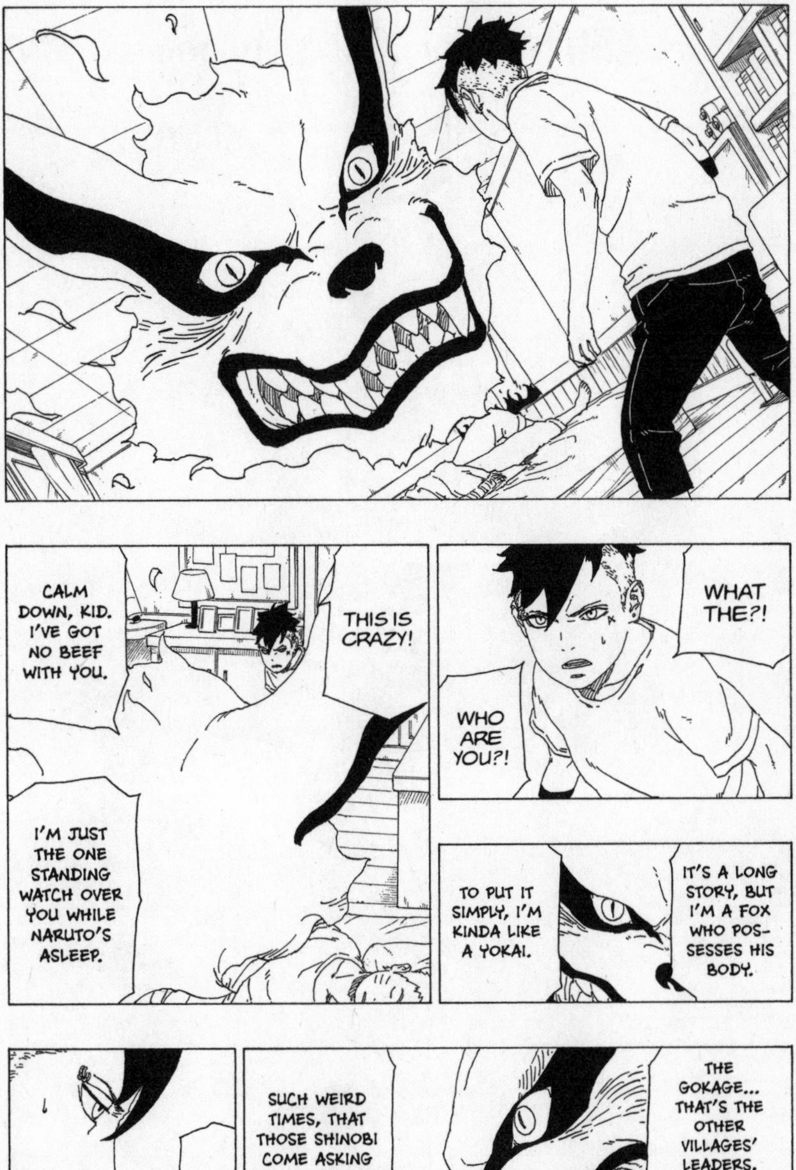
WHAT THE?!
WHO ARE YOU?!
IT'S A LONG STORY, BUT I'M A FOX WHO POS-SESSES HIS BODY.
TO PUT IT SIMPLY, I'M KINDA LIKE A YOKAI.
THIS IS CRAZY!
CALM DOWN, KID. I'VE GOT NO BEEF WITH YOU.
I'M JUST THE ONE STANDING WATCH OVER YOU WHILE NARUTO'S ASLEEP.
THE GOKAGE... THAT'S THE OTHER VILLAGES' LEADERS, ASKED ME TO AS WELL.
SUCH WEIRD TIMES, THAT THOSE SHINOBI COME ASKING FAVORS OF ME.
...

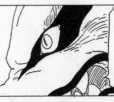

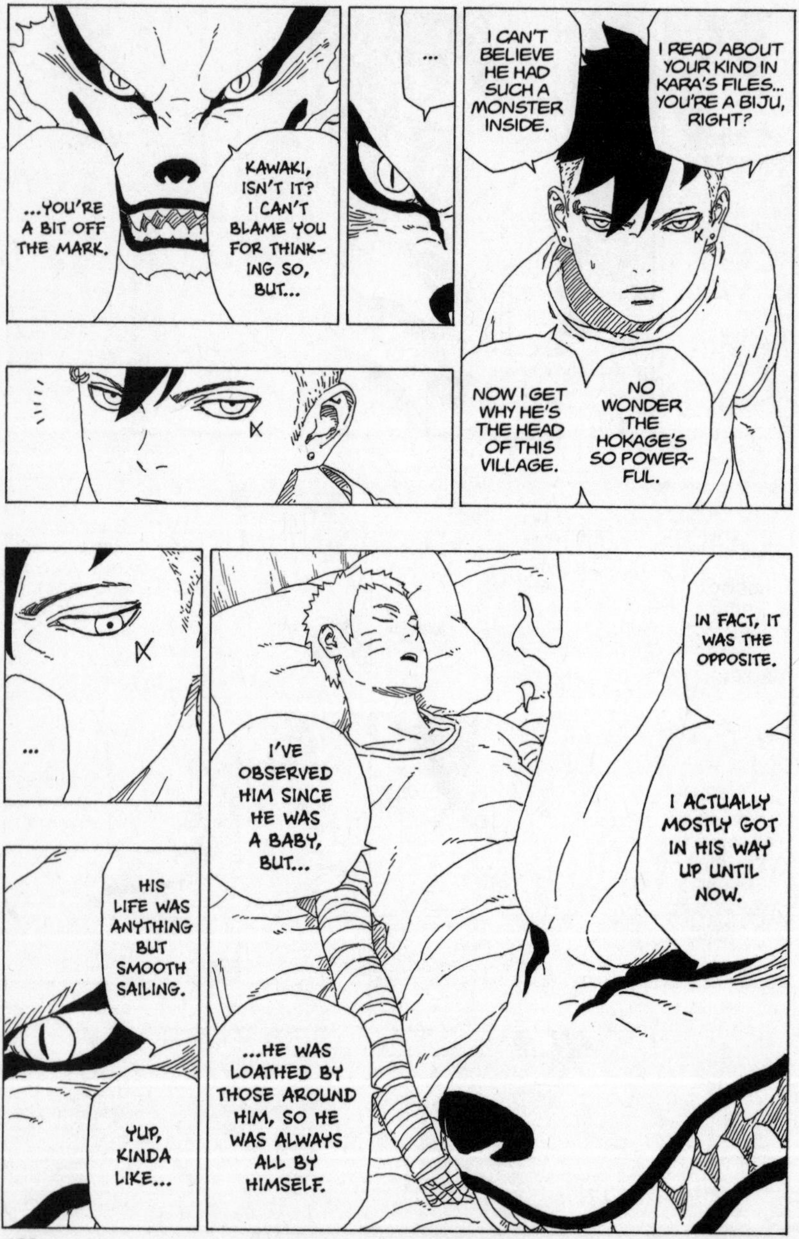
I READ ABOUT YOUR KIND IN KARA'S FILES... YOU'RE A BIJU, RIGHT?
I CAN'T BELIEVE HE HAD SUCH A MONSTER INSIDE.
NO WONDER THE HOKAGE'S SO POWERFUL.
NOW I GET WHY HE'S THE HEAD OF THIS VILLAGE.
...
KAWAKI, ISN'T IT? I CAN'T BLAME YOU FOR THINKING SO, BUT...
...YOU'RE A BIT OFF THE MARK.
IN FACT, IT WAS THE OPPOSITE.
I ACTUALLY MOSTLY GOT IN HIS WAY UP UNTIL NOW.
I'VE OBSERVED HIM SINCE HE WAS A BABY, BUT...
...HE WAS LOATHED BY THOSE AROUND HIM, SO HE WAS ALWAYS ALL BY HIMSELF.
...
HIS LIFE WAS ANYTHING BUT SMOOTH SAILING.
YUP, KINDA LIKE...

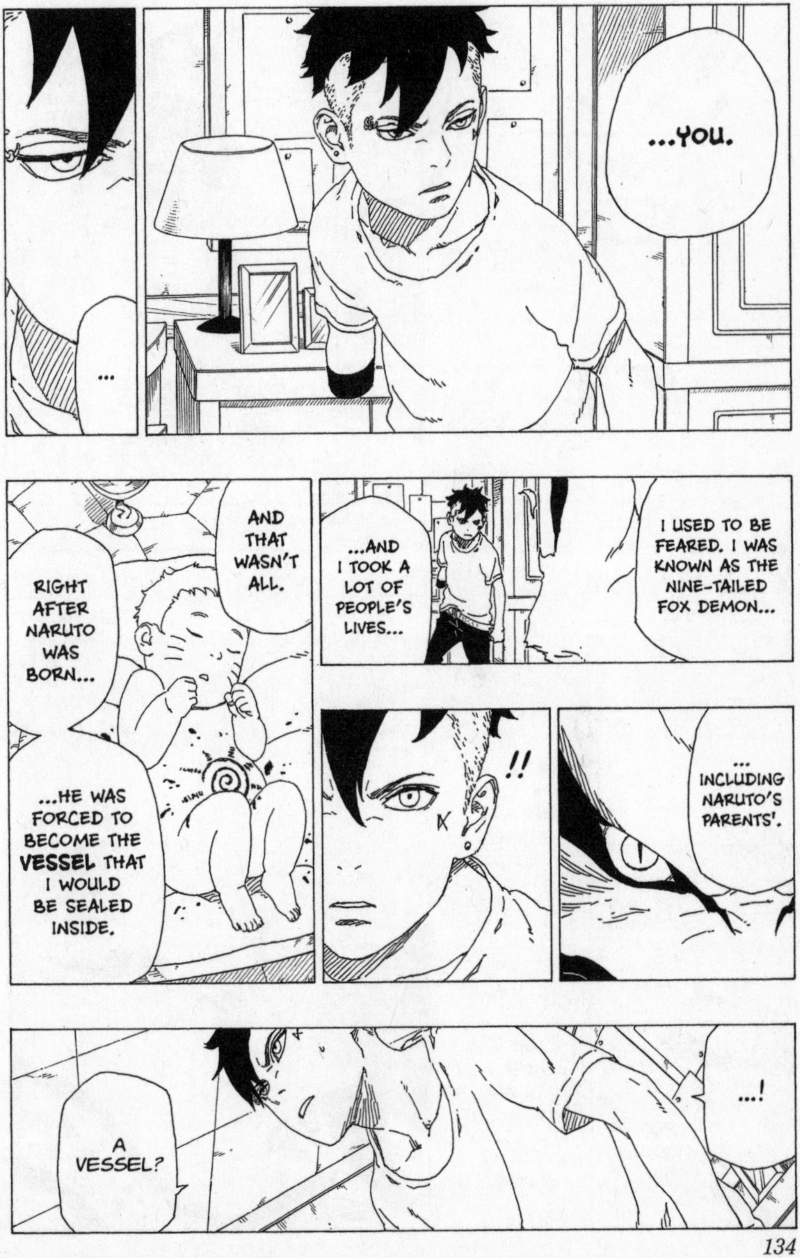

...YOU.
...
I USED TO BE FEARED. I WAS KNOWN AS THE NINE-TAILED FOX DEMON...
...AND I TOOK A LOT OF PEOPLE'S LIVES...
... INCLUDING NARUTO'S PARENTS'.
!!
AND THAT WASN'T ALL.
RIGHT AFTER NARUTO WAS BORN...
...HE WAS FORCED TO BECOME THE VESSEL THAT I WOULD BE SEALED INSIDE.
...!
A VESSEL?

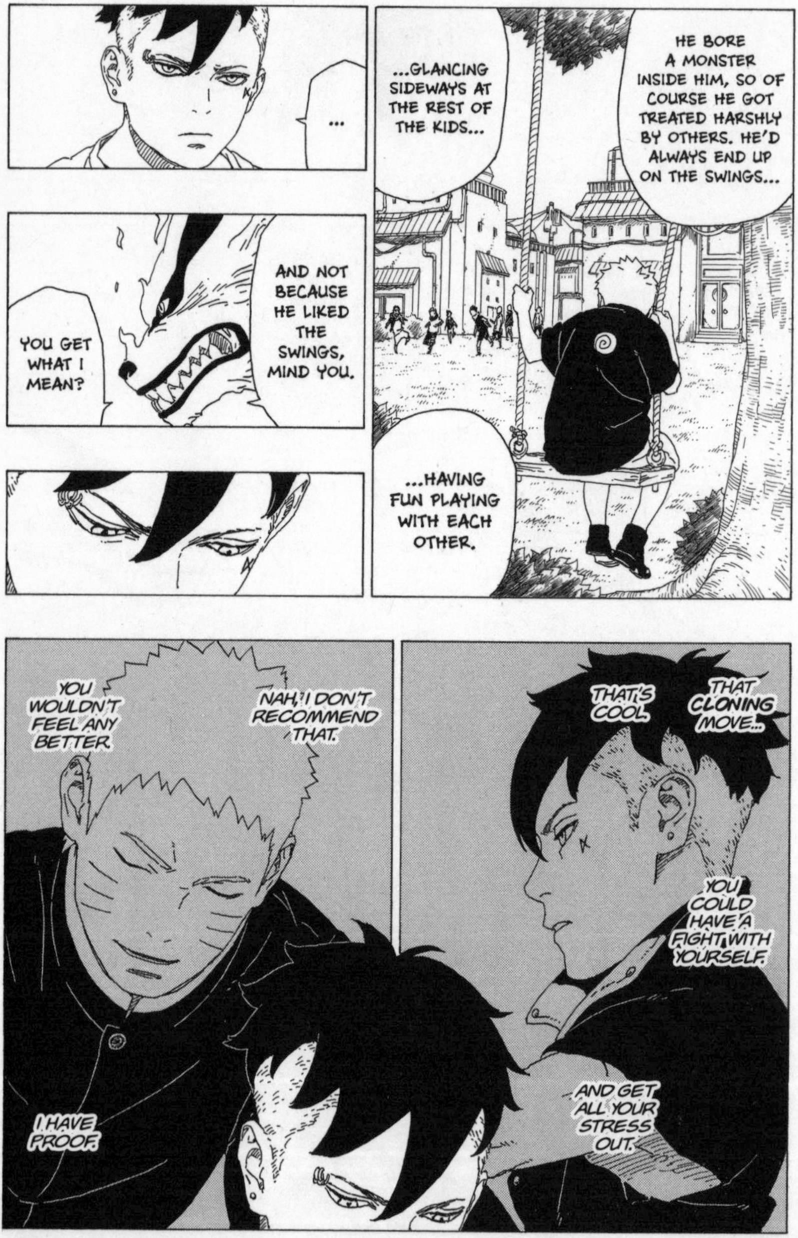
HE BORE A MONSTER INSIDE HIM, SO OF COURSE HE GOT TREATED HARSHLY BY OTHERS. HE'D ALWAYS END UP ON THE SWINGS...
...GLANCING SIDEWAYS AT THE REST OF THE KIDS...
...HAVING FUN PLAYING WITH EACH OTHER.
...
AND NOT BECAUSE HE LIKED THE SWINGS, MIND YOU.
YOU GET WHAT I MEAN?
THAT CLONING MOVE...
THAT'S COOL.
YOU COULD HAVE A FIGHT WITH YOURSELF.
AND GET ALL YOUR STRESS OUT.
NAH, I DON'T RECOMMEND THAT.
YOU WOULDN'T FEEL ANY BETTER.
I HAVE PROOF.

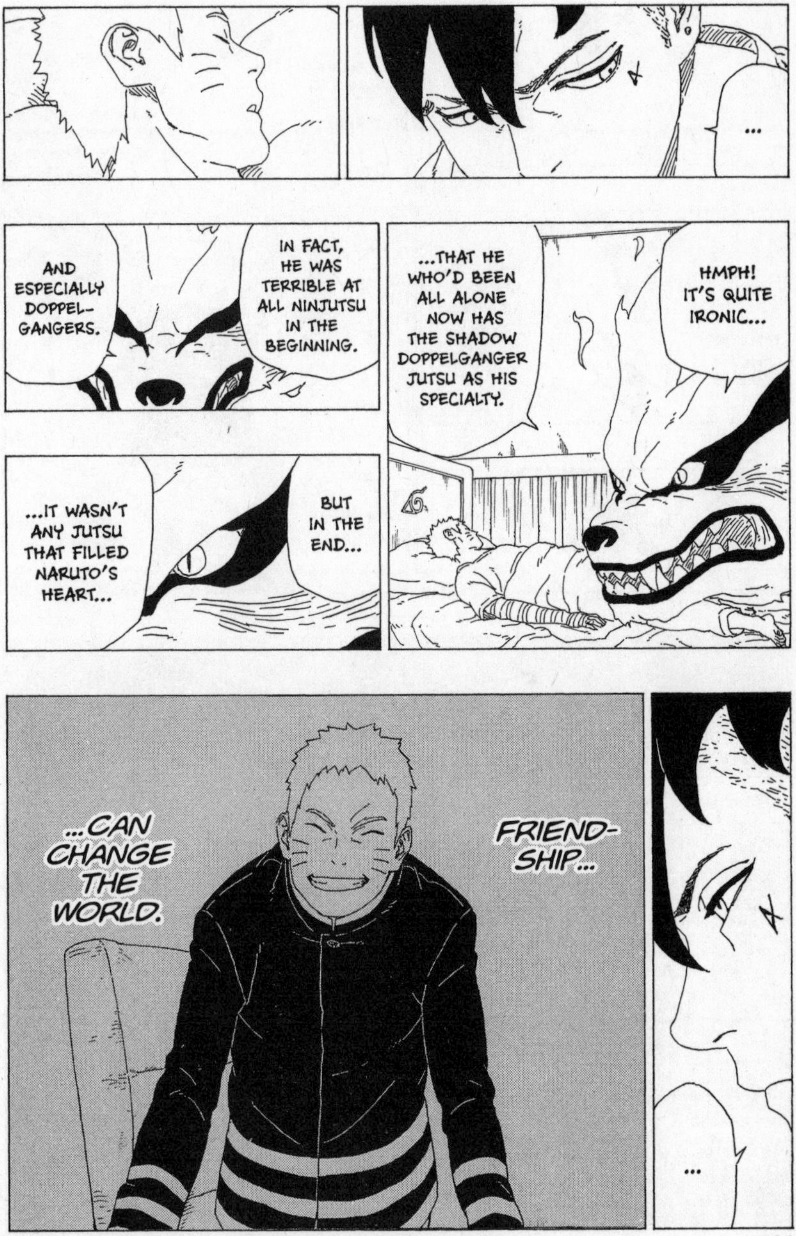
...
HMPH! IT'S QUITE IRONIC...
...THAT HE WHO'D BEEN ALL ALONE NOW HAS THE SHADOW DOPPELGANGER JUTSU AS HIS SPECIALTY.
IN FACT, HE WAS TERRIBLE AT ALL NINJUTSU IN THE BEGINNING.
AND ESPECIALLY DOPPEL-GANGERS.
BUT IN THE END...
...IT WASN'T ANY JUTSU THAT FILLED NARUTO'S HEART...
...
FRIEND-SHIP...
...CAN CHANGE THE WORLD.

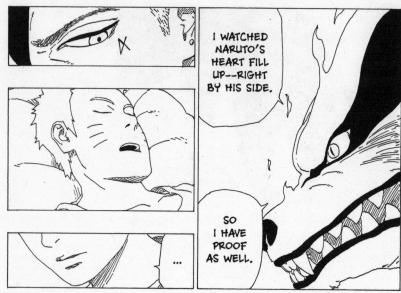

I WATCHED NARUTO'S HEART FILL UP--RIGHT BY HIS SIDE.

SO I HAVE PROOF AS WELL.

...

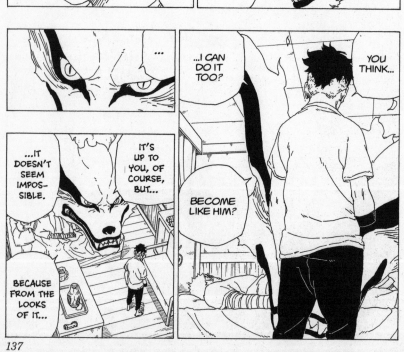

...

YOU THINK...

...I CAN DO IT TOO?

BECOME LIKE HIM?

IT'S UP TO YOU, OF COURSE, BUT...

...IT DOESN'T SEEM IMPOS-SIBLE.

BECAUSE FROM THE LOOKS OF IT...

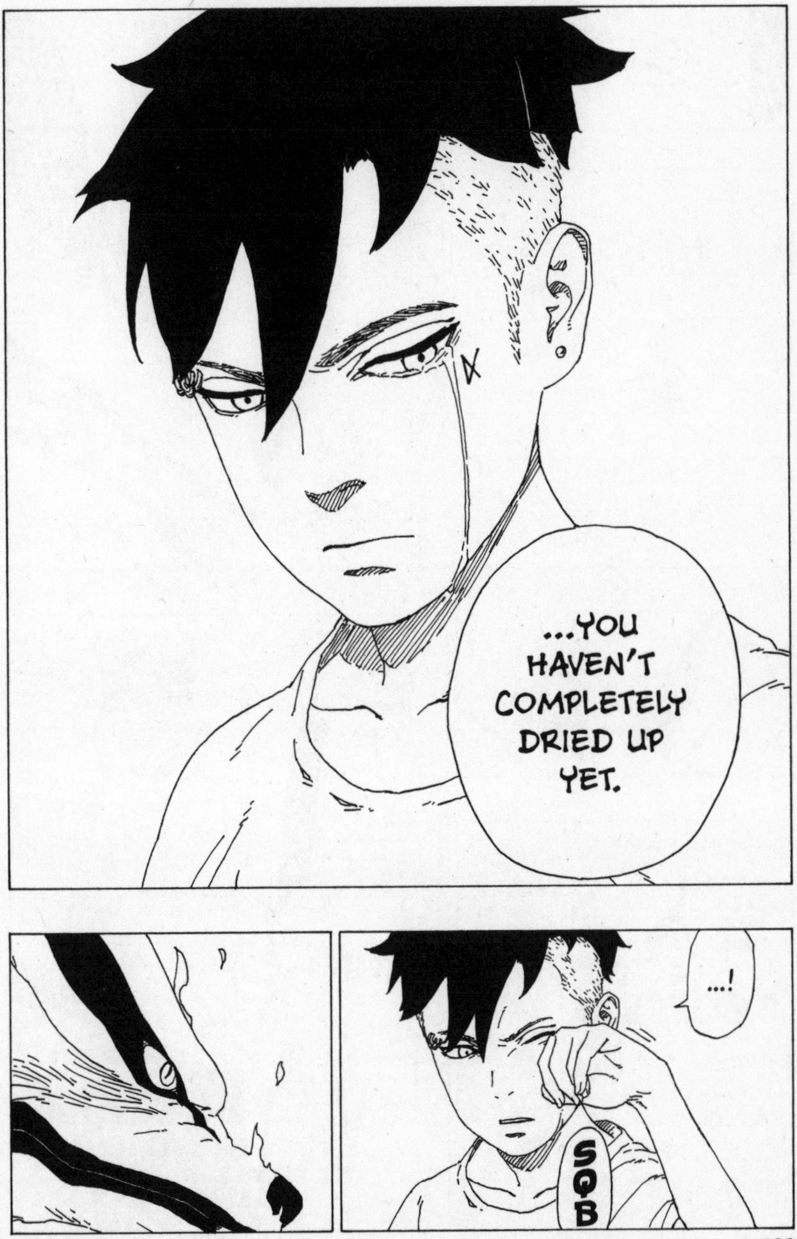
...YOU HAVEN'T COMPLETELY DRIED UP YET.
...!
SOB

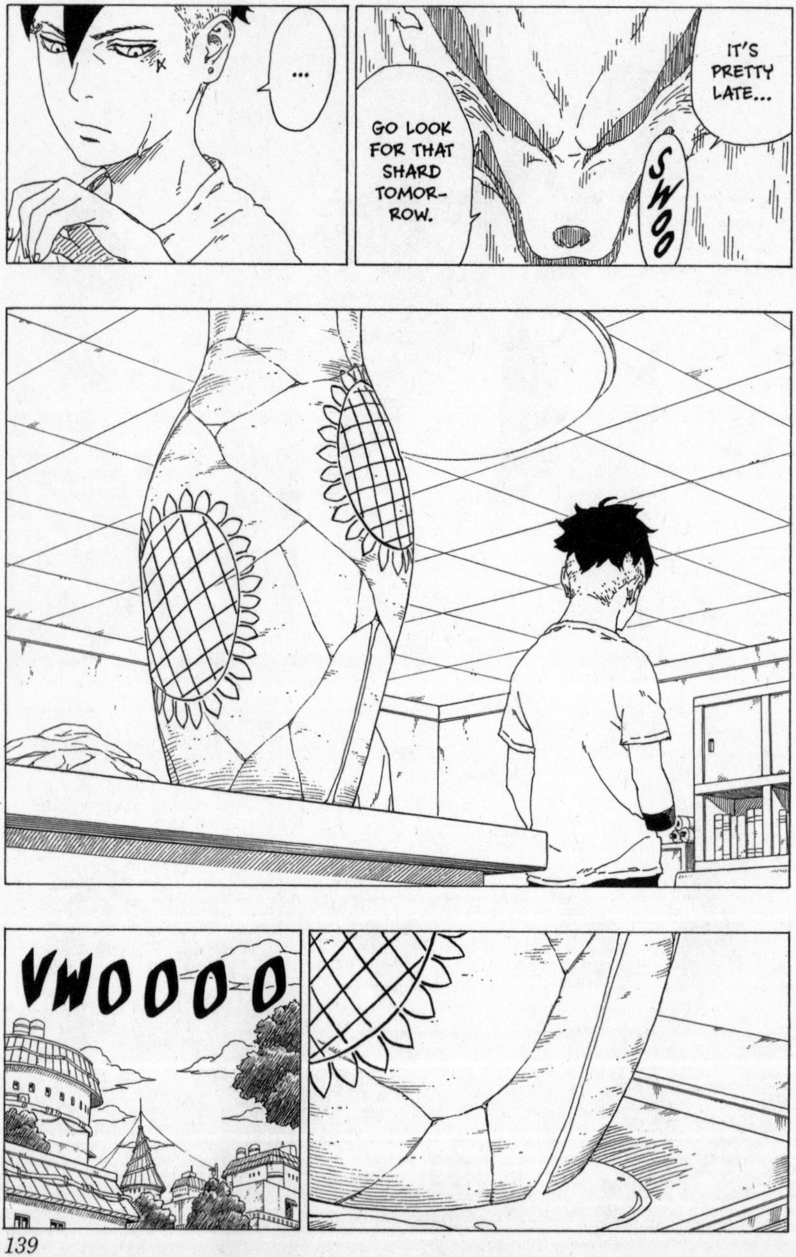
IT'S PRETTY LATE...
SWOO
GO LOOK FOR THAT SHARD TOMOR-ROW.
...
VWOOOO

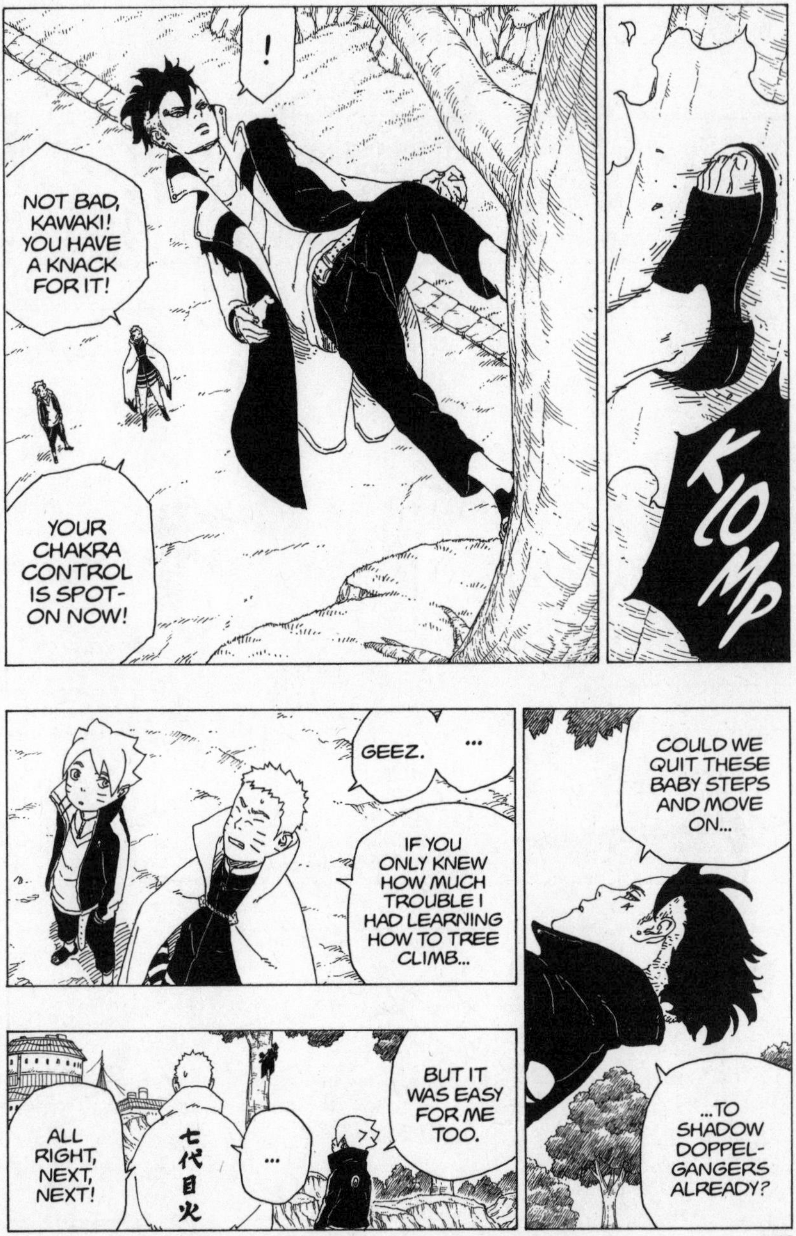
KLOMP
!
NOT BAD, KAWAKI! YOU HAVE A KNACK FOR IT!
YOUR CHAKRA CONTROL IS SPOT-ON NOW!
COULD WE QUIT THESE BABY STEPS AND MOVE ON...
...TO SHADOW DOPPEL-GANGERS ALREADY?
...
GEEZ.
IF YOU ONLY KNEW HOW MUCH TROUBLE I HAD LEARNING HOW TO TREE CLIMB...
BUT IT WAS EASY FOR ME TOO.
...
七代目火
ALL RIGHT, NEXT, NEXT!

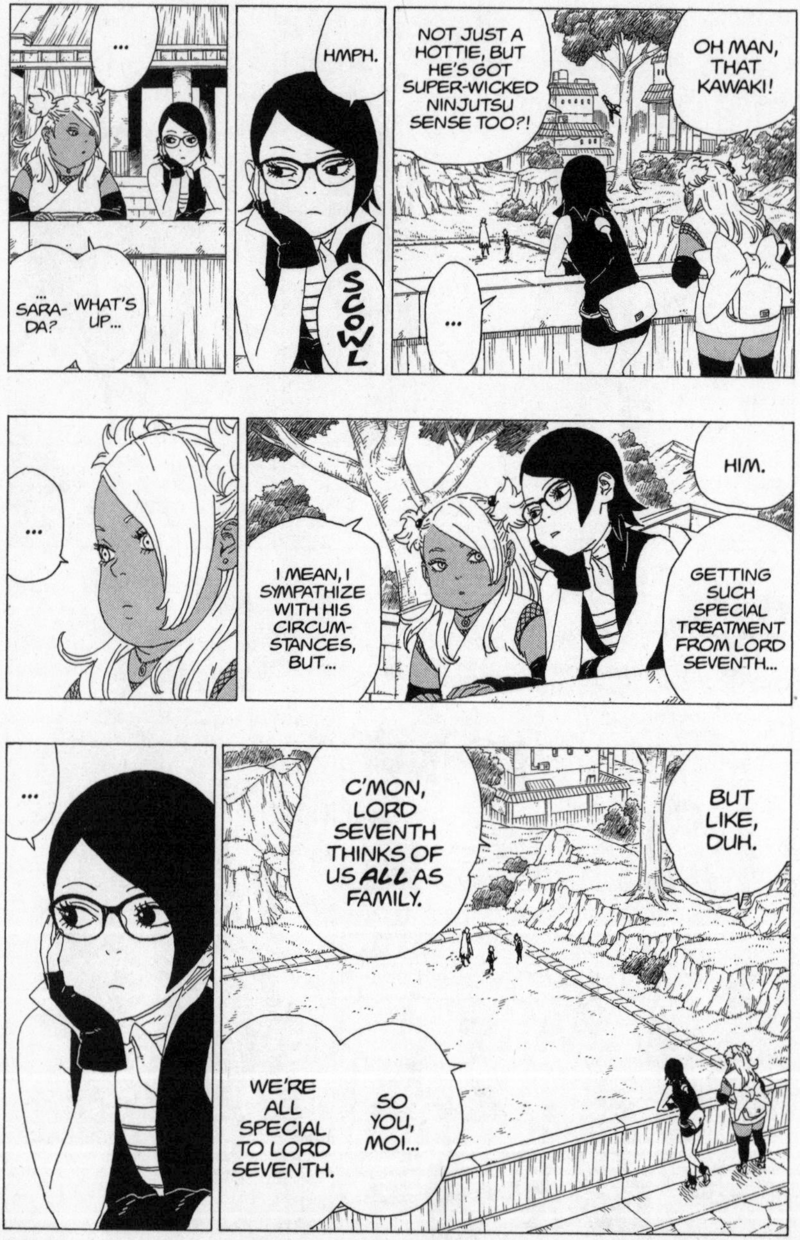
OH MAN, THAT KAWAKI!
NOT JUST A HOTTIE, BUT HE'S GOT SUPER-WICKED NINJUTSU SENSE TOO?!
...
HMPH.
SCOWL
...
WHAT'S UP...
... SARA-DA?
HIM.
GETTING SUCH SPECIAL TREATMENT FROM LORD SEVENTH...
I MEAN, I SYMPATHIZE WITH HIS CIRCUM-STANCES, BUT...
...
BUT LIKE, DUH.
C'MON, LORD SEVENTH THINKS OF US ALL AS FAMILY.
SO YOU, MOI...
WE'RE ALL SPECIAL TO LORD SEVENTH.
...

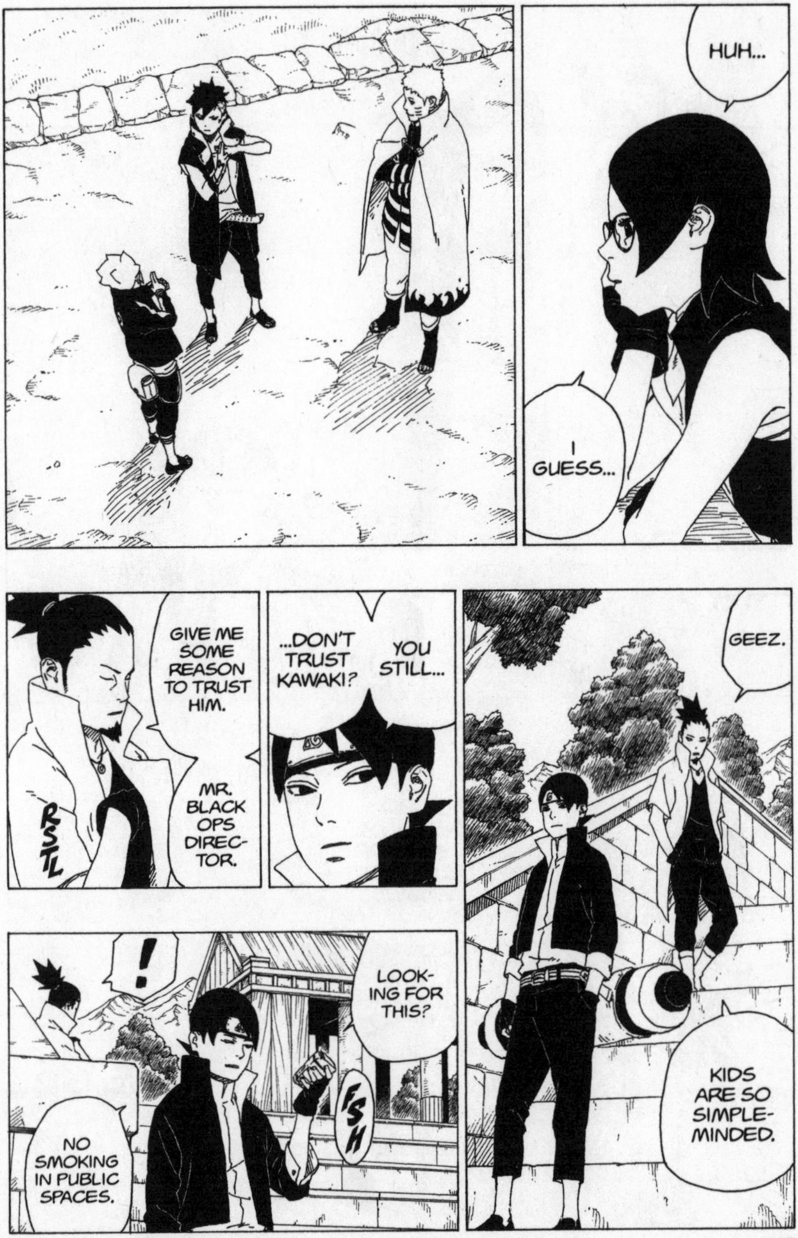
HUH...
I GUESS...
GEEZ.
KIDS ARE SO SIMPLE-MINDED.
YOU STILL...
...DON'T TRUST KAWAKI?
GIVE ME SOME REASON TO TRUST HIM.
MR. BLACK OPS DIRECTOR.
RSTL
!
LOOKING FOR THIS?
FSH
NO SMOKING IN PUBLIC SPACES.

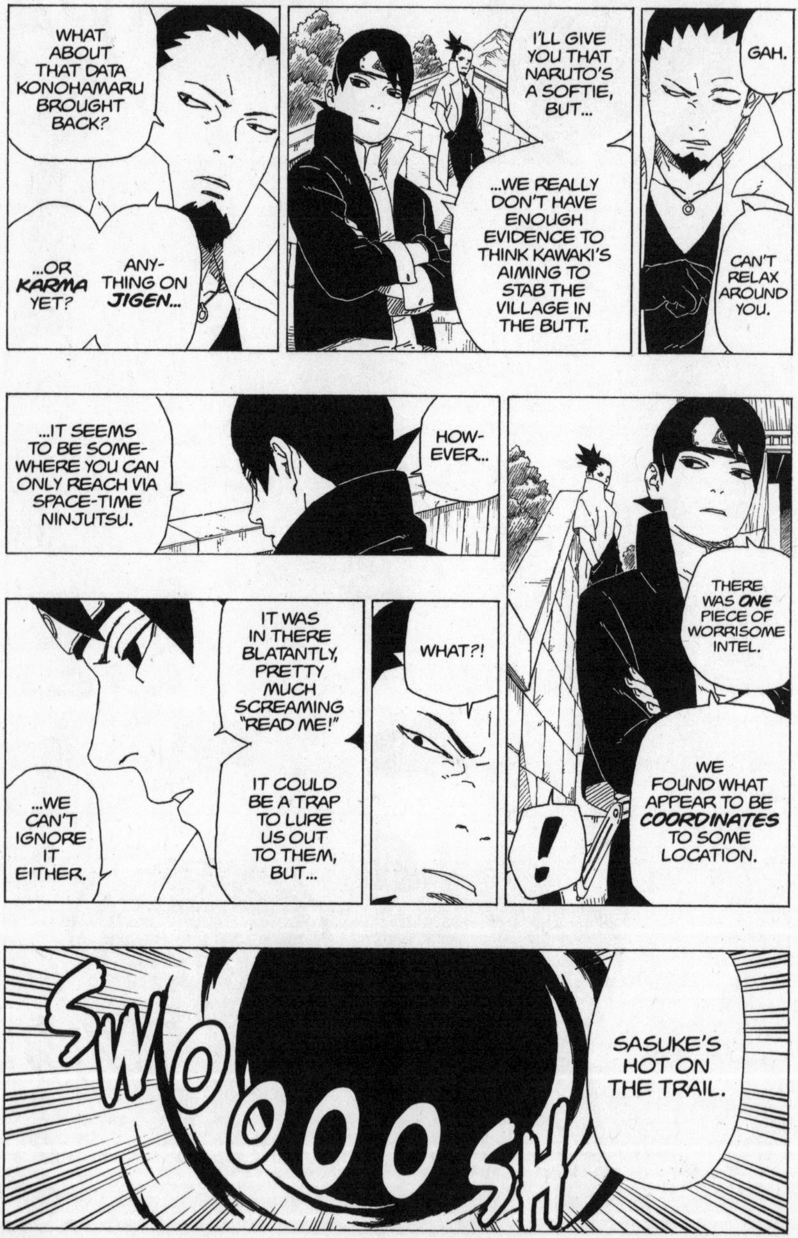
GAH.
CAN'T RELAX AROUND YOU.
I'LL GIVE YOU THAT NARUTO'S A SOFTIE, BUT...
...WE REALLY DON'T HAVE ENOUGH EVIDENCE TO THINK KAWAKI'S AIMING TO STAB THE VILLAGE IN THE BUTT.
WHAT ABOUT THAT DATA KONOHAMARU BROUGHT BACK?
ANYTHING ON JIGEN...
...OR KARMA YET?
THERE WAS ONE PIECE OF WORRISOME INTEL.
WE FOUND WHAT APPEAR TO BE COORDINATES TO SOME LOCATION.
!
HOW-EVER..
...IT SEEMS TO BE SOME-WHERE YOU CAN ONLY REACH VIA SPACE-TIME NINJUTSU.
WHAT?!
IT WAS IN THERE BLATANTLY, PRETTY MUCH SCREAMING "READ ME!"
IT COULD BE A TRAP TO LURE US OUT TO THEM, BUT...
...WE CAN'T IGNORE IT EITHER.
SASUKE'S HOT ON THE TRAIL.
SWOOOOOSH

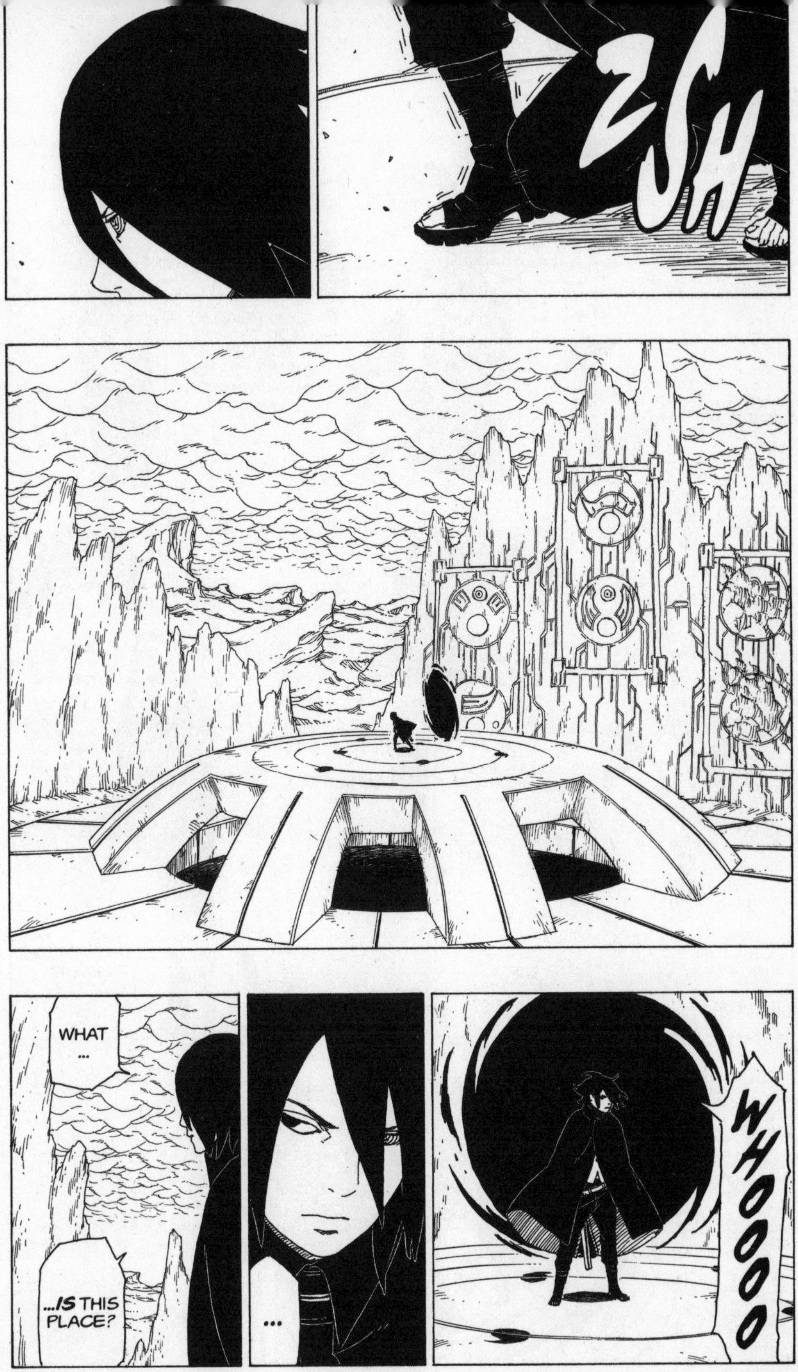
ZSH
WHOOOO
...
WHAT ...
...IS THIS PLACE?

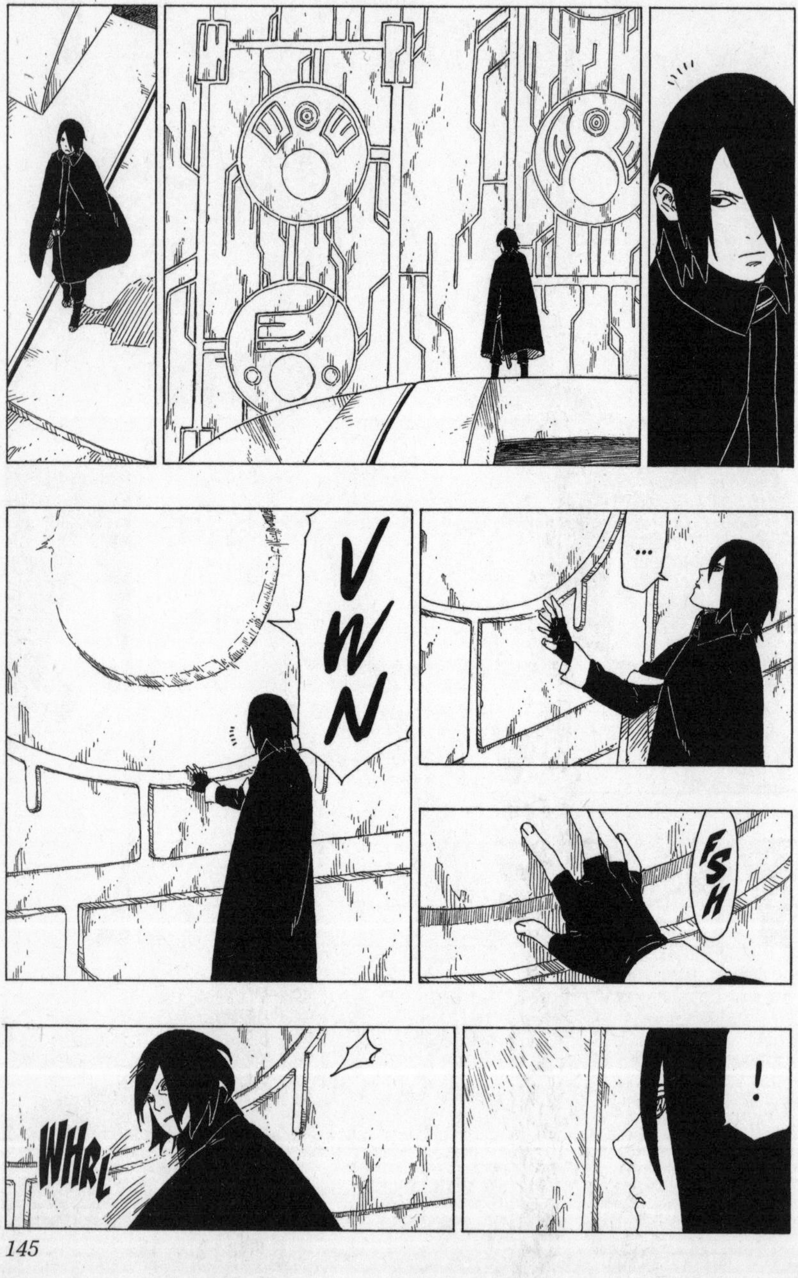
...
FSH
VWN
!
WHRL

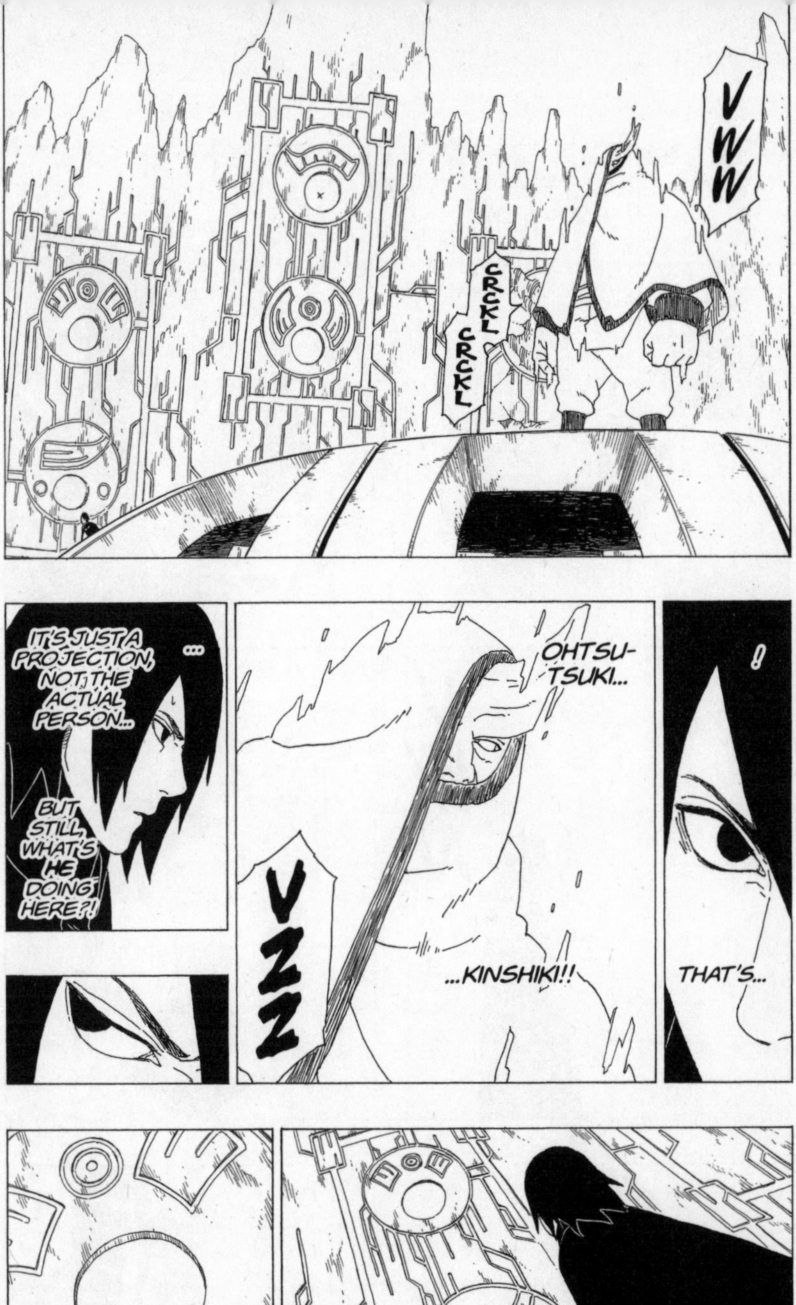
VWW
CRCKL CRCKL
!
THAT'S...
OHTSU-TSUKI...
...KINSHIKI!!
VZZ
...
IT'S JUST A PROJECTION, NOT THE ACTUAL PERSON...
BUT STILL, WHAT'S HE DOING HERE?!

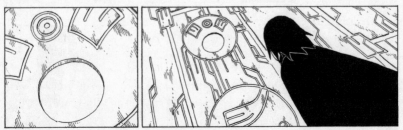

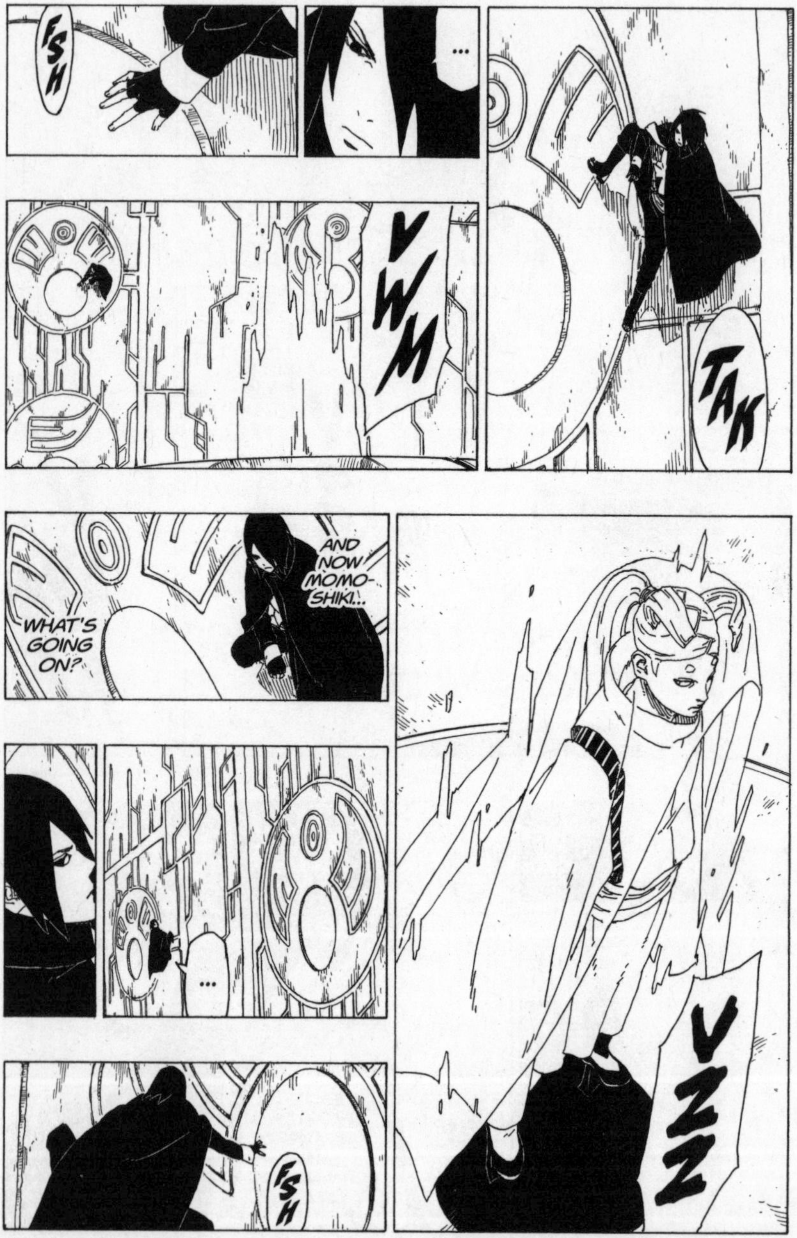
TAK
...
FSH
VWM
VZZ
AND NOW MOMOSHIKI...
WHAT'S GOING ON?
...
FSH

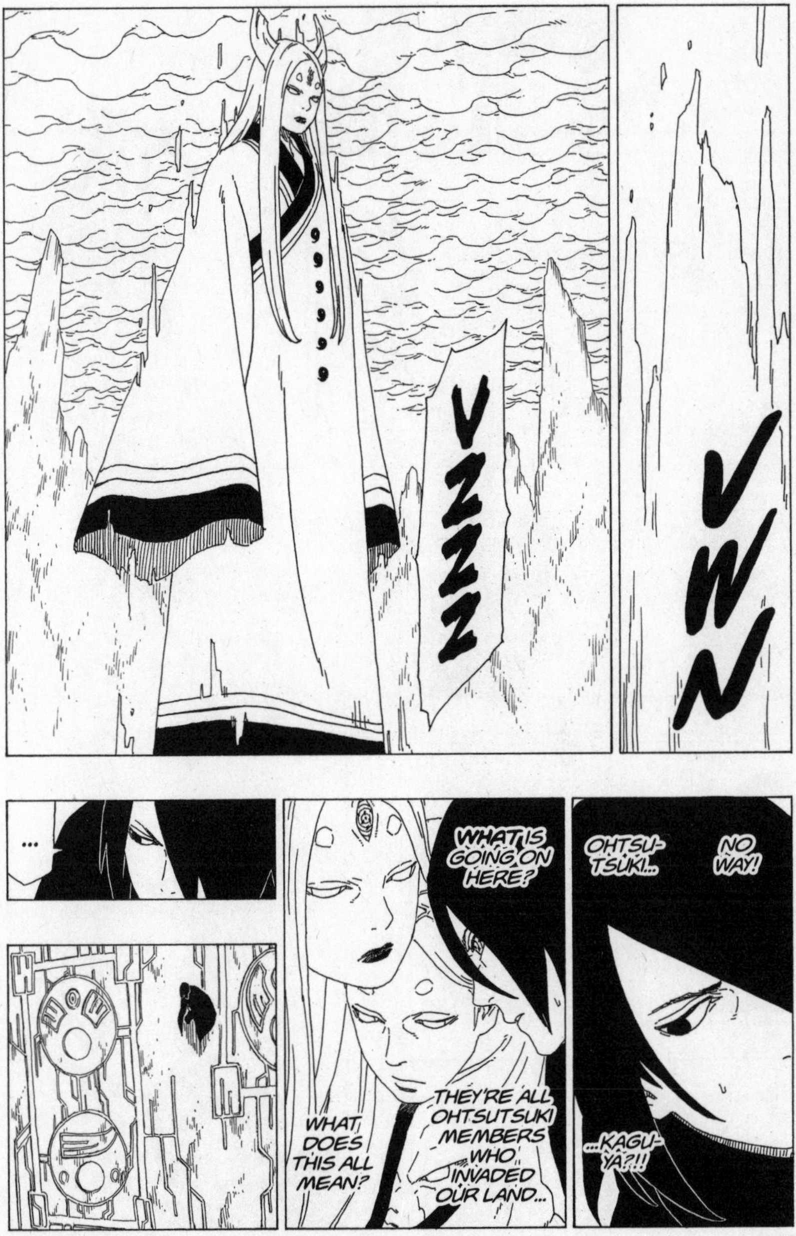
VWN
VZZZ
NO WAY!
OHTSU-TSUKI...
...KAGU-YA?!!
WHAT IS GOING ON HERE?
THEY'RE ALL OHTSUTSUKI MEMBERS WHO INVADED OUR LAND...
WHAT DOES THIS ALL MEAN?
...

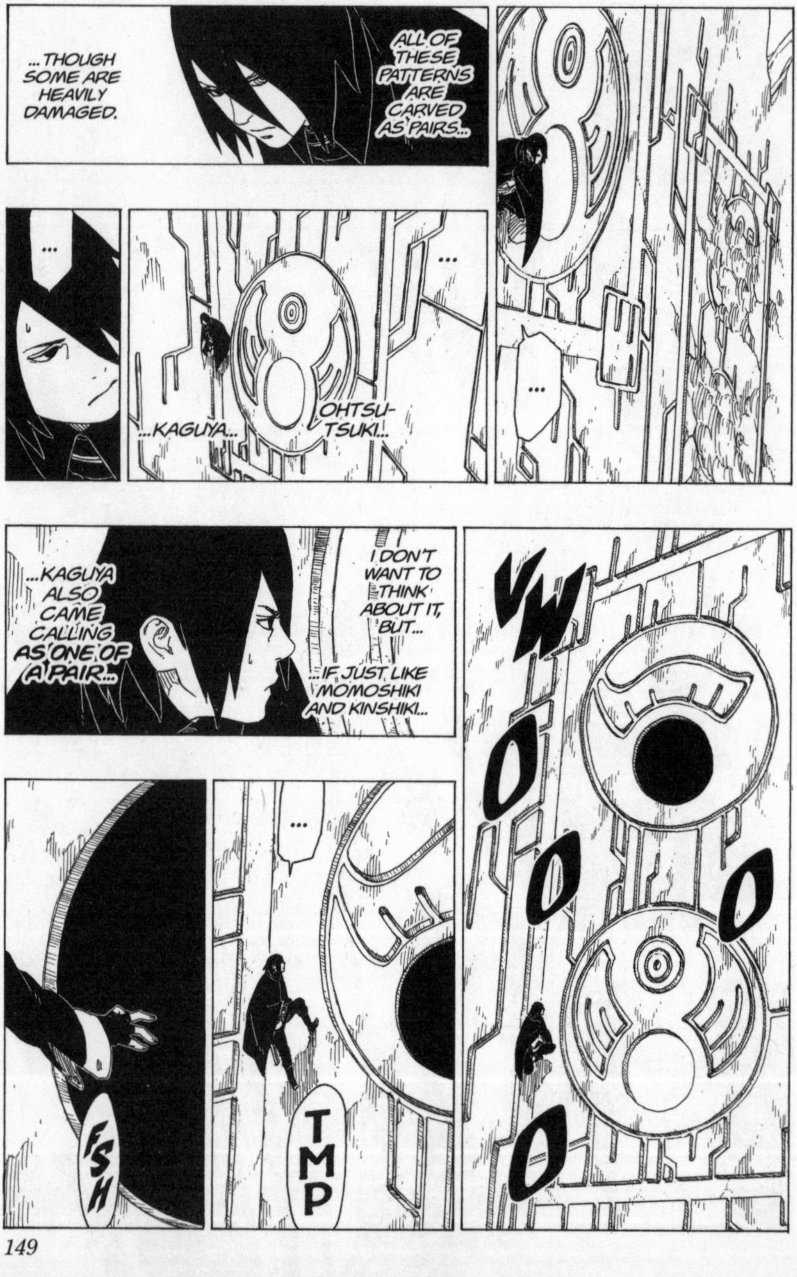
...
ALL OF THESE PATTERNS ARE CARVED AS PAIRS...
...THOUGH SOME ARE HEAVILY DAMAGED.
...
OHTSU-TSUKI...
...KAGUYA...
...
VWOOOO
I DON'T WANT TO THINK ABOUT IT, BUT...
...IF JUST LIKE MOMOSHIKI AND KINSHIKI...
...KAGUYA ALSO CAME CALLING AS ONE OF A PAIR...
...
TMP
FSH

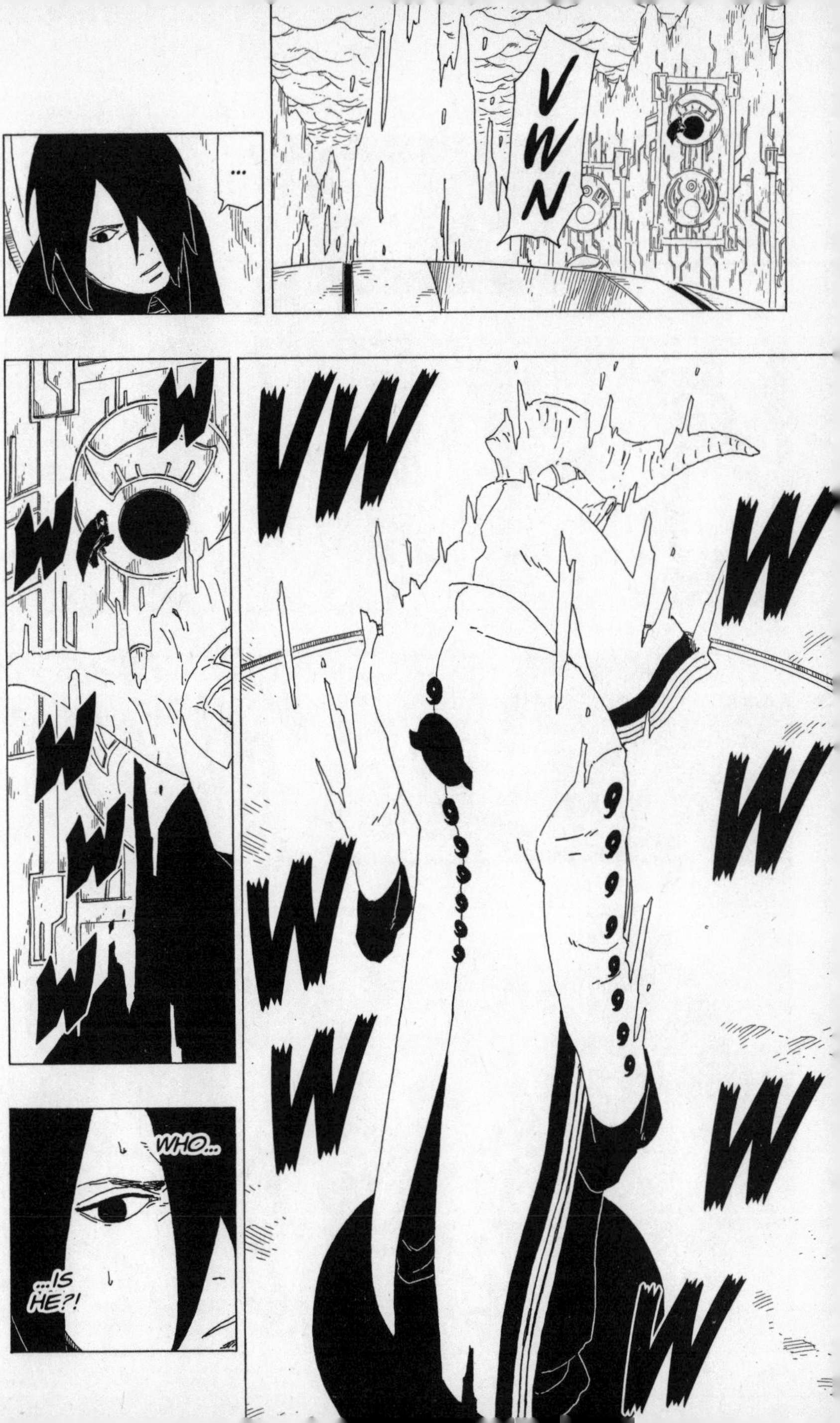

VWN
...
VWWWWWW
WWWWW
WHO...
...IS HE?!

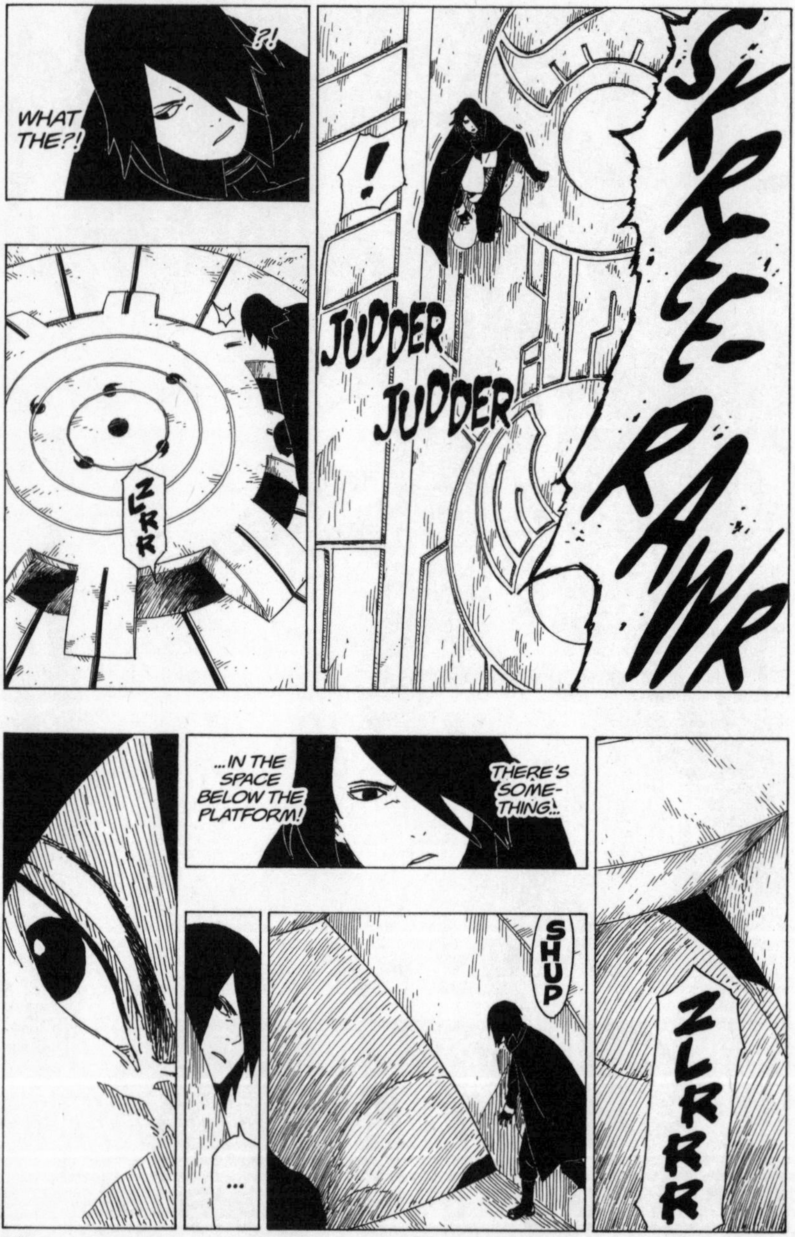

SKREEE-RAWR
!
JUDDER
JUDDER
?!
WHAT THE?!
ZLRR
ZLRRR
THERE'S SOME-THING...
...IN THE SPACE BELOW THE PLATFORM!
SHUP
...

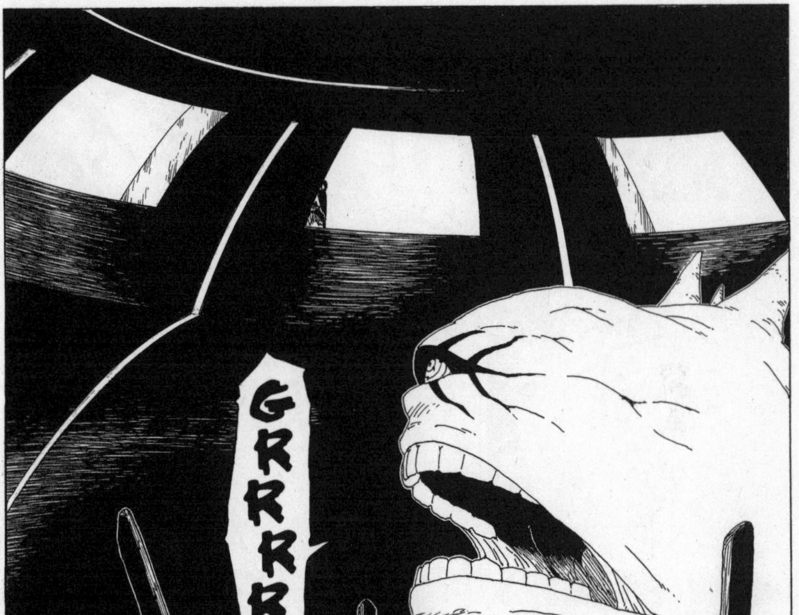
GRRRR

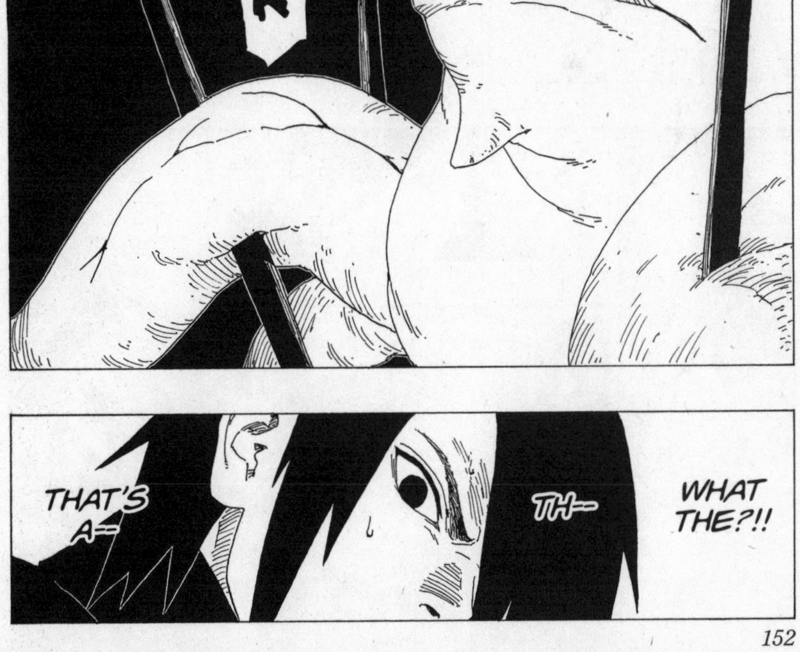
WHAT THE?!!
TH--
THAT'S A--

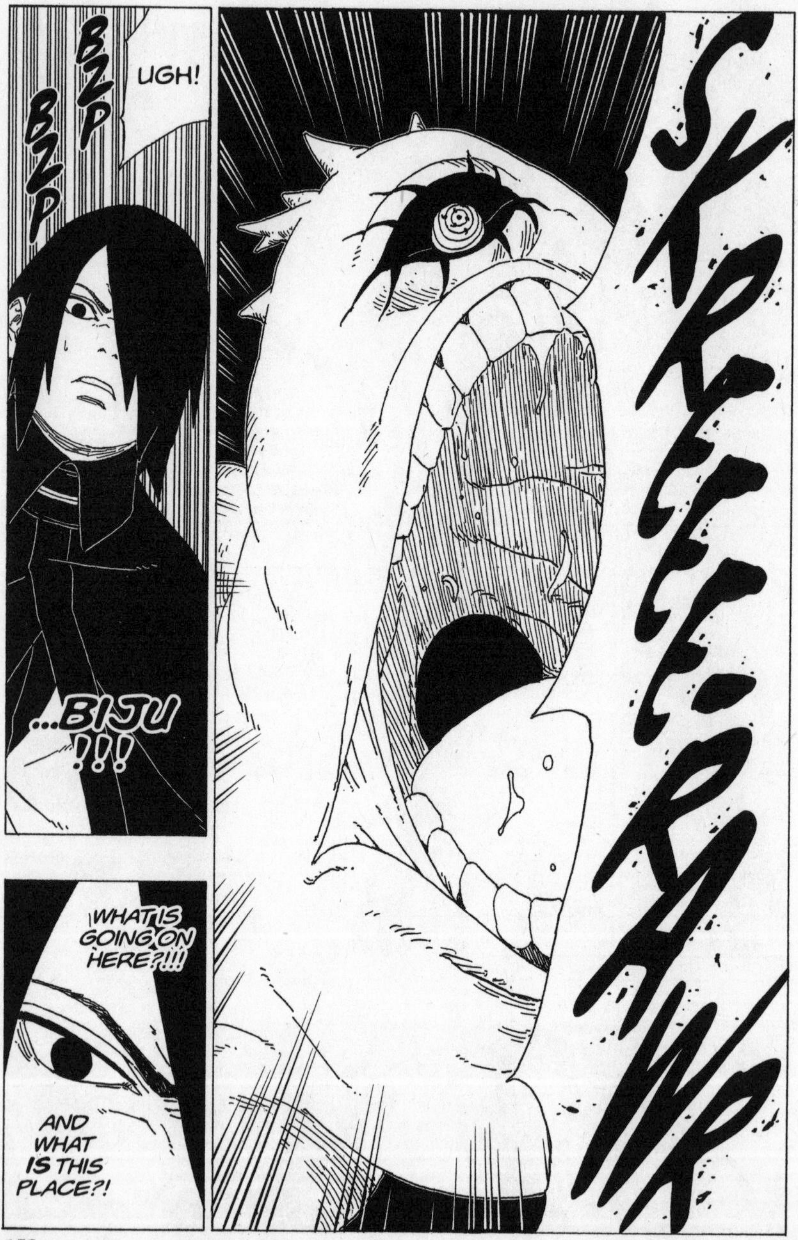
SKREEEERAWR
BZZP BZZP
UGH!
...BIJU!!!
WHAT IS GOING ON HERE?!!!
AND WHAT IS THIS PLACE?!

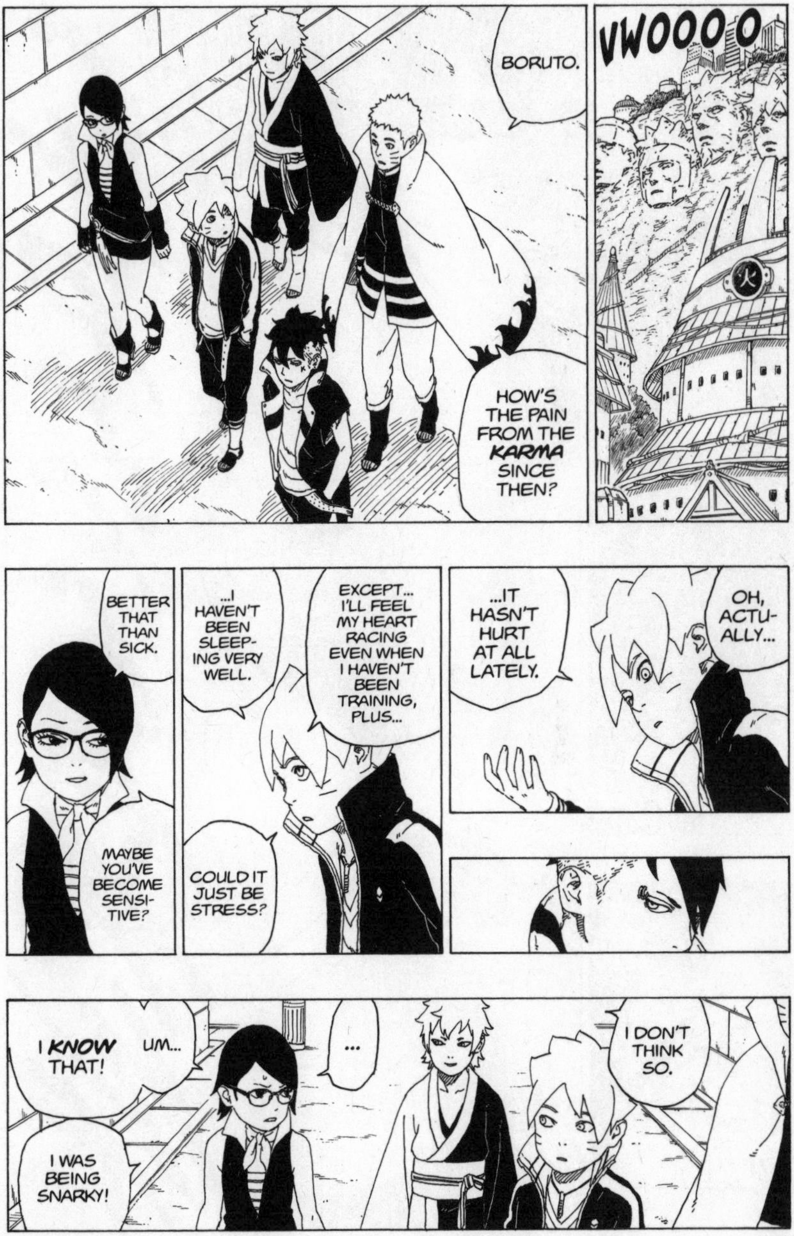
VWOOOO
BORUTO.
HOW'S THE PAIN FROM THE **KARMA** SINCE THEN?
OH, ACTUALLY...
...IT HASN'T HURT AT ALL LATELY.
EXCEPT... I'LL FEEL MY HEART RACING EVEN WHEN I HAVEN'T BEEN TRAINING, PLUS...
...I HAVEN'T BEEN SLEEPING VERY WELL.
COULD IT JUST BE STRESS?
BETTER THAT THAN SICK.
MAYBE YOU'VE BECOME SENSITIVE?
I DON'T THINK SO.
...
UM...
I **KNOW** THAT!
I WAS BEING SNARKY!

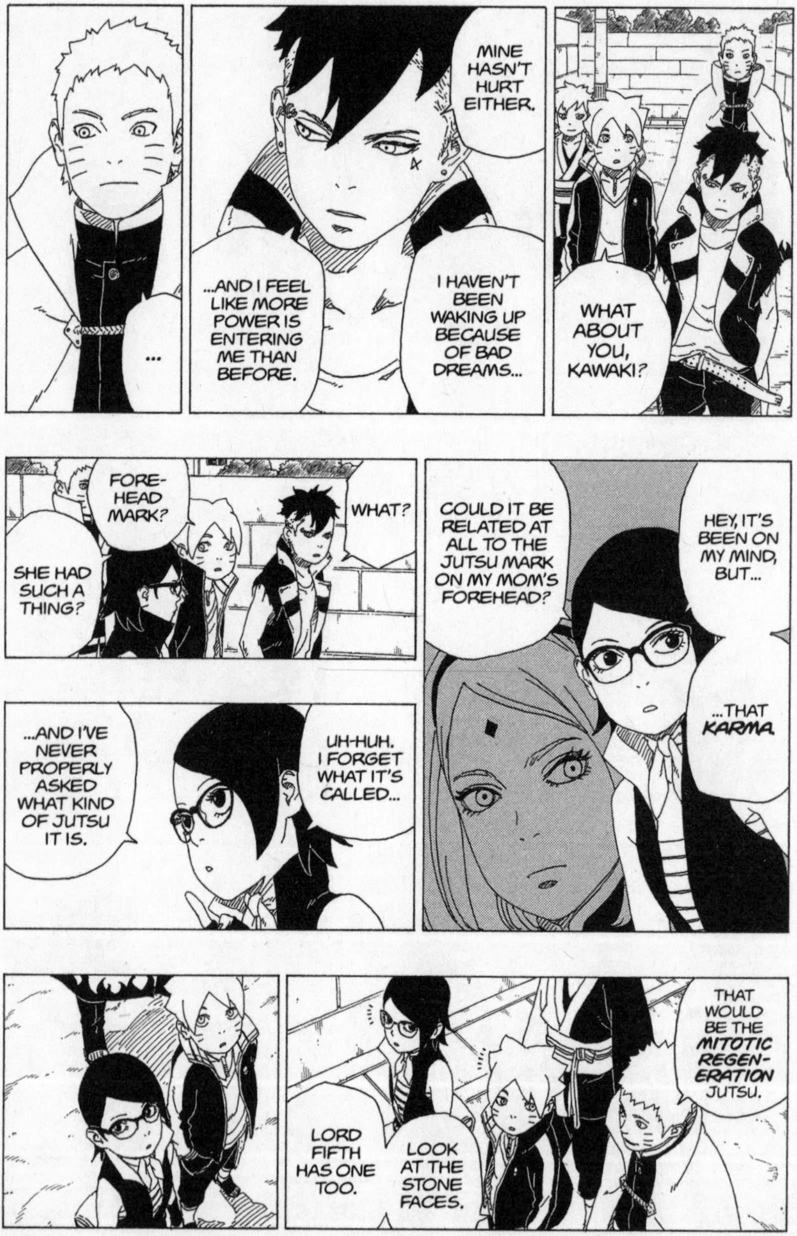
WHAT ABOUT YOU, KAWAKI?
MINE HASN'T HURT EITHER.
I HAVEN'T BEEN WAKING UP BECAUSE OF BAD DREAMS...
...AND I FEEL LIKE MORE POWER IS ENTERING ME THAN BEFORE.
...
HEY, IT'S BEEN ON MY MIND, BUT...
COULD IT BE RELATED AT ALL TO THE JUTSU MARK ON MY MOM'S FOREHEAD?
...THAT *KARMA.*
WHAT?
FORE-HEAD MARK?
SHE HAD SUCH A THING?
UH-HUH. I FORGET WHAT IT'S CALLED...
...AND I'VE NEVER PROPERLY ASKED WHAT KIND OF JUTSU IT IS.
THAT WOULD BE THE *MITOTIC REGEN-ERATION* JUTSU.
LOOK AT THE STONE FACES.
LORD FIFTH HAS ONE TOO.

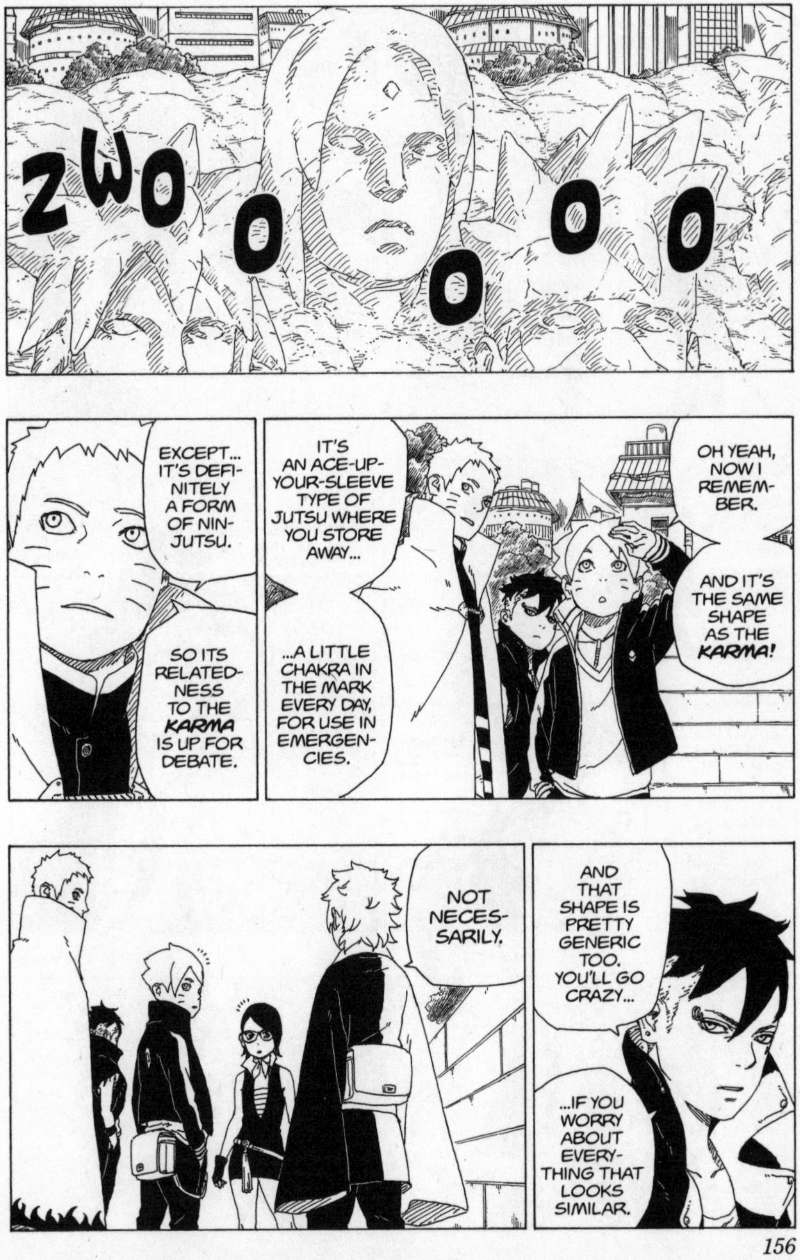
ZWOOOOOO
OH YEAH, NOW I REMEMBER.
AND IT'S THE SAME SHAPE AS THE *KARMA!*
IT'S AN ACE-UP-YOUR-SLEEVE TYPE OF JUTSU WHERE YOU STORE AWAY...
...A LITTLE CHAKRA IN THE MARK EVERY DAY, FOR USE IN EMERGENCIES.
EXCEPT... IT'S DEFINITELY A FORM OF NINJUTSU.
SO ITS RELATEDNESS TO THE *KARMA* IS UP FOR DEBATE.
AND THAT SHAPE IS PRETTY GENERIC TOO. YOU'LL GO CRAZY...
...IF YOU WORRY ABOUT EVERYTHING THAT LOOKS SIMILAR.
NOT NECESSARILY.

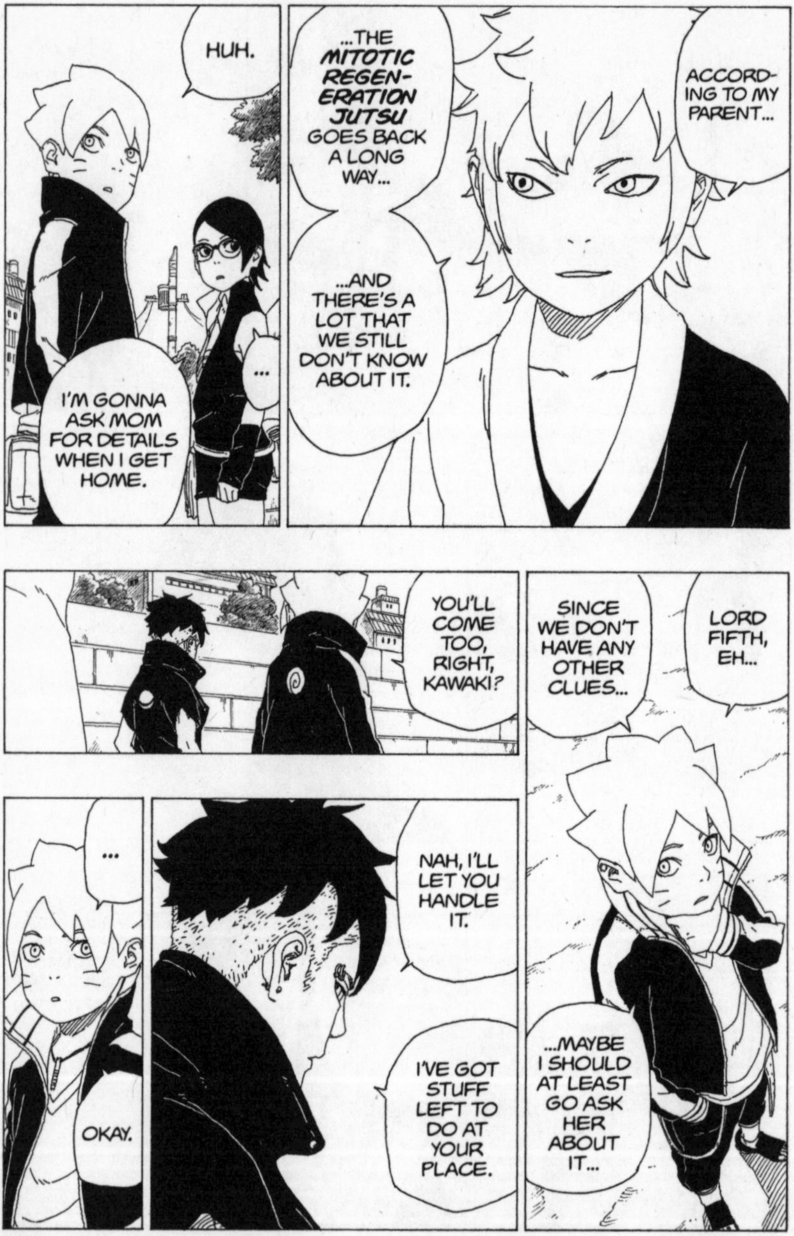
ACCORDING TO MY PARENT...
...THE MITOTIC REGENERATION JUTSU GOES BACK A LONG WAY...
...AND THERE'S A LOT THAT WE STILL DON'T KNOW ABOUT IT.
HUH.
...
I'M GONNA ASK MOM FOR DETAILS WHEN I GET HOME.
LORD FIFTH, EH...
SINCE WE DON'T HAVE ANY OTHER CLUES...
...MAYBE I SHOULD AT LEAST GO ASK HER ABOUT IT...
YOU'LL COME TOO, RIGHT, KAWAKI?
NAH, I'LL LET YOU HANDLE IT.
I'VE GOT STUFF LEFT TO DO AT YOUR PLACE.
...
OKAY.

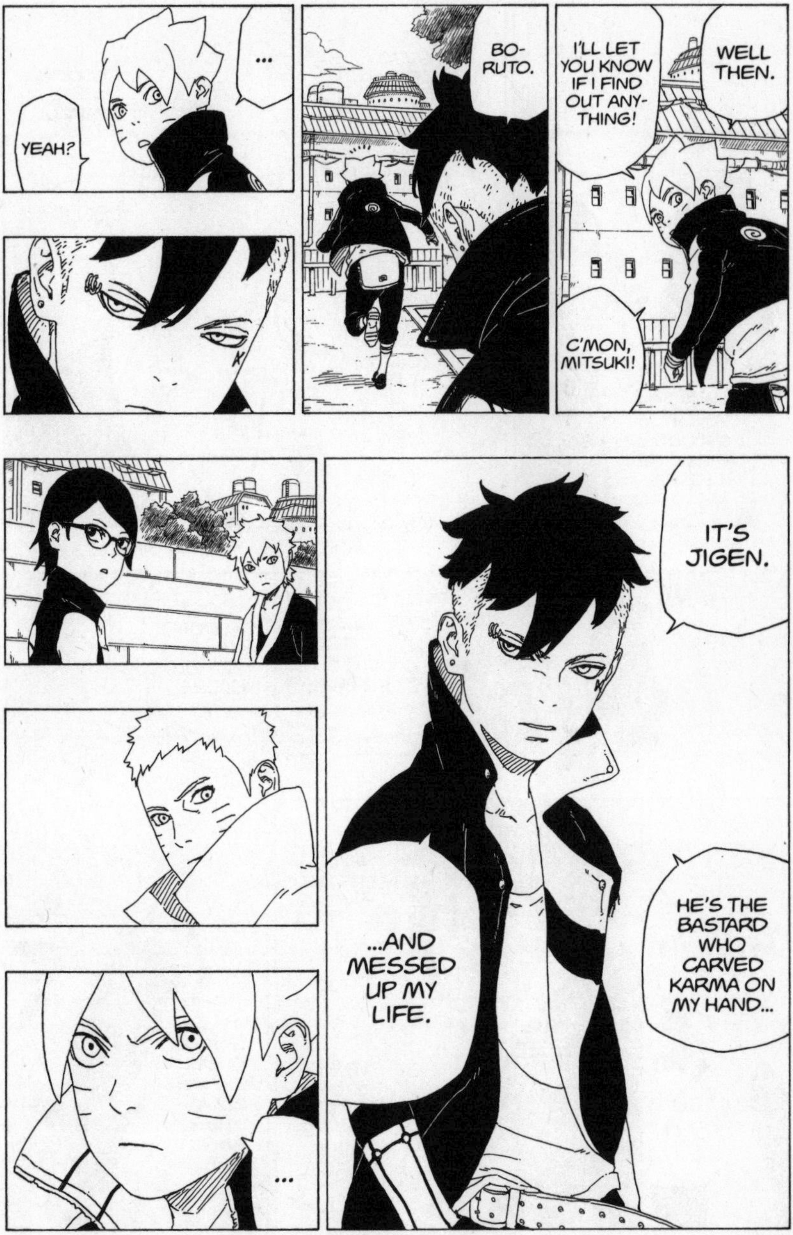
WELL THEN.
I'LL LET YOU KNOW IF I FIND OUT ANYTHING!
C'MON, MITSUKI!
BO-RUTO.
...
YEAH?
IT'S JIGEN.
HE'S THE BASTARD WHO CARVED KARMA ON MY HAND...
...AND MESSED UP MY LIFE.
...

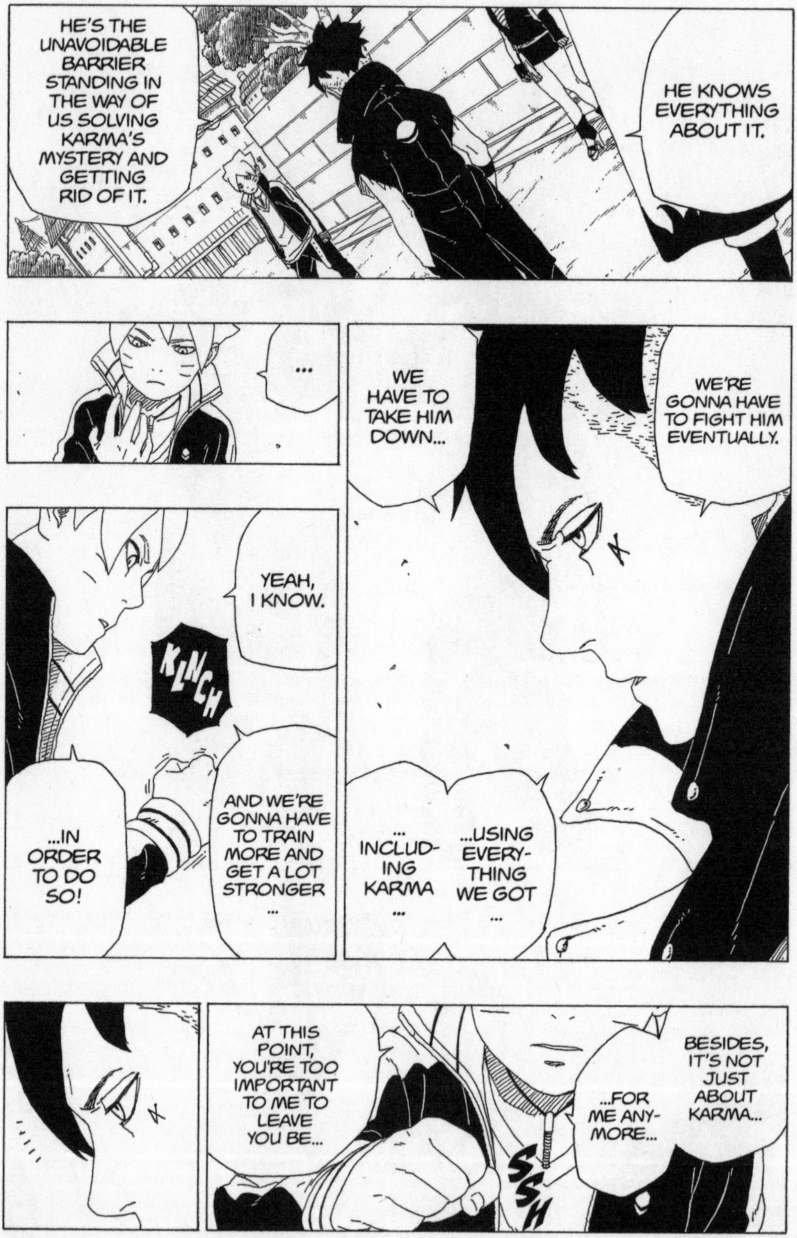
HE KNOWS EVERYTHING ABOUT IT.
HE'S THE UNAVOIDABLE BARRIER STANDING IN THE WAY OF US SOLVING KARMA'S MYSTERY AND GETTING RID OF IT.
WE'RE GONNA HAVE TO FIGHT HIM EVENTUALLY.
WE HAVE TO TAKE HIM DOWN...
...USING EVERY-THING WE GOT...
...INCLUD-ING KARMA...
...
YEAH, I KNOW.
KLNCH
AND WE'RE GONNA HAVE TO TRAIN MORE AND GET A LOT STRONGER...
...IN ORDER TO DO SO!
BESIDES, IT'S NOT JUST ABOUT KARMA...
...FOR ME ANY-MORE...
SSH
AT THIS POINT, YOU'RE TOO IMPORTANT TO ME TO LEAVE YOU BE...

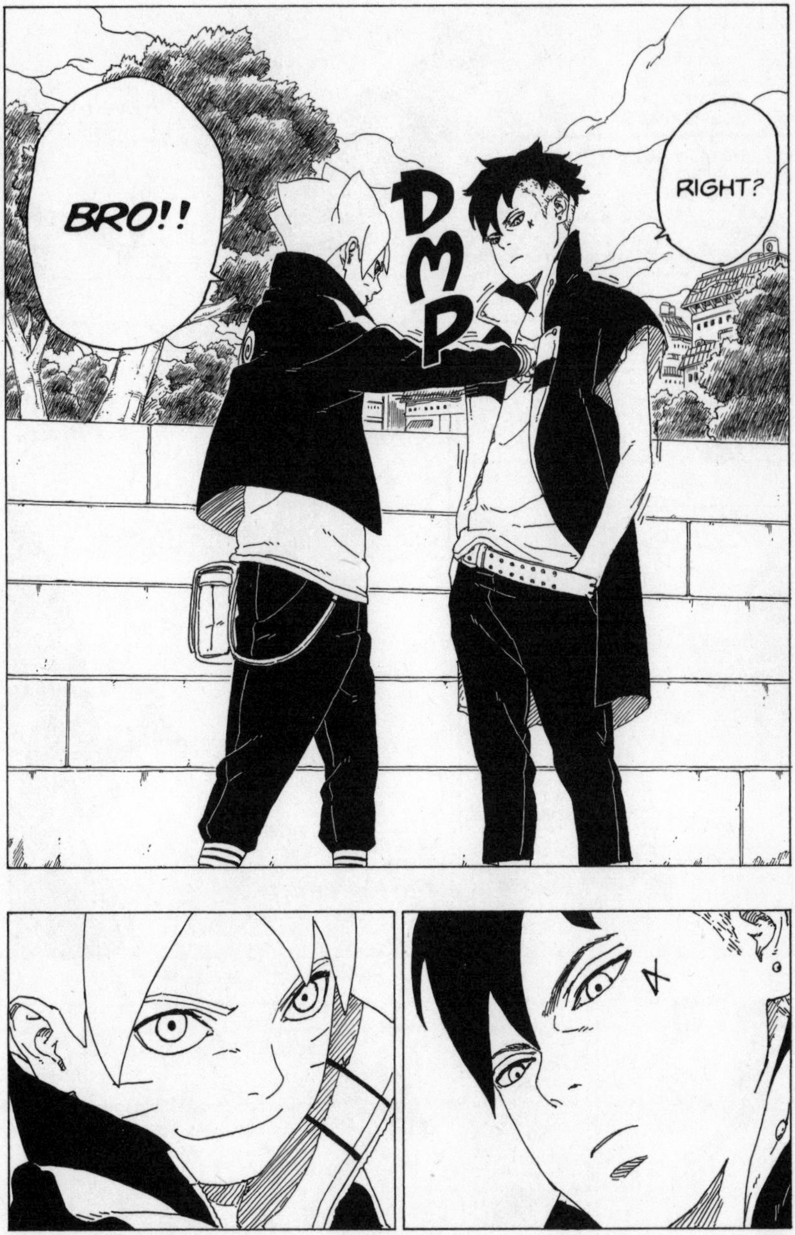
RIGHT?
DMP
BRO!!

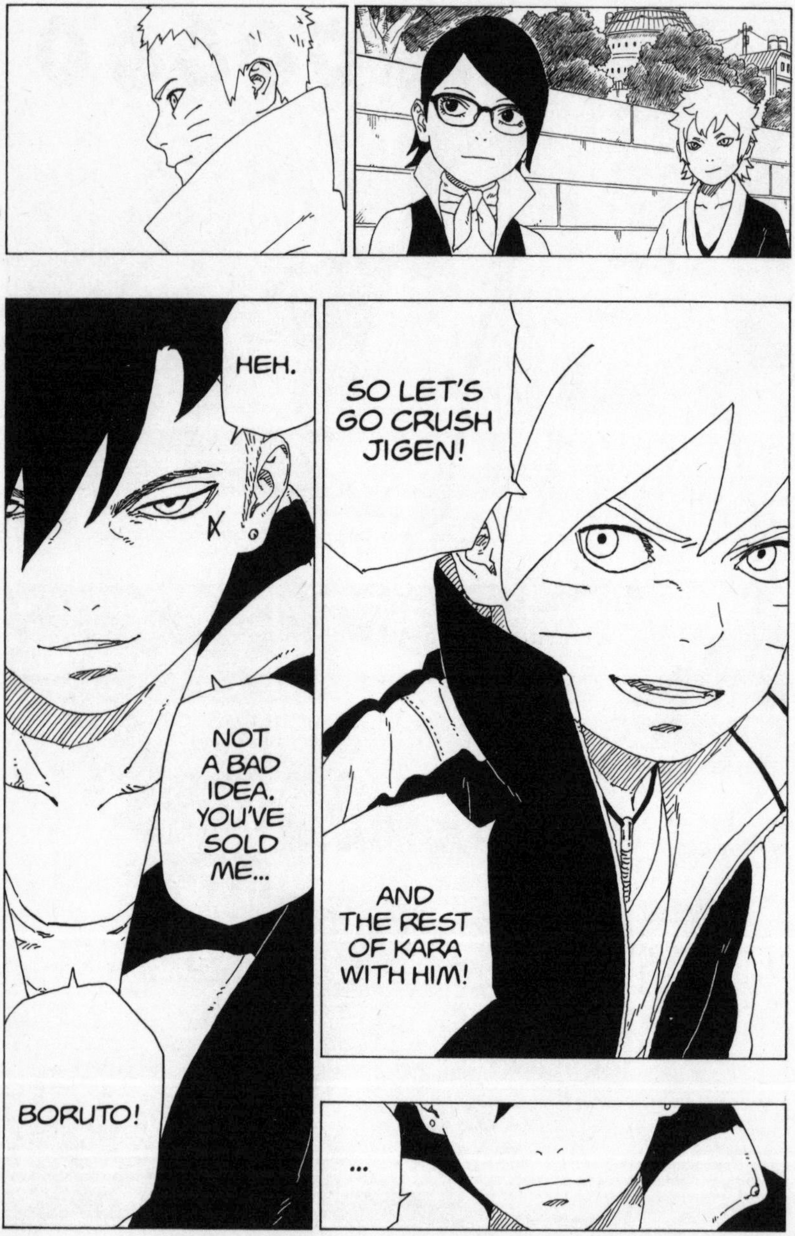
SO LET'S GO CRUSH JIGEN!
AND THE REST OF KARA WITH HIM!
...
HEH.
NOT A BAD IDEA. YOU'VE SOLD ME...
BORUTO!

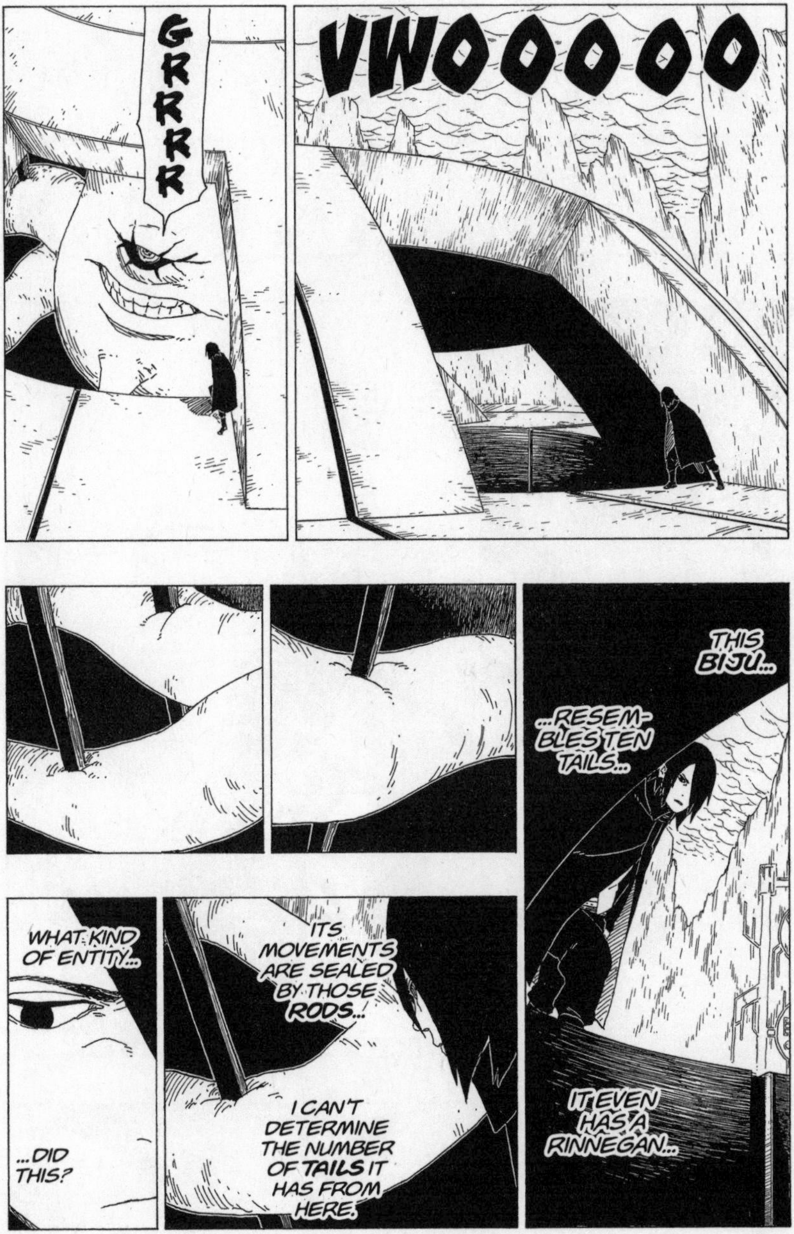
VWOOOOO
GRRRR
THIS BIJU...
...RESEMBLES TEN TAILS...
IT EVEN HAS A RINNEGAN...
ITS MOVEMENTS ARE SEALED BY THOSE RODS...
I CAN'T DETERMINE THE NUMBER OF TAILS IT HAS FROM HERE.
WHAT KIND OF ENTITY...
...DID THIS?

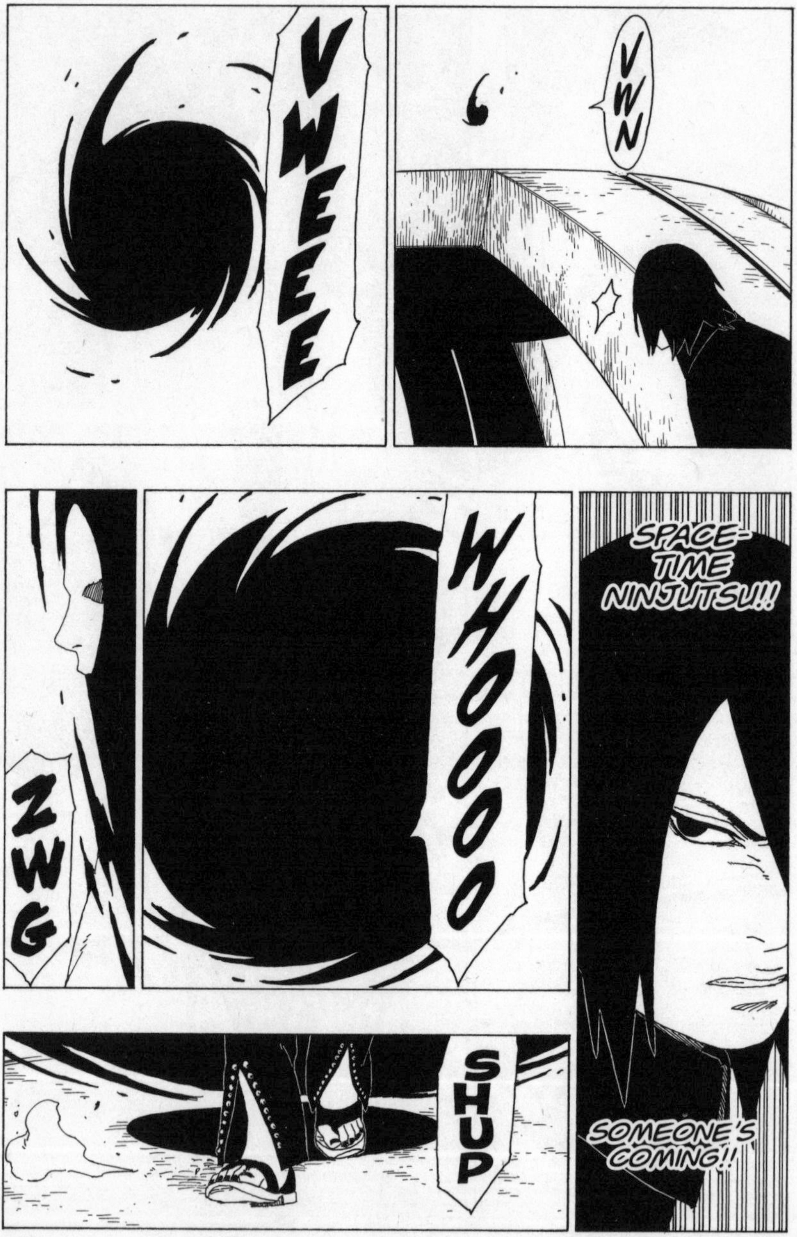
VWN
VWEEEE
SPACE-TIME NINJUTSU!!
SOMEONE'S COMING!!
WHOOOO
ZWG
SHUP

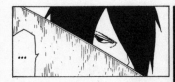

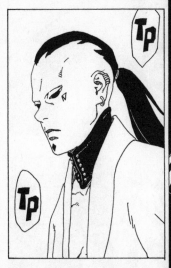

...
TP
TP
A KARMA ON HIS CHIN!
IT'S CONSISTENT WITH BLACK OPS' INTEL.
THAT HAS TO BE JIGEN!
KVSSH

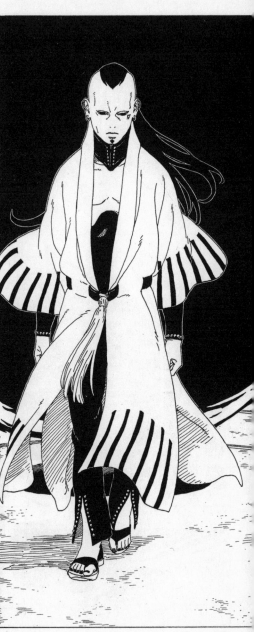

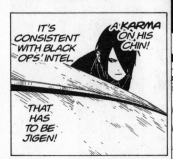

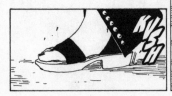

TP
TP
TP
SWSH
...
GRRR
WAFT

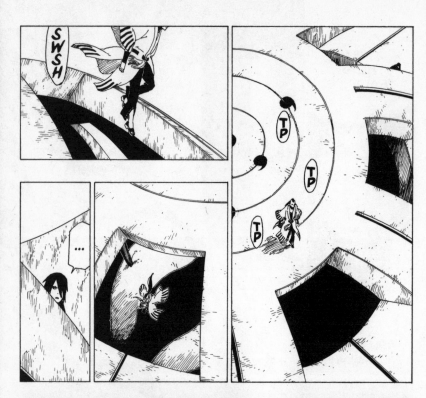

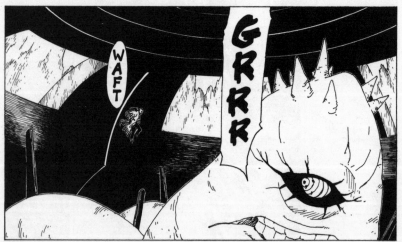

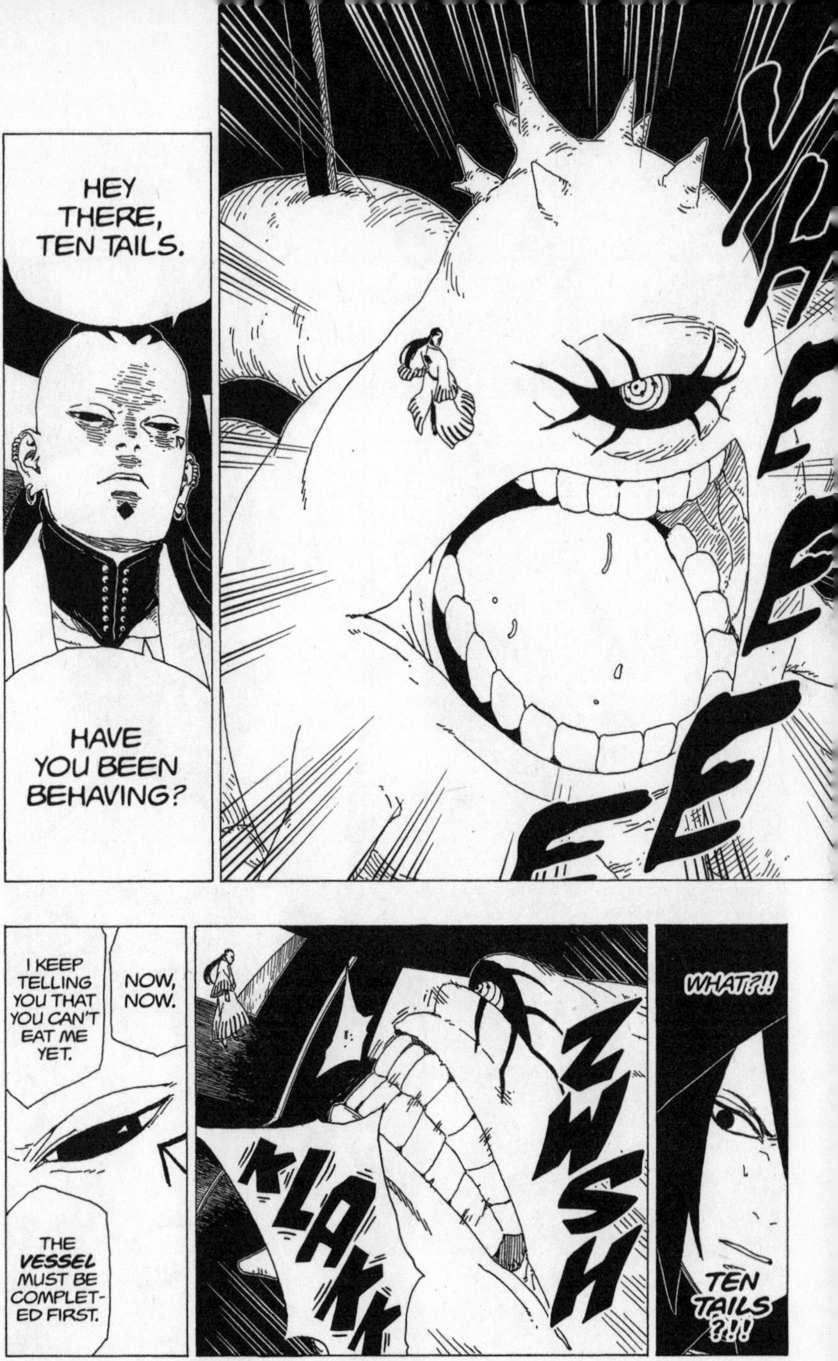
HEY THERE, TEN TAILS.
HAVE YOU BEEN BEHAVING?
WHAT?!!
TEN TAILS?!!
KLAKK
NOW, NOW.
I KEEP TELLING YOU THAT YOU CAN'T EAT ME YET.
THE ***VESSEL*** MUST BE COMPLETED FIRST.

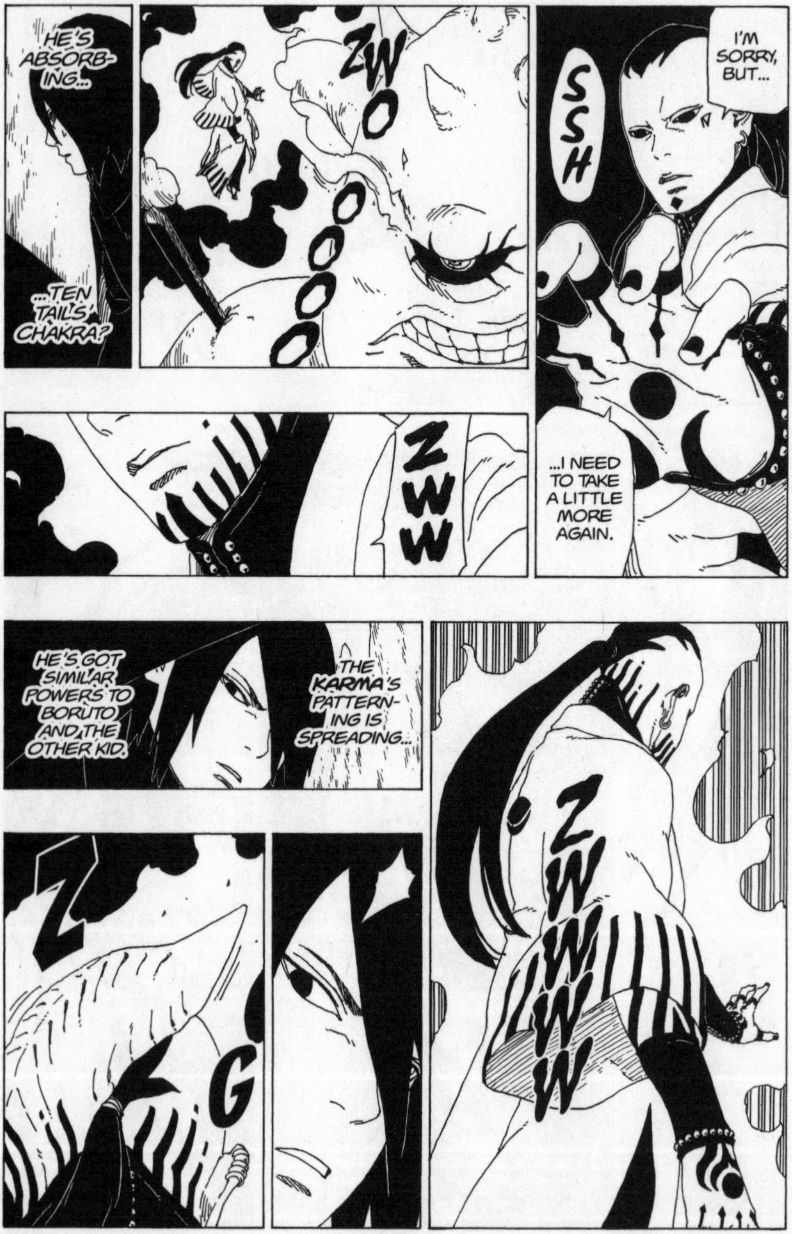
I'M SORRY, BUT...
SSH
...I NEED TO TAKE A LITTLE MORE AGAIN.
ZWOOOOOOO
HE'S ABSORBING...
...TEN TAILS' CHAKRA?
ZWW
ZWWWWWW
THE KARMA'S PATTERNING IS SPREADING...
HE'S GOT SIMILAR POWERS TO BORUTO AND THE OTHER KID.
ZG

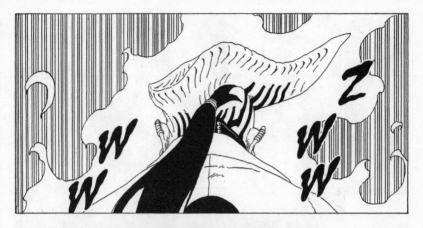

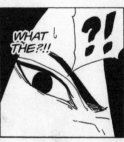

WHAT THE?!!

?!!

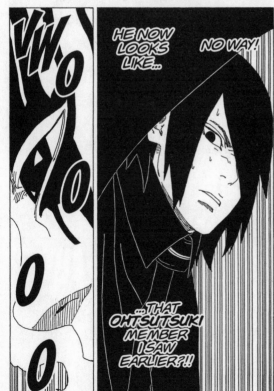

HE NOW LOOKS LIKE...

NO WAY!

...THAT OHTSUTSUKI MEMBER I SAW EARLIER?!!

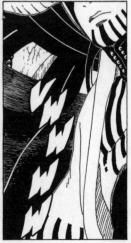

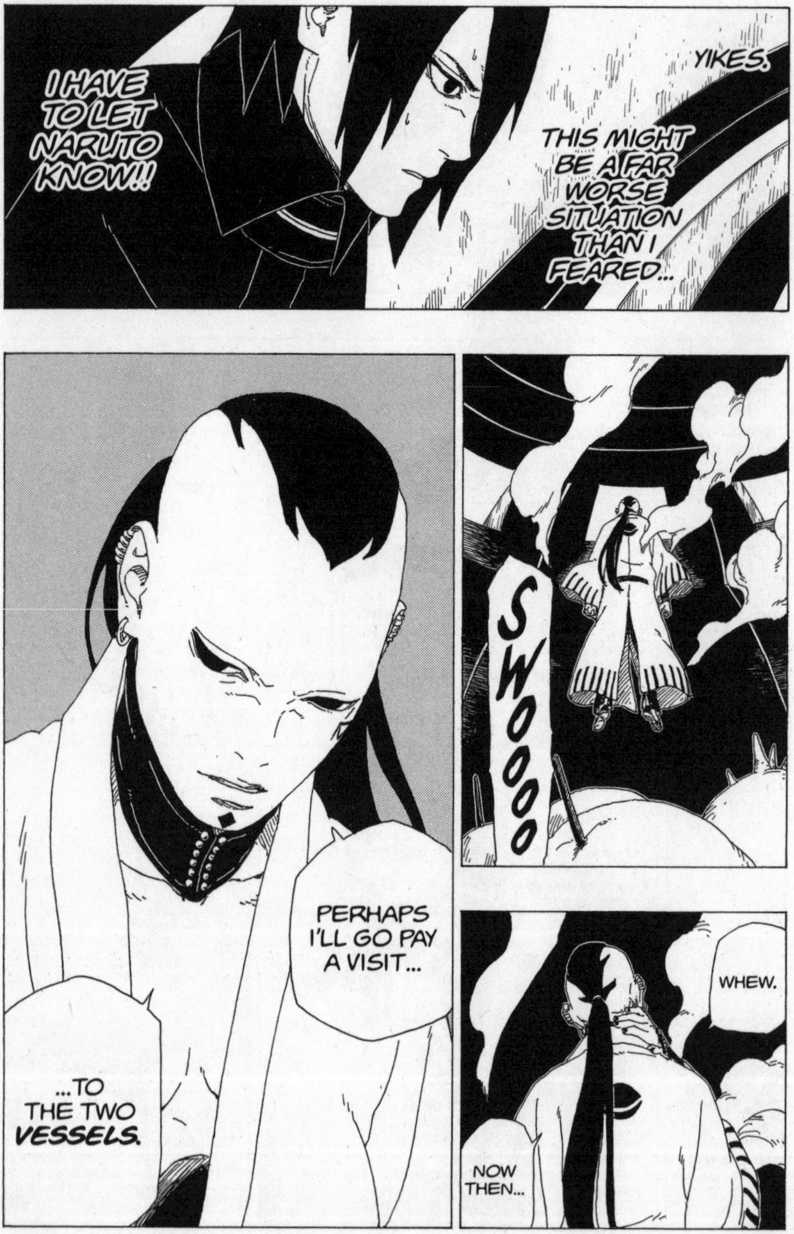
YIKES.
THIS MIGHT BE A FAR WORSE SITUATION THAN I FEARED...
I HAVE TO LET NARUTO KNOW!!
SWOOOO
WHEW.
NOW THEN...
PERHAPS I'LL GO PAY A VISIT...
...TO THE TWO VESSELS.

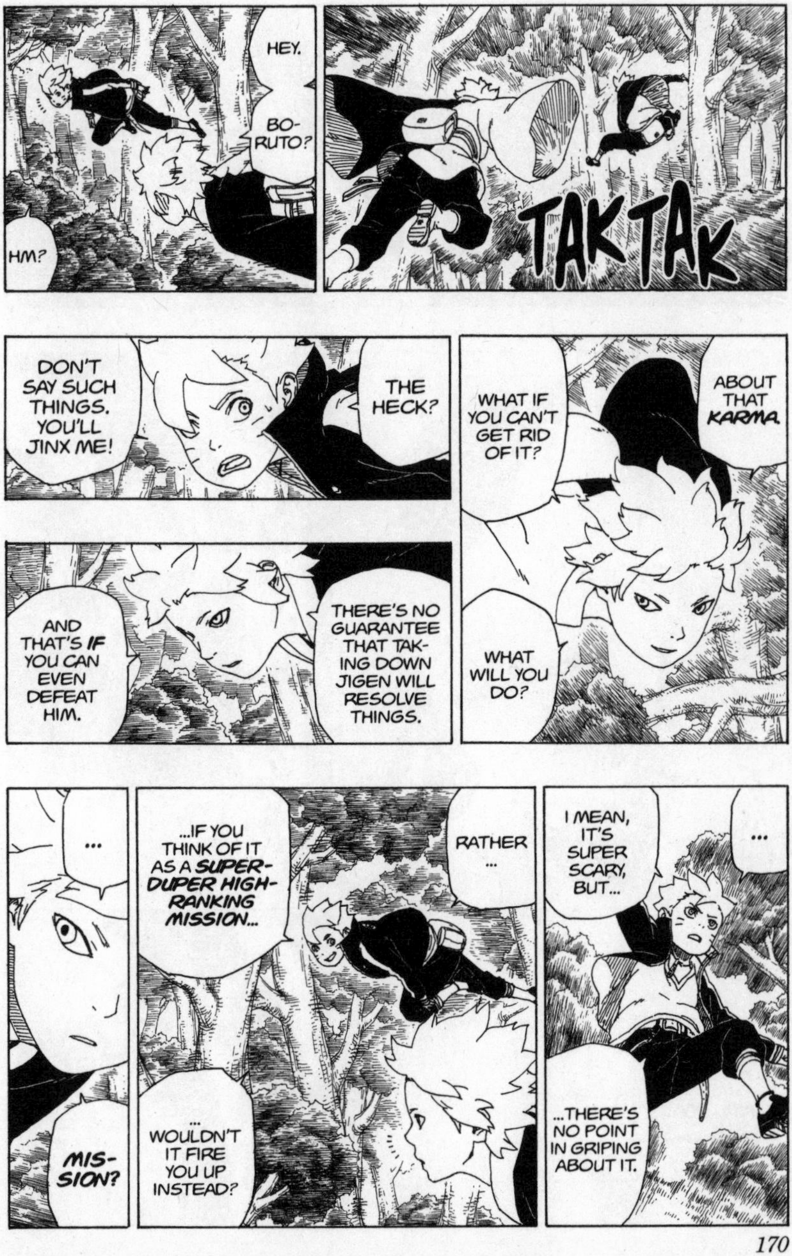
TAKTAK
HEY.
BO-RUTO?
HM?
ABOUT THAT ***KARMA.***
WHAT IF YOU CAN'T GET RID OF IT?
WHAT WILL YOU DO?
THE HECK?
DON'T SAY SUCH THINGS. YOU'LL JINX ME!
THERE'S NO GUARANTEE THAT TAK-ING DOWN JIGEN WILL RESOLVE THINGS.
AND THAT'S ***IF*** YOU CAN EVEN DEFEAT HIM.
...
I MEAN, IT'S SUPER SCARY, BUT...
...THERE'S NO POINT IN GRIPING ABOUT IT.
RATHER...
...IF YOU THINK OF IT AS A ***SUPER-DUPER HIGH-RANKING MISSION...***
... WOULDN'T IT FIRE YOU UP INSTEAD?
...
MIS-SION?

YEAH.
EVEN IF THE OBJECTIVE'S A BIT CRAZY, IF IT'S A ***MISSION***...
...YOU'LL PUT ALL YOU'VE GOT INTO IT NO MATTER WHAT, RIGHT?
...
GOTCHA.
ESPE-CIALLY CUZ...
TMP
...I'M SASUKE'S STUDENT ...
...AND THE HOKAGE'S SON...
TAK
...AND A ***NINJA!***

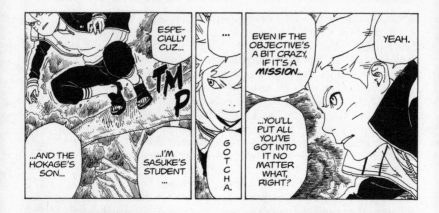

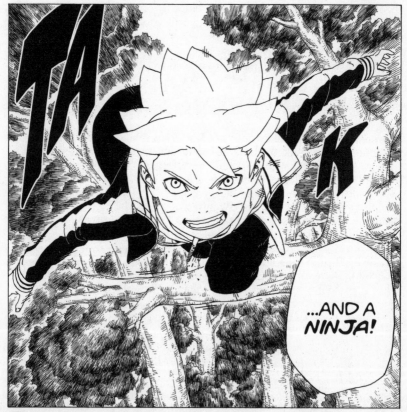

Shinobi Hiden Column 4: Shinobi and Their Bureaucratic Institution

An institution requires a vast support organization to maintain itself. By and large, five bureaucrats per one combatant is regarded as the rule, and the larger in scale and more sophisticated an institution is, the less it can be avoided. Ninja are no exception. They need people who will pay their wages, people in charge of their rearward supply trains, people who mobilize their weapons and ninja tools, people who maintain the Village and training facilities, staff such as medic ninja and educator ninja, etc. In general, it is said that for every one ninja on the frontline like Boruto, at least five bureaucrats are necessary. The trouble lies in where to position such bureaucrats in the institution, these ninja whose status within the organization should have already been decided based on their competency as a ninja and merits as a covert operative. In many Villages, alienation of the entire institution from the essence of being ninja is avoided by specially promoting ninja who possess above average talent as elders while still young, in an elitist manner.

However, this intrinsically does not lead to burying the gap between the consciousness of those in the field and those in the rear. The reason why Gaara, who has become Kazekage, struggled to have control over his Village is solely because its bureaucratic institution was under the thumb of the old guard. Conversely, one could also point out the historical example where, in Konoha Village, the runaway Black Ops was thwarted due to the Third Hokage tightly holding the bureaucrats in check. The presence of bureaucrats does not weaken the institution, of course. Boruto and Sarada are able to fight freely because there are people supporting them. For all that, decision-making in an institution by its very nature cannot avoid being slow. That is the reason for continuously lagging behind Akatsuki, a small

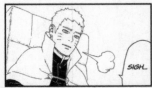

SIGH..

troop that did not require a support structure. The stability achieved by an institution's expansion, versus the expediency of the elite few. This dilemma faced by all institutions is not irrelevant to ninja as well.

The Complexification of Organizational Structure

It could be said that the discernment of a Village's organizational structure by outsiders is the biggest danger to the institution of ninja. So long as ninja remain a group of specialists, their numbers cannot be easily replenished. A Village's greatest assets are its ninja. For example, the collapse of the Uchiha Clan, a professional occupation group, is still having negative consequences on Konoha Village many years later. Hence, it is difficult to comprehend the institution of ninja from the outside. The reason why various terms such as Division, Section, and Clan are used, and why it is not instantly apparent which is higher in rank than another, is to disallow spies who have infiltrated from other nations to glean the organizational structure; and furthermore to not make it obvious to ninja on the inside either. This is because if insiders find out, confession, collusion and betrayal become possible. However, it is clear, even without needing to look at Danzo and the Uchiha Clan, or Katasuke's rampage, that this begets a hotbed of secretiveness. An institution always makes its own existence its top objective. This is especially true of a secret organization.

Within a complexified power hierarchy, each department always puts pursuing its own survival before the interests of the entire Village. This is unavoidable. For that reason, skills of watchfulness and coordination, in short, personal virtue-like qualities, are sought in leaders, starting with the Gokage. It is crucial to make each department feel that selecting leaders, then providing them with inside information, leads to their own survival. You cannot make people obey solely through fear, nor will people follow just logic either.

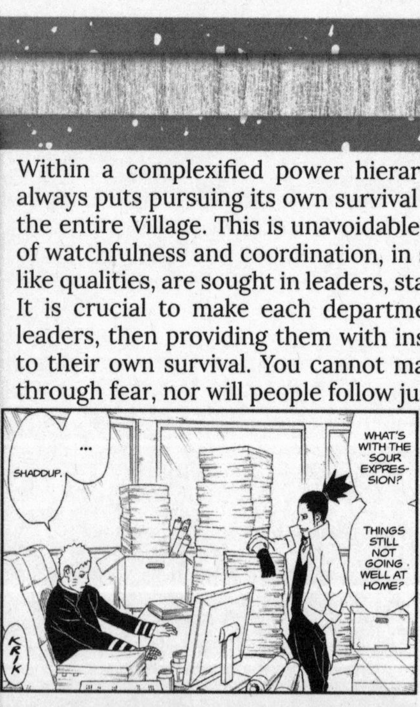
WHAT'S WITH THE SOUR EXPRESSION?
THINGS STILL NOT GOING WELL AT HOME?
...
SHADDUP.
KRIK

Then again, profit alone will lead to instant betrayal. So long as full freedom of information is not possible, the troubles of the ninja will be everlasting.

Black✤Clover

STORY & ART BY YŪKI TABATA

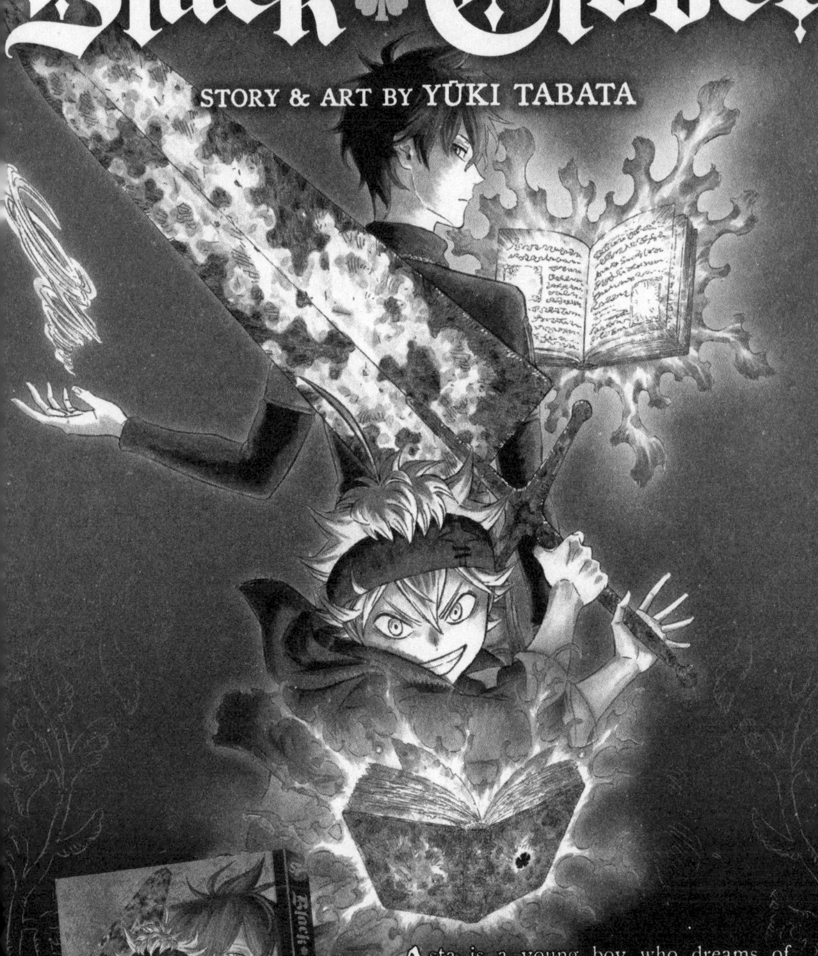

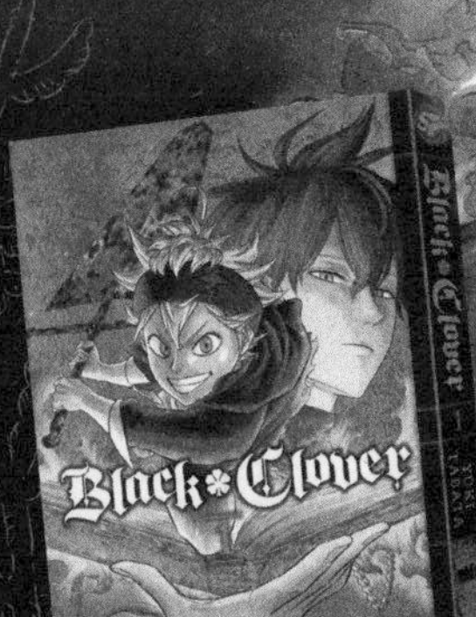

Asta is a young boy who dreams of becoming the greatest mage in the kingdom. Only one problem—he can't use any magic! Luckily for Asta, he receives the incredibly rare five-leaf clover grimoire that gives him the power of anti-magic. Can someone who can't use magic really become the Wizard King? One thing's for sure—Asta will never give up!

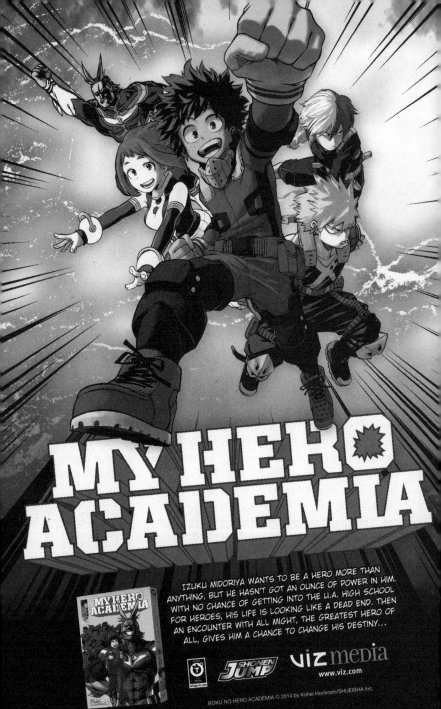

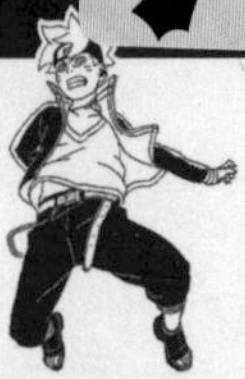

YOU'RE READING
IN THE
WRONG DIRECTION!!

WHOOPS! Guess what? You're starting at the wrong end of the comic!

...It's true! In keeping with the original Japanese format, **Boruto** is meant to be read from right to left, starting in the upper-right corner.

Unlike English, which is read from left to right, Japanese is read from right to left, meaning that action, sound effects and word-balloon order are completely reversed... something which can make readers unfamiliar with Japanese feel pretty backwards themselves. For this reason, manga or Japanese comics published in the U.S. in English have sometimes been published "flopped"—that is, printed in exact reverse order, as though seen from the other side of a mirror.

By flopping pages, U.S. publishers can avoid confusing readers, but the compromise is not without its downside. For one thing, a character in a flopped manga series who once wore in the original Japanese version a T-shirt emblazoned with "M A Y" (as in "the merry month of") now wears one which reads "Y A M"! Additionally, many manga creators in Japan are themselves unhappy with the process, as some feel the mirror-imaging of their art alters their original intentions.

We are proud to bring you **Boruto** in the original unflopped format. Turn to the other side of the book and let the ninjutsu begin...!

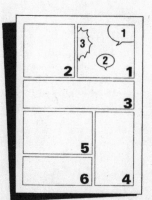

—Editor

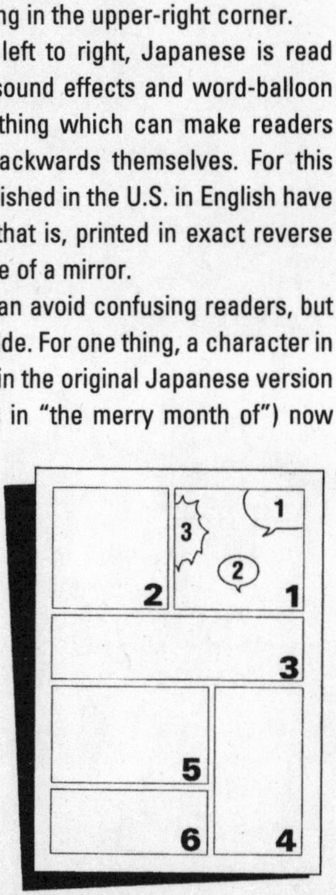